Ravensbrück

Everyday Life in a Women's
Concentration Camp 1939-45

Ravensbrück

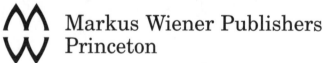
Markus Wiener Publishers
Princeton

Everyday Life in a Women's Concentration Camp 1939-45

JACK G. MORRISON

To
my mother, Bess
my wife, Betty
and
my daughter, Lisa

Copyright © 2000 by Jack G. Morrison

For information write to: Markus Wiener Publishers
231 Nassau Street, Princeton, NJ 08542

Library of Congress Cataloging-in-Publication Data

Morrison, Jack G. (Jack Gaylord), 1937–
    Ravensbrück: everyday life in a women's concentration camp,
        1939–45/Jack G. Morrison.
    Includes bibliographical references and index.
    ISBN 1-55876-218-3 (paperback)
    ISBN 1-55876-219-1 (hardcover)
    1. Ravensbrück (Concentration camp)   2. World War, 1939–1945—
        Prisoners and prisons, German.   3. Women prisoners—
        Germany.   I. Title
    D805.G3M6143 2000
    940.53'1743157—dc21   99-085963

Markus Wiener Publishers books are printed in the
United States of America on acid-free paper,
and meet the guidelines for permanence and durability
of the committee on production guidelines for book
longevity of the council on library resources.

Contents

Preface

This book is an attempt to reconstruct the workings of every-day life of the concentration camp at Ravensbrück, the only camp in the Nazi system designed for women. It is primarily a study of the social dynamics of the women prisoners, their relationships with each other, and, to a lesser extent, with their SS masters. As such, it encompasses a whole range of issues and activities, from bartering to storytelling, from political maneuvering to coping with body lice. It discusses their work, for Ravensbrück was a labor camp (*Arbeitslager*) rather than an extermination camp (*Vernichtungslager*), and work was mainly what absorbed the women's time. And, of course, it addresses the issues of sickness, death, and killing, which were undeniable parts of the concentration camp experience. This book is most decidedly NOT a study in the psychology of women concentration camp inmates. However valuable such a study might be, I am not the one to write it, and I have not attempted it here.

This study has its origins in a fortuitous visit I made to the Ravensbrück Memorial (*Gedenkstätte*) in 1993. Having read Germaine Tillion's memoir-monograph[1] years before, I knew about the camp, but had never visited the site. The Russian army, which had liberated the camp in 1945 and then moved into its facilities, was still there in 1993, using about 95 percent of the former concentration camp as a military post. But they were preparing to leave the following year, and as they did so, the German historians at the Memorial and the Brandenburg Historical Commission were formulating plans for the future of Ravensbrück. From what I learned, it seemed like a monumental, but fascinating and challenging, undertaking, and I volunteered to help. My offer was accepted, and I returned in the fall of 1994, having been awarded a sabbatical leave from Shippensburg University for this purpose. I'm not sure that I was really of much

assistance, but I enjoyed working with the *Gedenkstätte* staff, and
I learned quite a lot about the women's concentration camp. I
returned to Ravensbrück in 1997 and again in 1998 to pursue my
own research. This study is the result of those visits, as well as
other research.

Originally, I had planned to write a much shorter monograph,
but I changed my approach for two reasons. First, working in the
Ravensbrück Archives, and particularly in reading the many
Erlebnisberichte (Reports of Experience—most written shortly
after the end of the war by survivors) made me realize how much
more material there was on this topic than I had earlier suspected (or dared to hope).[2] Second, I had all along wanted to write a
study that was aimed at a general audience as well as at scholars.
In pursuing this goal, I soon realized that I could not describe the
workings of everyday life in a women's concentration camp and
have it make sense, unless I described the context in which much
of this took place. Among other things, this meant including considerably more material on the SS, the anti-Jewish program, the
wartime economy, and concentration camps in general.

It occurred to me to subtitle this study "An Anecdotal History."
I didn't do this because it's unnecessary; anyone who reads even a
few pages in the sections on everyday life will quickly see that my
main sources are anecdotal: memoirs, reports of experience, and
oral histories. A book of this nature could not be written without
these kinds of sources. The SS at Ravensbrück destroyed virtually their entire holdings of official records in the closing stages of
the war, leaving tremendous gaps in our knowledge. Not only do
we not have many of the official records concerning inmates, but
we don't know the rationale for many SS actions and policies.
However, even if we had the SS records, we would still need to use
many personal accounts to get at the details of everyday life.

The effort to reconstruct the everyday life of women prisoners
at Ravensbrück has been a daunting task. I take some comfort in
the advice given by Erika Buchmann, a survivor of Ravensbrück,
to a budding playwright, Hedda Zimmer, about 1960. When asked
by Zimmer if she thought that somebody who had never personal-

ly experienced incarceration in a concentration camp could ever
understand what it was really like, Buchmann responded:
"Perhaps you could understand it even better than somebody who
was there but who only knew that little part which she herself had
experienced."[3] Buchmann's candidness is refreshing. In reading
the plentiful survivor literature, one is reminded of the allegory of
the blind men describing an elephant. Each survivor had her own
perspective, but sometimes these differed so greatly that one had
to wonder whether they were describing the same camp.
Ravensbrück, by the midpoint of the war, had become a sizable
and complex operation, and it would have been difficult for any
one person, particularly an inmate, restricted in mobility as she
was, to comprehend the entire system.

A Note Concerning the Photographs

Scattered throughout this volume are a number of contempo-
rary photographs, most of them showing women prisoners at various workplaces around Ravensbrück. These photographs must be
viewed with extreme caution, for they were intended to give a mis-
leading impression of life and work in the camp. The photographs
were part of an album conceived, created, and assembled by the
SS in the period 1940–1941. Their purpose was to show visiting
delegations, such as the Red Cross, how benign and pleasant
working conditions were and how healthy and well cared for were
the women prisoners. It is obvious that the photographs were
staged. Only robust and healthy-looking inmates are pictured,
appearing quite contented as they go about their work, seemingly
under conditions that were uncrowded and free of stress.[4] As we
shall see, these images did not realistically portray living and
working conditions at the camp, at least not in general. Nevertheless, they are the only photographs known to have been taken
at Ravensbrück, and when viewed with appropriate wariness
have considerable value for this study.

Acknowledgments

Ravensbrück: Everyday Life in a Women's Concentration Camp, 1939–45 owes its existence to many people and institutions on both sides of the Atlantic. Shippensburg University, where I have taught for many years, generously provided me with sabbatical leaves in 1994 and 1997; without this support, the basic research for this volume could not have been undertaken, and I am grateful to my university and to the taxpayers of Pennsylvania for this funding. I would like to thank the History Department of the University of Iowa and the Deutscher Akademischer Austauschdienst who many years ago took a chance on me and invested in my training as a central European historian.

It is, for me, a long-awaited pleasure to acknowledge the help and encouragement given me by the staff of the Mahn- und Gedenkstätte at Ravensbrück, who went out of their way to treat me as a colleague and who afforded me every conceivable courtesy as I pursued my research. In particular, I wish to acknowledge the assistance given me by Dr. Sigrid Jacobeit, Frau Monika Herzog, and Frau Christa Schulz. Their patience with my interminable questions expressed in less-than-perfect German was truly remarkable, and their willingness to share their insights and expertise helped me enormously to conceptualize issues and focus my research. I wish to add a special thanks to Frau Schulz for allowing me to quote poems from her edited work, *Der Wind weht weinend über die Ebene.*

Were it not for the many drawings made by prisoner-artists that I have been allowed to reproduce in the following pages, the value of this work would be much diminished. I am therefore pleased and honored to acknowledge the following persons who have granted me permission to use their copyrighted works: Madame Violette Rougier-LeCoq (Paris) for permission to use her drawings from *Témoignages*; Miss Dunya Breur (Amsterdam) for allowing me to use her mother's drawings from *Een verborgen herinnering*, as well as for providing me with commentaries on these drawings through telephone conversations. I wish to thank the Stadtgeschichtsmuseum Schwerin for their kind permission to reprint works from Helen Ernst; I am again indebted to the Mahn- und Gedenkstätte Ravensbrück for permission to reproduce selected drawings of Maria Hispanska, Nina Jirsikova, Yvonne Useldinger, Kveta Hnilickova, and Aat Breur. I also want to thank Frau Antonia Bruha for permitting me to reprint the untitled poem from her memoir, *Ich bin keine Heldin*, and for sharing with me other poems she has written.

I would like to thank the staffs of the Public Record Office in London, the U.S. Holocaust Memorial Museum Research Division in Washington, and the U.S. National Archives. Josie Fisher of the Gratz College Oral History Collection (Philadelphia) was extreme- ly hospitable, as were Rita Hofrichter, Rositta Kenigsberg, and Karen Oleet of the Holocaust Documentation and Education Center (Miami). Thanks also to Sybil Milton, not only for her careful and perceptive critique of the galley, but for sharing insights with me in telephone conversations. Closer to home, Diane Kalathas of the Shippensburg University Inter-Library Loan Department seemed never to fail in tracking down the many obscure volumes I requested, while Shelley Gross-Gray and Catherine Houghton of the University's Computer Services divi- sion patiently tutored me in the art of scanning. Several col- leagues in various academic departments at Shippensburg University read and critiqued all or parts of the manuscript. I especially want to thank the following: Jim Coolsen, Paul Gill, and Charles Loucks (History), Marty Dako (Philosophy), Eveline Lang (Speech), Hans Meuer (Modern Languages), John Taggart (English), Debra Zellner (Psychology), and Ellen Gigliotti. To my department colleagues: I can never hope to repay the debt I owe so many of you for the cooperation, affection, and encouragement shown to me over so many years.

I deeply appreciate the substantial help given me by my family.

My daughter, Lisa, gave the entire manuscript a thorough critique, pointing out numerous problem areas. My stepson, Vince, through his skills as a graphic artist, assisted me by making maps and charts and designing chapter headings. And my wife, Betty, deserves particular mention, not only for putting up with (and sharing in) what became an obsession, but for being my "first critic," carefully examining each chapter as it was written, then reviewing each revision. Moreover, our frequent discussions about Ravensbrück and women prisoners helped me tremendously in conceptualizing many of the issues involved in this project.

Finally, I would like to express a special thanks to the Wiese family of Fürstenberg: Herbert, Rhona, Robert, and especially Rotraud. Their friendship, generosity, and hospitality immeasurably brightened my various visits to Ravensbrück, in addition to acquainting me with the region and providing me with valuable contacts to townspeople.

INTRODUCTION

National Socialism and Women

Adolf Hitler, Rally at Bückeberg, 1935. Source: Cigaretten Bilderdienst.

Scenes of adoring German women thrusting bouquets at the *Führer's* passing motorcade or looking on enraptured as Hitler addressed them have become part of the iconography of twentieth-century history, captured forever on film. Ironically, the most important of the Nazi cinematographers to record these scenes was a woman, Leni Riefenstahl, arguably the only female to achieve significant recognition for her contributions to the Third Reich. However, beneath the surface of these carefully arranged and well-publicized special events, other German women were being arrested and incarcerated by the Nazis, not because they were women, but because they ran afoul of the new regime for any of a variety of reasons. Early on, this was often tied to membership in Communist or Socialist organizations; eventually, it could be anything from being "work-shy" to having relations with a non-German.

National Socialism (the official name was National Socialist German Workers Party or NSDAP, but everyone called them "Nazis") was from beginning to end a male-dominated system. It consciously lashed out at what it considered the perverted and gender-blurring world of the Weimar Republic, particularly the effort to "emancipate" women. Thus, those modern movements that sought to redirect women from their "natural" roles in order to "liberate" them had done society a disservice and distorted the very nature of women.

Women, the Nazis insisted, had physical and mental characteristics that were not only different from men, but were vastly inferior. Such notions were widespread among party leaders, and, as with much of Nazi thinking, the tone was set by Hitler himself. Speaking in private, particularly to his inner circle, Hitler often spoke contemptuously of women in general:[1]

> Women have the talent, which is unknown to us males, for giving a kiss to a woman-friend and at the same time piercing her heart with a well-sharpened stiletto. To wish to change women in this respect would be ingenuous. Women are what they are. Let's come to terms with their little weaknesses. And

if women really only need satisfactions of that sort to keep them happy, let them not deprive themselves! For my part, I prefer to see them thus occupied than devoting themselves to metaphysics. There is no greater disaster than to see them grappling with ideas.[2]

This kind of antifeminism, stressing as it did the "natural inferiority" of women and their supposed inability to handle ideas, functioned as a kind of "secondary racism."[3] It was women's purpose as well as their presumed inclination to serve men. This could best be achieved if women were to accept the traditional roles of mothers and homemakers, and indeed these roles were greatly emphasized in Nazi rhetoric and propaganda. But, in fact, the notion of the three K's—*Kinder, Kirche, und Küche* (children, church and kitchen)—represented a propaganda ploy rather than reality. Motherhood was stressed, but other types of "women's work" were always considered. This included domestic service, sales, secretarial work, nursing, elementary school teaching, social work, and, perhaps most important, farm work.[4] Hitler addressed this issue in general terms in a speech he gave to the National Socialist Women's Organization (*NS-Frauenschaft*, or *NSF*) in September 1935. After proclaiming that he would never send women to fight on the battlefield, he noted: "Women have their own battlefield. With every child that they bring into the world, they fight a battle for the nation. The man engages himself for the *Volk* exactly as the woman does for the family. Equal rights for a woman consists in experiencing the well-deserved respect which comes from involving herself in those realms for which nature has predisposed her."[5] "Those realms" could include a number of activities, and during the war, in fact, the notion of "women's work" proved to be a rather elastic concept. One thing which was inelastic, however, was politics. Wielding power, making decisions, managing systems—all these were the prerogatives of men.

Weimar Germany was, viewed in retrospect, a wonderland of *avant-garde* culture, sexual expressionism, political extremism, and mass movements for every kind of cause imaginable. Inevitably, issues concerning women gained prominence and even notoriety. One of the most controversial of these issues was sex reform. The issue had many aspects to it, from sex education through birth control to abortion. As one might expect, the left favored reform and the right opposed it. Conservative groups, for example, feared a more open approach to sexuality would lead to immorality, not to mention *Kulturbolschewismus* (cultural Bolshevism).[6]

Women's organizations in Germany were not new in the 1920s, but in the polarized atmosphere of the time they took on a new urgency. During Weimar, there was every variety of women's organization, from leftist ultrafeminist organizations, through bourgeois-conservative groups (which included a Jewish women's group, the JFB), to Catholic and Protestant groups, which rejected feminism and emphasized family issues.

1932 NSDAP election poster urging women to "rescue the German family" by voting for Hitler.

On the far right of the women's question, of course, were the National Socialists. Before 1933, women accounted for only five percent of the party membership, but almost half its votes.[7]

In 1933, membership in Nazi women's organizations soared; the NSF increased by 800 percent from January to December of that year.[8] One might legitimately ask: Why would any woman voluntarily join an organization dedicated to taking away her political rights and reducing her to second-class citizenship? Some have suggested that the answer to this question might be found in an analysis of the female psyche, even female sexuality.[9] As intriguing as this approach is, the answer is likely more mundane. We simply cannot overlook the fact that many German (and other European) women were profoundly traditional. For these women, many of whom had no political experience before joining the NSDAP, the idea of rigid separation between male and female domains was not an "escape from freedom" as much as it was a retreat into a world they knew and with which they were comfortable. The tumultuous and (for many) upsetting world of Weimar made the image of a secure and orderly home life, in which each member knew her or his place, immensely attractive. Coupled to this was a religious appeal: Hitler and the Nazis promised to restore morality and "positive Christianity" to Germany. Most of those who believed this were ultimately to be terribly disappointed, but in the 1920s and 1930s this hope was still there.[10] Finally, many German women would have had the same reasons as German men for supporting National Socialism. Hitler's program was indeed broadly-based, and many women were certainly not immune to appeals made to their sense of national pride.

The Nazis' approach to the "women's question" was two-pronged. First, they "coordinated" women's organizations into a single agency, the NSF, under state control. Second, women were excluded from certain professions and from all political positions. Almost all female civil servants were dismissed, along with all women judges and public prosecutors. By 1936, women could not practice law, and, in most cases, medicine. Further, many married women were dismissed from other fields, such as teaching, as the new regime put pressure on "double-earners."[11]

The government's exclusion of women from the labor force could only go so far before the negative economic consequences were disproportionate to the social and ideological gains. In spite of rowdyism by the SA (Storm Troopers or *Sturmabteilung*, the Nazi private army), designed to force employers to fire female employees, many employers held their ground and refused to dispense with cheap female labor.[12] In fact, the number of women employed increased significantly from 1933 to 1939 as the economic revival continued.[13] By the late 1930s, the government was rethinking some of its policies, particularly those excluding women from studying certain fields in the universities, such as medicine. The outbreak of the war in 1939 intensified the labor shortage as well as the reliance on women, as it became increasingly necessary to replace males who were sent to the army.

By the late 1930s, the women's movement, under the control of the state, had become fully "coordinated," meaning that its primary purpose was to direct the labor and activities of women towards whatever programs and goals the state required. Gertrud Scholtz-Klink, the chief (*Führerin*) of the NSF, oversaw the labor of 25,000 full-time female employees who, in their turn, supervised the efforts of some 8 million volunteers. These volunteers were especially instrumental in running the various social services sponsored by the government. Also, it was women from the NSF who were sent to work as guards in the early women's concentration camps, Moringen and Lichtenburg (but not Ravensbrück). Scholtz-Klink's management of a sizable bureaucratic apparatus appears to contradict the Nazis' own admonitions against women running things. But she was clever, and remained properly deferential to her male commanders.[14]

On another level, the League of German Girls (*Bund Deutscher Mädel* or BDM), the female equivalent of the Hitler Youth, essentially prepared girls for a lifetime of subordination to the state and to their male superiors. These young women were encouraged to report for voluntary labor service. In 1938, the Duty Year (*Pflichtjahr*) was introduced for single women under twenty-five. This attempted to force women into jobs in agriculture and domestic service, positions that many young women had been shunning because of the generally poor conditions and low pay.[15]

By 1940, the widespread use of female labor had become absolutely essential in order to keep the German wartime economy functioning at anywhere near sufficient levels of productivity. Huge numbers of women were being conscripted into the labor pool (that year more than a third of a million young women served their Duty Year, and many others were ordered to work also).[16] In addition, many married women, in the absence of their husbands, had to take over the management of shops, stores, and farms. Some of the conscripted women were assigned to them, especially if they had small children. But as the war continued, the numbers of German women (and men) available for work simply did not suffice. Thus it was that the regime turned to the conscription and exploitation of workers from Poland and other occupied territories. In addition, other marginalized groups—Jews, Gypsies, asocials, political dissidents—were numerous, cheap, and expendable,[17] all the more so if they were women.

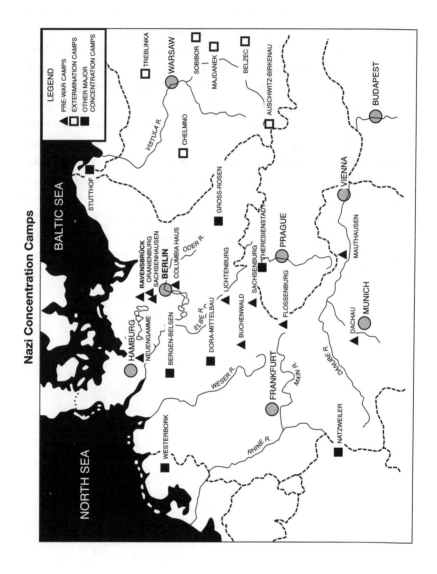

Nazi Concentration Camps

LEGEND

▲ PRE-WAR CAMPS
□ EXTERMINATION CAMPS
■ OTHER MAJOR CONCENTRATION CAMPS

NORTH SEA

BALTIC SEA

HAMBURG
NEUENGAMME
BERGEN-BELSEN
WESTERBORK
FRANKFURT
DORA-MITTELBAU
BUCHENWALD
WESER R.
RHINE R.
MAIN R.
NATZWEILER
DANUBE R.
MUNICH
DACHAU
MAUTHAUSEN
VIENNA
FLOSSENBURG
PRAGUE
THERESIENSTADT
SACHSENBURG
LICHTENBURG
ELBE R.
COLUMBIA HAUS
BERLIN
SACHSENHAUSEN
ORANIENBURG
RAVENSBRÜCK
ODER R.
GROSS-ROSEN
STUTTHOF
CHELMNO
VISTULA R.
WARSAW
TREBLINKA
SOBIBOR
MAJDANEK
BELZEC
AUSCHWITZ-BIRKENAU
BUDAPEST

The Women's Camp and the SS

Reichsführer-SS Heinrich Himmler inspects the female overseers at Ravensbrück. (SS Photo.) *Sammlungen Mahn- und Gedenkstätte Ravensbrück.* Courtesy U.S. Holocaust Memorial Museum Photo Archives.

The Early Concentration Camps and Women

On 27 February 1933, under circumstances that are still mysterious, the Reichstag building in Berlin was gutted by fire. The very next day, the new Nazi regime issued its "Emergency Decree for the Protection of the Nation and State," empowering the SA, the SS (*Schutzstaffel* or Protective Squad, originally Hitler's bodyguard detachment, by 1933 an elite military force within the party), and police to arrest persons and place them in "protective custody" (*Schutzhaft*) without a trial or even a hearing.[1] Within weeks, thousands were in custody, many of them in makeshift jails. Rudolf Diels, chief of the *Gestapo* (acronym for Secret State Police, by 1934 the main investigative branch of the SS), acknowledged that he, himself, was taken by surprise, as overzealous SA men took matters into their own hands: "No order and no instruction exists for the establishment of the concentration camps; they were not established, one day they were simply there. The SA leaders put up 'their' camps because they did not want to trust the police with their prisoners or because the prisons were overcrowded. No information about many of these *ad hoc* camps ever got as far as Berlin."[2]

Intraparty rivalries, particularly between the SA and SS, soon forced the issue of who was in control, and led to a greater standardization of the entire political detention system. Heinrich Himmler, head of the SS and by 1 April 1933 commander of the Bavarian police, used his positions to pre-empt his SA competition and begin the process of centralization. Under Himmler, Dachau, a few kilometers from Munich, became the first camp exclusively under SS control, and it shortly became a model for other camps throughout the country.[3]

In the first few months of the new regime, the number of political detainees quickly soared, reaching over 25,000 by July 1933. Then the numbers leveled off, as many prisoners were released upon satisfactory completion of a period of so-called political re-education. However, even as this was occurring, in mid-1934,

Himmler ordered Theodor Eicke, commandant of Dachau, to expand and reorganize the entire concentration camp system. The regime clearly had plans for going well beyond the temporary incarceration of political opponents.[4]

After June 1934, with the SA having been pushed out of the picture through the "blood purge," the SS was given a free hand to develop and expand the concentration camp system along lines in keeping with its political-racial worldview. Hitler's role in the creation of this system was apparently indirect and minimal, as he preferred to delegate authority and allow his top lieutenants, in this case Himmler, Goebbels, and Goering, to work out details. By 1935, the foundations of what would eventually become a mammoth enterprise were well established, with concentration camps operating at Dachau, Esterwegen, Oranienburg (shortly transferred to Sachsenhausen), Columbia-Haus at Berlin-Tempelhof, and Sachsenburg. The total prisoner population was then only about thirty-five hundred, but with construction under way for new camps at Buchenwald, Flossenburg, and Sachsenhausen, the system was obviously gearing up to accommodate many times this number.[5]

In the beginning, women were incarcerated for roughly the same reasons as men, primarily for political affiliations or criminal activity. But soon, some women whose husbands had fled or gone into hiding were arrested and held hostage. At first, women who were arrested were simply placed in regular jails, but in April 1933, the workhouse at Moringen, near Hanover, was converted into a detention center, which was quickly transformed into a camp exclusively for women. By November, 141 women were being held there.[6]

There are no indications that women sent to Moringen were mistreated; indeed, evenings were often spent in group discussions, part of the Nazis' self-styled re-education effort. In any case, most were there only a short time, a few weeks on average, before being returned to their families. Neither the SA nor SS had anything to do with this camp, and as a result only "light cases" were sent there. Most of the women held at Moringen were Communist Party members or suspects. (One woman was in detention for decorating the graves of Rosa Luxemburg and Karl Liebknecht.)[7] But in the mid-thirties, as the regime tightened its grip by defining new categories of enemies and criminals, a growing number of Germans, including women, were arrested and imprisoned.[8] The criminalization of abortion, the campaign against prostitution, and the outlawing of sexual relations between Germans and non-Germans all worked to significantly increase the number of females being incarcerated.

Except for Moringen, the early concentration camps held few female prisoners.[9] But in late 1937, the regime took a significant step by opening a camp for women at Lichtenburg, in Saxony. It functioned as a women's concentration camp for about a year and a half, essentially replacing Moringen. Moringen was closed in March 1938, and its roughly two dozen inmates were transferred to Lichtenburg. It was during this time that the Nazi state's growing intolerance for what it considered "asocial elements," and recalcitrant types like Jehovah's Witnesses, led to a swelling of the prisoner population. Unlike Moringen, the camp at Lichtenburg was run by the SS, and the overseers were all female. Its director was *SS Hauptsturmführer* Max Koegel, who had received his training at Dachau under Theodor Eicke, the creator of the concentration camp system.[10] Lichtenburg, a converted castle fortress, was not designed to hold the numbers of women who were being arrested by 1938, and it quickly became inadequate.

A word of explanation seems in order here, since all readers may not be familiar with the workings and development of the concentration camp system. There was no such thing as a typical concentration camp; each camp was unique, and it is therefore not easy to generalize about the range of activities and experiences that inmates went through. Nevertheless, it must be pointed out that these prewar camps in Germany were generally created to be detention centers, institutions for incarcerating political opponents of the regime and those who did not or would not adapt themselves to the National Socialist Folkish Community (*Volksgemeinschaft*) then being created. Under the guidance of the SS, these camps had the potential for evolving into something more sinister, and eventually they did. But they are not to be compared with later camps, such as Maidanek, Sobibor, or the most notorious of them all, Auschwitz. These later camps, constructed after German military conquests had brought many non-German peoples under their control, bear little resemblance to the earlier camps. Unlike the prewar camps, they had nothing to do with political detention or re-education, nor were they concerned with weeding out those who did not fit into the Folkish Community. Simply put, camps like Sobibor, Maidanek and Auschwitz were killing centers whose goal was the annihilation of "racial undesirables," particularly Jews. In pursuit of this goal, the SS virtually invented "assembly-line" procedures for murdering people in numbers that still numb the imagination.[11] Indeed, it is questionable whether a study such as this one on the everyday lives of Ravensbrück inmates could even be done on these killing centers. The comparatively brief duration of most prisoners' detentions, as well as the almost unfathomable horror of their experiences, virtually precluded any semblance of the kind of living that even some Ravensbrück prisoners thought of as normal, with its measures of predictability and routineness.[12] Camps such as Ravensbrück, run by the SS as they were, had many incidents of unchecked brutality and terror all along. Inmates' awareness of this, and the fear this engendered, were to a degree what kept the system going. But these camps were not part of the systematic effort to eradicate whole categories of people, at least not until the very end, after the genuine killing centers were liberated by the Russian army. This fundamental difference between German labor camp and Eastern European extermination center must be understood if we are to appreciate how prisoners at Ravensbrück were able to undertake all of the activities and enterprises which are examined in forthcoming chapters.

The Creation of Ravensbrück
Concentration Camp

By 1934 the state and the Nazi Party were making land purchases across the lake from the town of Fürstenberg, located in the lake district of Mecklenburg between Berlin and the Baltic. These purchases were being made in a settlement known as Ravensbrück, hardly more than a hamlet. What plans they had at that time for this property are not known, but in 1938 the SS also made land purchases here.[13] Later, in November of that year, five hundred male prisoners from Sachsenhausen Concentration Camp and an Advance Crew (*Vorkommando*) of women from Lichtenburg were brought in to begin construction on a new camp for women.[14] By then, several hundred acres of land (roughly 1 km by 3 km) lying to the east of the Havel River were in their possession.

It is not certain what were all the factors that influenced the SS's decision to create a concentration camp at Ravensbrück, but we can surmise that considerations such as the following must have played a role: Ravensbrück was in a secluded area with a rel-

View of the town of Fürstenberg from the concentration camp, across Schwedt Lake, 1997. Photograph by the author.

Ravensbrück Concentration Camp, 1944

Schwedt Lake

1. Commandant's Headquarters
2. Kitchens
3. Bunker
4. Crematorium
5. Gas chamber
6. SS canteen
7. Infirmary
8. Laundry
9. SS Textile Factory
10. Men's Camp
11. Waffen-SS storage
12. Kennels
13. Workshops
14. Barracks for SS-guards
15. Youth Camp–Uckermark
16. Gardens
17. Work and storage barracks
18. Barracks for Siemens civilian workers
19. Siemens factory
20. Siemens barracks
21. Water Treatment Plant
22. Political Department
23. Kitchen for Female Overseers
24. Barracks for Female Overseers
25. Single-Family houses for SS leaders
26. Two-Family houses for SS officers
27. Potato cellars
28. Armament workshops
29. Reed-Mat Weaving Plant
30. Barracks for civilian workers
31. Waffen-SS workshops and storage
32. Roll call grounds
33. Tent

atively small population; the Havel River and the lake (Schwedtsee) separated the area from the town of Fürstenberg and somewhat limited access to the camp; there were good rail connections to Berlin (about 90 km/55 miles away) and to Oranienburg (about 50 km/30 miles), where the SS had a major headquarters and where the Sachsenhausen Concentration Camp was already in operation; the system of lakes connected by canals and the Havel River allowed barges to transport heavy goods, such as coal, right to the perimeters of the concentration camp; and, finally, the Mecklenburg lake district, with its interconnected system of lakes, canals, and the Havel River, was (and still is) a boater's paradise, one of the loveliest areas in Germany (at least during the summer). This had to serve as an attraction to the SS, whose officers could look forward to bringing their families here and enjoying the surroundings. Not only the SS officers who were stationed at the camp would do this, but others as well. Oswald Pohl, who headed the SS's huge economic system, moved his family to an estate near Ravensbrück. To accommodate the staff and their families, a sizeable SS housing development just to the north of the main camp was begun, not long after the construction on Ravensbrück had started. The SS leadership was not expected to live a spartan existence.

On 18 May 1939, the first transport, containing 867 female prisoners, was brought from Lichtenburg to Ravensbrück, and the camp officially began its operations. By the end of June, just over a thousand women had been brought in, and a year later, this number had tripled. There were twenty barracks, called "Blocks" (a block referred to a place as well as its residents), each designed to house about 200 inmates. Thus, the theoretical capacity of the original camp was around 4,000. This figure was reached within a year and a half. In November 1940, the prisoner population stood at 4,100, and some barracks began to experience overcrowding.[15] In 1942, twelve new barracks were added as part of a major expansion of the camp. The barracks in the "new camp" were larger than the original ones, but by the time they were completed, the

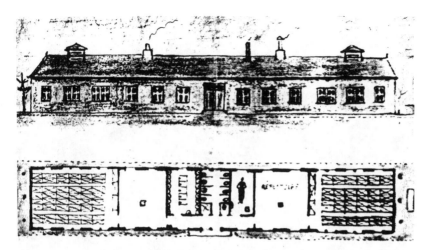

France Audoul, Drawing of a small barracks. From *Ravensbrück: 15,000 Femmes en Enfer.*

prisoner population had grown to the point that they were already inadequate.

Each barracks had two wings, an "A" side and a "B" side, each with its own sleeping area and day room. In the middle of the barracks, separating the wings, was the washroom (twenty sinks) and toilet area (ten lavatories). Located in this area, also, was the overseer's room, which was actually used more by prisoner officials, especially the block senior, than by the overseer. In the early years, by most accounts, these accommodations were at least adequate. Margarete Buber-Neumann had been brought to Ravensbrück in August 1940 from a Stalinist camp in Kazakhstan as part of a prisoner exchange. By comparison, her new home "seemed like a palace" to her.[16] Here each barracks had toilets and showers, electricity and heat, and each prisoner had her own bed with a straw mattress and blankets. But Buber-Neumann had arrived at Ravensbrück during its "idyllic period,"[17] when conditions were still relatively tolerable. By late 1944, she was writing that Ravensbrück was no better than a Stalinist gulag.[18]

Barracks at Ravensbrück, about 1940. (SS Photo.)
Dokumentationsarchiv des Österreichischen Widerstandes. Courtesy
USHMM Photo Archives.

Barracks at Ravensbrück, about 1940. (SS Photo.)
Dokumentationsarchiv des Österreichischen Widerstandes. Courtesy
USHMM Photo Archives.

The SS Administration

By the time Ravensbrück opened in 1939, there were already six major concentration camps in operation. The procedures and mechanisms for running the camps had become reasonably well established, and it was mainly a matter of adapting these to the special needs of a women's camp. In its structure and methods of operation, Ravensbrück was certainly very similar to the other camps in Germany.

Ravensbrück was essentially run through the efforts of two overlapping hierarchies, a prisoner hierarchy and an SS hierarchy. To a surprising extent, the actual day-to-day running of the camp was in the hands of the prisoners themselves, and some of the prisoner officials wielded considerable influence. Nevertheless, there was never any question about where ultimate authority and real decision-making power lay. Such power was in the hands of the SS, and prisoners needed no reminder of that fundamental fact.

At the top of the camp hierarchy was the commandant (*Kommandant*). *SS Hauptsturmführer* Max Koegel, who had been director of the women's camp at Lichtenburg, was brought in for this post. Ravensbrück only had two commandants in its six-year history. *SS Hauptsturmführer* Fritz Suhren succeeded Koegel in 1942, and served until the end of the war. The commandant was responsible for the overall operation of the camp and its dependent subcamps. It was a weighty position, comparable in today's terms to the CEO of a major corporation. Perhaps he was even more powerful, since not only did he oversee the daily functioning of the camp, including its huge inmate labor force, but he was also in charge of disciplining and punishing personnel, both prisoners and staff.[19]

Following the organizational pattern set by the already existing concentration camps, Ravensbrück had five major subdivisions (*Abteilungen*), including the office of commandant. The others were the Camp Leader for Protective Custody, the Political

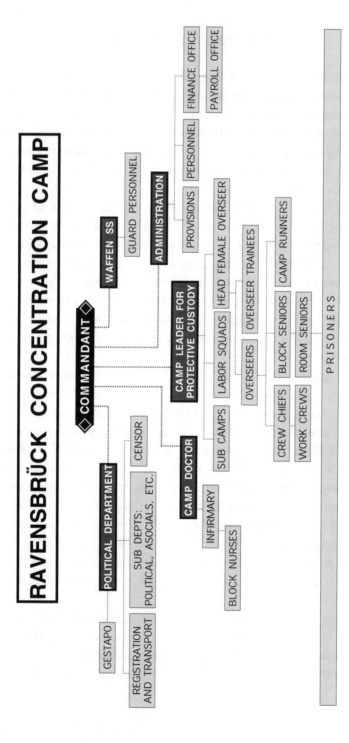

RAVENSBRÜCK CONCENTRATION CAMP

◇ COMMANDANT ◇

WAFFEN SS

GUARD PERSONNEL

ADMINISTRATION

PROVISIONS

PERSONNEL

FINANCE OFFICE

PAYROLL OFFICE

CAMP LEADER FOR PROTECTIVE CUSTODY

HEAD FEMALE OVERSEER

LABOR SQUADS

OVERSEER TRAINEES

OVERSEERS

BLOCK SENIORS

CAMP RUNNERS

CREW CHIEFS

ROOM SENIORS

WORK CREWS

SUB CAMPS

POLITICAL DEPARTMENT

CENSOR

SUB DEPTS: POLITICAL, ASOCIALS, ETC.

GESTAPO

REGISTRATION AND TRANSPORT

CAMP DOCTOR

INFIRMARY

BLOCK NURSES

PRISONERS

Organizational Chart of the Ravensbrück Concentration Camp

Department, the Administrative division, and the office of Camp Doctor.[20] Each of these four was responsible to the commandant's office, although the Political Department, tied in as it was with the Gestapo, had somewhat more autonomy.

The *Schutzhaftlagerführer* (inmates understandably shortened this to *Lagerführer* or camp leader, and we shall do the same) was a particularly influential officer because he oversaw the whole range of concerns dealing with the prisoners. Most important, the Camp Leader directed prisoner labor through the office of Labor Squads (*Arbeitseinsatz*). In addition, he was directly superior to the Head Female Overseer (*Oberaufseherin*) who was in charge of the overseers in the camp. They had the closest dealings of any agency with the prisoners and with the daily operations of the camp.

The Political Department, sometimes called *Abteilung II* (Department II), registered incoming and outgoing prisoners and maintained offices for the separate categories of inmates such as Political, Criminal, and so on, keeping its own records on them. In doing this it at least partially duplicated what the Personnel Office in the Administration was doing, but this duplication of function was a relatively common feature of Nazi Germany. The Political Department also was in charge of checking and censoring mail, both incoming and outgoing, for all the prisoners. Finally, the Political Department represented the Gestapo at the camp, and thus was empowered to run internal investigations, not only on prisoners (whom they could send for punishment), but also on conditions in the camp as well as fellow SS personnel. Inevitably, this led to tensions between Gestapo and camp officials.[21]

The Administrative Office directed the provisioning of the camp as well as its financial affairs. The physical domain of the camp was under its control, including the continued expansion of the camp's barracks and work areas. In addition, this office handled personnel records for prisoners and the female overseers (but not for the SS men). Some indication of the scope and growth of the administration is shown by the testimony of a prisoner, Maria

Plura. She had been at Ravensbrück since March 1941, but in April 1944 she was "promoted" to a job as steno-typist in the Payroll Office. This office handled the payroll records of all the female overseers in all the concentration camps. By late 1944, this included more than 3,000 individual accounts. When Plura began working in that office, there were only two steno-typists. A year later, there were twenty.[22]

The office of Camp Doctor was headed by the Garrison Doctor (*Standortartzt*) who supervised the functioning of the infirmary and its staff. Beginning in 1942, he also played a major role in the medical experiments performed on Ravensbrück prisoners and

France Audoul, "Main entrance of the camp, viewed from inside."
From *Ravensbrück: 15,000 Femmes en Enfer.*

directed the "selections," determining which prisoners were "work-capable" and which were not. A few of the doctors and many of the nurses were inmates. They were part of an elite group within the camp and were *de facto* under the authority of the camp doctor rather than the overseers.

There was also a large number of support staff. Prisoners did nearly all of the actual work in the internal running of the camp, but non-prisoners were used in other capacities, such as drivers, technical supervisors, and guards. Many of these, particularly the guards, were *Waffen SS* personnel assigned to Ravensbrück and housed in barracks just outside the camp. Male guards from the *Waffen SS* patrolled the perimeters of the camp and also acted as a backup force for the female overseers inside the camp. They were also placed in charge when prisoners needed to be moved anywhere outside the camp, most often between the main camp and subcamps. By 1943–1944, there were some nine hundred men from the *Waffen SS* stationed at Ravensbrück and its subcamps.[23] A number of them were older men who were considered incapable of combat. Many were *Volksdeutsche* (ethnic Germans) from Romania, Hungary, and points east.[24]

The Female Overseers

Without exception, the overseers at Ravensbrück were women. They were called *Aufseherinnen* (Female overseers. The German language can indicate female gender with a simple suffix: "*in*." Since there were no male overseers at Ravensbrück, I shall refer to them as "overseers") Prisoners were instructed to address them as "Frau Aufseherin" ("Madame Overseer") without using a last name, and in fact many prisoners did not know their last names.[25] French and Spanish prisoners, employing a phonetic system, called them "*Officierines*"[26] and "Officierinas"[27] (literally, female officers), respectively. Since these sounded so similar to the German, nobody bothered about this. In casual conversation, most prisoners gave them nicknames or just called them "SS-women." Technically, however, the overseers were not *bona fide* members of the SS, which was an all-male organization. They belonged to the SS Women's Auxiliary (*weibliche SS-Gefolge*).[28]

There were about 150 overseers at Ravensbrück by 1944, not counting trainees. Each block or barracks was headed by an overseer called a block leader (*Blockleiter*), and the prisoners had their closest contact with her, for she supervised roll calls, meals, and other activities taking place in and around the barracks. But by far the greatest number of overseers were employed to supervise the work crews. Each work crew, whether it operated outside or inside the camp, was headed by at least one overseer. In the larger factories, each hall would have several. Each administrative office where prisoners worked had an overseer. The only workplace that seems to have been relatively free of supervision by overseers was the infirmary; prisoner doctors and nurses were directed more by SS doctors than by overseers. But elsewhere they were an omnipresent element. Their job was to see that the camp regulations (*Lagerordnung*) were followed, and if they were not, then a formal, written Report was to be made.

Overwhelmingly, the overseers were young German women of modest backgrounds and little education who either were conscripted or saw the opportunity for improving their circumstances during the war.[29] A few came in as genuine volunteers, attracted by the promise of "light physical work" and good pay.[30] Erna Dorn, who had training and experience as a secretary, was encouraged by her father to apply.[31] Help-wanted advertisements in the newspapers were used, but these never mentioned concentration camps.[32] Many young women were recruited, sometimes with the added incentive of pressure from SS officials. Anna David was a young woman working on the assembly line at the Heinkel aircraft factory in Berlin when the SS chief there ordered her to choose between continuing indefinitely in her menial position or joining the SS. He promised that if she joined the SS and took the training to become an overseer, she would earn more money and not work as hard.[33] In 1944, a twenty-five year old unmarried overseer would earn about RM 185 a month, compared to an unskilled female textile worker, who would earn about RM 76.[34] This was, of course, considerably less than what a male would earn in a comparable position. But it represented a decent salary, and in many cases upward mobility for the young women.

Evidence suggests that by 1942, with the expansion of the female concentration camp population, the SS began to launch a major recruitment effort for female overseers.[35] However, voluntary recruitment, even when accompanied by pressure, did not bring in sufficient numbers, and the regime then turned increasingly to conscription. By 1943, the Reich Labor Ministry was empowered to conscript women between seventeen and forty-five years of age (between sixteen and sixty-five for men) for labor service. Although it was relatively easy for women from the middle and upper classes to secure exemptions, the overall effort did bring in large numbers of female workers. By late 1943, the great majority of women reporting for overseer's training were conscripts.[36]

Once drafted or recruited, the prospective SS overseer was sent to Ravensbrück for orientation and training. Apparently there were few qualifications beyond a healthy body and a background free of a criminal record. After 1942, Ravensbrück served as the main training center for female overseers, and about thirty-five hundred were trained here. Trainees spent anywhere from a week to half a year at the camp, at first being given systematic instruction by the Head Overseer. They were given a detailed grounding in the *Lagerordnung*, the standardized regulations for all the concentration camps. They were taught how to detect sabotage and work slowdowns, how to prevent escapes, and how to punish prisoners within the parameters of the camp regulations.[37] Above all, it was drummed into them that they were to have no dealings of a personal nature, not even conversations, with the prisoners. The last half of the course, roughly, was a form of internship, closely supervised, in which these "overseer helpers" (*Hilfsaufseherinnen*) assisted Ravensbrück overseers in carrying out their duties. Upon satisfactory completion of the course, the new *Aufseherinnen* would be sent out somewhere into that massive and complex system of concentration camps and subcamps, the German version of the Stalinist gulags.

As a group, the overseers were not highly regarded by the women inmates, who often had educational and cultural levels well above any of their supervisors. The feeling ran fairly deeply that most overseers were rather stupid types whose only claim to superiority was their uniform.[38] Their training had taught them to take a hard attitude toward the prisoners, and for some of them this attitude and the arrogance that came from wielding such power led almost effortlessly into a kind of mindless, almost juvenile, type of brutality. Gudrun Schwarz, author of a penetrating study of the female overseers, has observed: "A goal of the instruction and training of the female overseers was inconsiderateness and a readiness to use force toward the inmates. Only those female overseers who were brutal and not reluctant to use force gained the recognition of their SS colleagues and only they were rapidly promoted."[39] Survivor recollections overflow with examples of overseers boxing their ears, punching them at roll call, kicking at them or pulling their hair, all for minor misdeeds. In theory, overseers were not to punish prisoners themselves, but were only to send in Reports on them. In practice, however, they did punish inmates, not only by petty actions like these, but also in far more harmful ways. On one occasion, a prisoner named Friedel Kubitzka made an offhand remark that the overseer, Johanna Brach, found offensive. Brach told Kubitzka to take off her glasses, whereupon she used her riding whip to beat her across the face, causing bruises and swelling, as well as permanent scars. Yet there were no repercussions.[40]

This incident was anything but an isolated event. One of the most ordinary occurrences was for an overseer to turn her dog (overseers of work crews frequently walked with German shepherds on a leash) on a prisoner who offended her or broke the rules.[41] Infirmary workers have testified that dog bites were among the most common prisoner injuries in the camp.[42]

Prisoners' loathing of overseers was general, but not universal. Some overseers were decent and even respectful to prisoners, and their subordinates very much appreciated them. In mid-1942, the Political Department was assigned a new overseer named Krüger, about twenty years old. She treated the prisoners well, sometimes getting food from the SS pantries and sharing it with her mostly Polish workers. Privately, she admitted to them that she was ashamed of what she was learning about conditions and practices at Ravensbrück. When the Forestry Crew got a new overseer in 1944, a Bavarian named Brigitte, crew members were at first apprehensive. But she was friendly, and quickly got acquainted with everyone. Even though she herself was not well educated, she told them: "I am really proud to have so many well-educated women in my crew." The women responded in kind: "We saw in her, not an official of the Third Reich, but a woman who, like us, had been torn away from her normal life and, like us, longed to return to it." Unfortunately, she served as their overseer for only a few days, then was transferred.[43]

These young women were taking risks by being so solicitous and friendly to prisoners. Whether they were eventually punished or removed is not known, although perhaps they were discreet and survived indefinitely. They appear to have represented a more widespread phenomenon than the SS was willing to tolerate. In November 1944, *SS Obergruppenführer* Richard Glücks, the head of concentration camps, sent an order to all camp commandants directing them to remind all female overseers that "under no circumstances" were they to have any personal dealings with inmates.[44] This had always been part of camp regulations, but apparently in the late stages of the war there were sufficient numbers of violations to warrant its reiteration. There doesn't appear to have been a comparable reminder sent to the men's camps.

Up to this point we have primarily discussed the camp leadership, the SS, and the kinds of structural and institutional support

systems put in place to make a concentration camp like Ravensbrück function. All of this was their creation, and they maintained
a firm grip on the controls. But there was another factor in this
increasingly involved equation, introduced by the SS themselves,
and that, of course, was the female prisoners.

Even had Ravensbrück remained the kind of protective custody
camp for German women it started out to be in 1939, it would
have been a complex operation. But as it grew in size and scope,
as new categories of women from many different nations were
brought in, and as new functions and goals were added and superimposed over old ones, this became ever more true. By the end of
the war, Ravensbrück had become unrecognizable from what it
had been at the start. Inevitably, these transformations directly
affected the relations between the SS and prisoners and between
different groups of prisoners, the work routines, the health and
living conditions of nearly all the prisoners. These transformations, in short, affected the grass-roots issues of life and survival
in the camp.

2

Arriving

Violette LeCoq, "Welcome" and "Two Hours Later." From LeCoq,
Témoignages . . . Courtesy Mme. Violette Rougier-LeCoq.

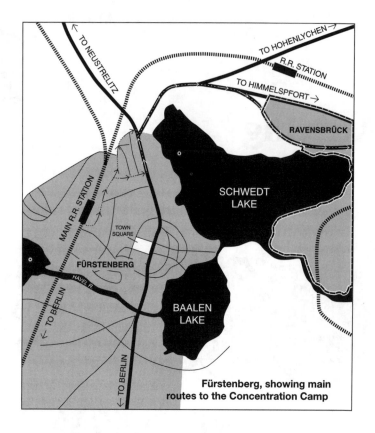

Fürstenberg, showing main routes to the Concentration Camp

In early June 1939, Elisabeth Sabo-Ewert wrote to her sister, Minna, about the wonderful drive by automobile she had just enjoyed from the women's prison at Lichtenburg "through the blooming landscape of Saxony" to Ravensbrück.[1] The experience of these early arrivals in the recently opened women's concentration camp, those arriving by automobile, was apparently unique. Subsequent arrivals all talk of traveling by train, although until 1944 most prisoners rode in regular passenger cars, rather than cattle or freight cars. When they arrived at the Fürstenberg railroad station, they were met by SS men and female overseers, who directed their disembarking, then accompanied them on the roughly three kilometer (two mile) trip to the camp. Occasionally, they were taken there in trucks, but most often they were marched, sometimes carrying their luggage.[2]

First Impressions

The new prisoners were generally marched on a back street shortcut, but sometimes they were taken right through town. Carmen Buatell, from Spain, described being marched through "a pretty little village full of flowers, with white gardenias on the window sills. Fürstenberg. Is there really a prettier village on earth?"[3] Many times these marches occurred at night, but when they happened in daylight, they inevitably attracted the attention of the townspeople. One Fürstenberger who was a young boy at the time remembered the sight: female overseers with big dogs driving hordes of women through the village streets.[4] Most prisoners did not note any particular response other than curiosity. However, in January 1944, as a group was being marched through town, Lolf Heinecke later recalled that children threw stones at them and townspeople spat at them, pointing fingers and yelling "traitors."[5] It was not the only time such an incident occurred.[6]

After passing through the village, the throng had to make a broad right turn in order to go around the lake (Schwedtsee). Continuing, they marched past "pretty little cottages, spread through the pine trees, which gave the place a resort look."[7] Indeed, Fürstenberg and the surrounding area had long been a resort area, popular with the boating crowd, who still today enjoy its location on Mecklenburg's chain of lakes.

After a few more minutes marching, with a nice view of the lake on the right and the homes of the SS officers on the left, the camp came into view. There was no "Work Makes You Free" sign above the gate,[8] but what most impressed new arrivals were the high walls, "so high you could not see the sky" according to one survivor.[9] They were perhaps not that high, but they were four to five meters (12–15 ft.), and for those inside they quite effectively blocked out any view of the surrounding countryside.

At this point, the new prisoners were just inside the gate, on the edge of what they would soon come to know as the roll-call grounds (*Appelplatz*). Antonia Bruha has left us this description of her first impressions:

A high, thick wall surrounds the camp. On it is stretched barbed wire. We later learned that this wire was electrically charged, day and night, in order to make escape impossible. On the one side lay a long wooden barracks, separated from the roll-call area by barbed wire. Through the open window we could see SS men and female overseers sitting. [This was the SS canteen.]

On the right-hand side stood a wooden barracks, into which we, one after the other, were summoned. A little further ahead we could see large cooking pots and we surmised that that must be the kitchen. To our left began a wide street that was bordered on both sides by wooden barracks. In the distance, above the wall, one could see treetops.[10]

The Trauma of Processing

If the newcomers were lucky, as Bruha's group was, they would be processed quickly, at least the same day. If not, they would wait. Nearly all prisoners arriving in the evening had to wait, standing, until the next day, and some waited even longer. At length, however, their processing would begin by their undressing and turning in everything: clothes, jewelry, money, suitcases—whatever they had brought with them. This would all be registered, but in reality they were unlikely to ever see their belongings again, "except in a few cases we saw our own clothes being worn by some of the higher-up prisoners."[11] This was particularly true for prisoners from Eastern Europe, for whom keeping this record was mostly *pro forma*.[12]

Following this, a pleasant surprise: showers. But then the nightmare really began. Each newcomer was inspected for lice, and at the slightest suggestion of their presence, the prisoner's head and body hair were shaved. Some women recalled how brusquely their pubic area was shaved, often leaving cuts and scratches.[13] The inspection and shaving was done by veteran inmates, most often Jehovah's Witnesses.[14] For nearly all the women, it was a traumatic experience; many of them cried.

Monica Jene, a French prisoner, admitted that the horror of having her head shaved "was greater than all the physical and psychological horrors which still awaited her."[15] Sara Tuvel, recently arrived with a transport of Jews from Budapest, could not sleep the first night in the camp, still preoccupied with what had happened to her. "Who was I without my hair?" she asked herself.[16] A group of French women cried at first, but then laughed and gave each other silly nicknames: "Sugar Loaf Dome," "Dobbin's Nobbin."[17] Certain categories of female inmates such as Gypsies and Jews were more likely than others to be shaved, whereas when a group of Norwegian women came in, none had their heads shaved.[18] But for some women the humiliation was simply too profound. Erika Buchmann, a perceptive observer of her surroundings, noted that one of the main reasons women committed suicide by throwing themselves on the electrically charged barbed wire was because they had just had their heads shaved.[19]

The most humiliating part of the processing was yet to come, and understandably many of the women remember their medical exam with a great deal of bitterness. To make matters worse, the women were often kept waiting for hours, naked, for the doctor(s) to arrive. Modern-day readers perhaps need to be reminded of the sense of modesty that prevailed at the time. If many Europeans have become open and relaxed about nudity in the later years of the twentieth century, this was decidedly not so in its earlier years. Many grandmothers had never been seen naked by their own granddaughters, let alone strangers. One young woman was so traumatized by having to go to the toilet in front of other people on the journey to Ravensbrück that she held it back as much as possible, and the result was that she arrived sick.[20] Many of the women cried as they were made to parade naked before not only SS doctors, but also SS soldiers. Many of the older women walked with heads lowered, not looking at anyone. They were frequently the butt of crude remarks by the on-looking *Herrenmenschen* (master-race types).[21] A Spanish prisoner, Neus Català, remembered that the medical examination involved the most humiliating

France Audoul, "Plundered and Shorn." From *Ravensbrück: 15,000 Femmes en Enfer.*

vaginal examination imaginable. It was as much a search for hidden valuables as it was a medical exam. Moreover, the same instrument was used on all the women without being disinfected.[22] Sometimes the examinations were substantive, and other times perfunctory. Fanny Marette remembered waiting for eight hours for the doctor to arrive, and all he did was check their teeth: "Who else but a German would strip 1,500 women, in the open air, at five o'clock in the morning, for the sole purpose of opening their mouths at one o'clock in the afternoon?"[23] Obviously, the SS were playing mind games, trying to break the will and spirit of the prisoners. In such a situation, Antonia Bruha's existential approach seems most appropriate: "What these men in their ostentatious uniforms say and do doesn't concern me, I say to myself. I'm not taking part in this. I'm not standing here naked with many others. It's all theater."[24]

France Audoul, "Waiting for the Dentist." From *Ravensbrück: 15,000 Femmes en Enfer.*

Theater, perhaps. But the play went on. Once a prisoner had been shaved, inspected, and sufficiently humiliated, she was issued a uniform (at least until 1943), placed in a category, given a number, and then assigned to the quarantine barracks for an unspecified period, typically about two to three weeks.

The period of quarantine was a vulnerable time for the new inmates. In theory, they could not leave their barracks and others could not come in, but in practice, there were experienced thieves who knew how to take advantage of inexperienced prisoners. Inmates quickly learned that they had to guard their few possessions constantly, even sleeping with their shoes under their heads, or they would be stolen by morning.[25]

It was at this point, too, that inmates would be contacted by one of several groups, most notably the international Communist organization.[26] They were particularly interested in establishing ties with women who had prior associations with Communism or who had sympathies with the organization and possessed useful skills. They could often secure favorable work and barracks assignments for women who met their qualifications.[27]

For any unfortunate woman who came into the camp already sick, the period of quarantine was especially dangerous. Unless she was a Special Prisoner (*Sonderhäftling*) she was unlikely to be given medical treatment. Moreover, given the unique characteristics of a group of newly arrived prisoners—depressed, homesick, confused—there were not yet the personal ties or support networks that might help sick and desperate individuals. The result, predictably, was that many sick newcomers did not survive more than a few days in the camp.[28]

The period of quarantine was also used by the camp administration to acquaint the newcomers with the rules and regulations of the camp. It was the responsibility of the Admissions Block Senior to explain these things, along with many other essential pieces of information, such as how to address superiors, how to make a bed properly, and how to wear one's kerchief.[29] Confounding the difficulties was that these orientation sessions were given mainly in German, and thus many foreign women remained somewhat confused about these matters until they had been in the camp for quite some time.

After a few weeks, the quarantine ended, and the women were assigned to a regular block or barracks, and generally, but not always, to a regular job. For most of the women, what they had been through was the most demeaning and humiliating episode of their lives. But for one newcomer, Hardy Kupferberg, a Jewish woman from Berlin who had spent months in hiding, being sent to Ravensbrück was a bit of a relief. She wasn't alone anymore. She was no longer in hiding. And, she remembered, "I was not hungry anymore."[30]

3

Green and Black Triangles: Criminals, Asocials and Gypsies

Aat Breur, "Gypsy Girl." From *Een verborgen herinnering*. Courtesy Dunya Breur.

Categories

One of the most important components of the processing of new prisoners was their placement into one of several distinct categories. Largely this was accomplished through information already received, which had been entered on the prisoner's personnel record. However, many women were given a brief interview at the time of their medical examination that corroborated data or could fill in gaps. The extent of some interviews was "Why are you here?"[1]

There were no borderline cases; the prisoner fit into one category or another. A woman incarcerated for killing her husband was a Criminal and would be assigned a green triangle. A prostitute was classified as an Asocial and would be given a black triangle. Socialists and Communists were Politicals and proudly wore the red triangle. Jehovah's Witnesses who refused to renounce their faith wore, equally proudly, a lavendar triangle.

Two other categories, blue for returning emigrants and pink for homosexuals, played no role at Ravensbrück. Nazi loathing of homosexuals appears to have been largely confined to male homosexuals. The records do not indicate that any Ravensbrück prisoner was ever assigned a pink triangle.[2]

Finally, Jews were assigned a yellow triangle, and over this was superimposed a second triangle for one of the above-mentioned categories or for "race defilement" (having had sex with an Aryan). Thus, Jews, unlike other prisoners, often had two categories (although many Jews were simply issued two yellow triangles). In any case, it was their categorization as Jews that really mattered and determined their placement in the camp.[3]

The assignment of a prisoner to one category or another was, in fact, subjective, and reflected both the whims of politics and the idiosyncracies of the Nazi state. "Special prisoners" were nearly always made Politicals, giving them access to the better blocks and work assignments. Nazi women and wives of Nazis who were arrested for fraud or embezzlement were not given a green triangle, but a red one, and were given quite preferential treatment.[4]

The assignment to a certain category was permanent, but not immutable. Two German sisters, Amelie and Gertrud Phillip, came into the camp as Politicals and were given comfortable jobs in the Payroll Office of the administration, handling the payroll acounts of the female overseers. But a few weeks into their new jobs it was learned that their father was Jewish. They were then ordered to wear the yellow triangle along with the red, and they lost their desirable positions.[5] The recategorization of prisoners was a constant procedure in the camp, a result of investigations as well as material supplied by informants, both of which worked to continually update a prisoner's personnel file. In August 1942, Margot Sara Motteck, who had been a Political Jew, was relabeled a race-defiling Jew. In November of that year, in an apparent flurry of recategorizing activity, some women who had been Asocials became Jehovah's Witnesses and vice versa, and a few Poles and ethnic Germans got their designations switched.[6] After working at the Siemens factory for a year and a half, Esther Bejarano was reclassifed from Jew to Political when it was learned that her grandmother was not Jewish. She was still a *Mischling* (of mixed race), but exchanging a yellow triangle for a red one allowed her to receive packages.[7]

In addition to one's triangle or "badge" (most inmates referred to it as a *Winkel*, meaning "chevron" or "stripe"), the prisoner was also assigned a number. This number went directly above the badge, and both were worn on the upper left sleeve. Since the numbers were assigned in order of date of arrival, they gave an immediate indication of seniority. For example, a prisoner who had been at Ravensbrück before 1941 would have a number no higher than 5,338, the last number assigned in 1940.[8] There was some prestige in having a low number. Other prisoners would sometimes remark: "Ah, she's an 8,000" . . . or 19,000, or whatever.[9] Seniority was sometimes translated into preferential treatment by SS personnel and fellow prisoners. Everyone, especially newcomers, valued experience.

Criminals

During the Weimar Republic, there had been a heated debate in Germany, prompted by some sensational mass murders, concerning the nature of criminals and the most appropriate methods to deal with crime and criminals. And like everything else in that short-lived democracy, the issue became polarized and politicized. In general, the left argued that criminality was a sickness and that lawbreakers could be rehabilitated. Conversely, the right took the position that criminals were born, not made by society, and that efforts to rehabilitate them were by and large a hopeless cause.[10]

On the level of public policy, the issue was settled by the coming to power of Adolf Hitler and the National Socialists in early 1933. The new regime acted quickly to purge society, not only of its violent offenders, but also of lower-level habitual criminals, especially those who had spent some years in prison. By the start of the war, green-triangle prisoners had become the largest single group in several of the concentration camps in Germany, including Dachau and Mauthausen.[11]

The campaign to round up criminals and isolate them from decent society, along with the criminalization of prostitution and abortion, greatly increased the number of women being incarcerated in the 1930s in Germany. The laws against abortion, which had been on the books since 1871, but had been only leniently enforced during the Weimar period, were tightened in 1933 and then enforced according to racial criteria. This meant that "Aryan women" who obtained or even sought abortions, along with medical doctors, midwives, nurses, or other health care professionals who aided them, were all engaged in criminal acts.[12] So were those who dispensed birth control information or operated clinics for the treatment of sexual dysfunction. Germany, and Berlin in particular, which had been the center for the international movement for sex research and sex reform, in early 1933 lost its status overnight. The practitioners and advocates of this movement for sexual enlightenment and female liberation who, incidentally, were disproportionately Jewish, mostly emigrated or were arrested. Not surprisingly, a significant number were women.[13]

This rising female prisoner population was a key factor in the regime's decision to create a concentration camp for women at Ravensbrück. When the camp opened, one of the first Prisoner-Strength Reports (*Gefangenen Stärkemeldung*) dated 24 June 1939, showed 124 criminals out of a total camp population of 1,048, nearly 12%. While the absolute number of criminals at Ravensbrück would rise steadily for the next few years, proportionately it would never again come close to being even 10%.[14] Wanda Kiedrzynska, whose statistical study of 25,028 women prisoners at Ravensbrück is considered a definitive work, noted that only 506 of the total, or 2% were criminals.[15]

These figures for criminals at Ravensbrück would need to be revised slightly upward, since most women arrested for prostitution or abortion were placed, not in the Criminal category, but among the Asocials. Nevertheless, it is clear that Ravensbrück never had anywhere near the proportion of criminals that many of the other camps had; they were always a small minority.

However, in its initial stages, Ravensbrück followed the model established by the existing camps, that of encouraging the criminal element to play key roles in the prisoner administration, allowing them to act as a kind of surrogate force of terror for the SS. Whether they were directly recruited by the SS to serve in these positions, as they were in other camps, is not known with certainty, but such was probably the case. This predominance lasted until about 1942, ending around the time that decisions were made to change Ravensbrück from a protective custody labor camp into more of a slave-labor economic enterprise. Denise Clark no doubt spoke for many women when she noted, "The worst fellow prisoners, of course, were the German criminals."[16] Others thought them to be crude and undisciplined, always fighting, and stealing even from each other.[17]

But if living with them was horrible, having to serve under a "green-badge" block senior was hell. In one block, a "Green Blockova" forced "non-Green women" to sleep with "*Schmuckstücke*"[18] (filthy, diseased women — see chapter 14). In the Admissions Block, the long time block senior was an Austrian criminal, "Goldhansi," called that both because of her teeth, as well as her habit of stealing gold and jewelry from newcomers. Eventually she was shot by the SS when her gold hoard was discovered, but not until she had caused the deaths of quite a few women and made miserable the lives of many more.[19]

Erika Buchmann, a Political and sometime block senior, has given us the fullest description we have of any green badge at Ravensbrück. This was a professional criminal named Martha, a woman of about fifty. Martha "was a stranger to no vice," but she was quite enterprising and far from stupid. She would often be seen surrounded by a small audience whom she lectured on how to steal, swindle fellow inmates, and generally live well without doing much actual work. For this bit of instruction, her trainees paid her with small pieces of wurst or margarine. Her job in the block was cleaning the toilets. Here she "pursued lesbian opportunities," again for a price. "In this connection, she knew the individual wishes of the girls quite precisely." In addition, she was the "Postman of Love" (*Postillon d'amour*), organizing secret exchanges of letters between the women's and men's camps, a highly risky venture for all involved, but it allowed Martha to considerably improve her standard of living in the camp. Eventually, Martha killed another inmate and was executed by the SS, reportedly by being hanged.[20]

Partly because the criminals were so hated and despised, little is really known about them. None of them, to my knowledge, wrote a memoir, and none appears to have been the subject of a biography. A 1994 exhibit at the Ravensbrück memorial that chronicled the lives of over two dozen Ravensbrück inmates totally omitted any discussion of this category of prisoner.

Asocials

Betty Leue had had a hard life. When she was a child, her mother died, the victim of spousal abuse. When her father remarried, her stepmother repeatedly abused her until she left home as a teenager. She wandered around, but had difficulty holding jobs. While she was pregnant, the father of her unborn child drowned. After her child was born, in a Berlin jail cell, she again took to the streets. She later married, and had two more children, but her alcoholic husband could not support her. The family lived on public welfare, supplemented by what little she could earn by doing odd jobs or begging. After losing custody of her children and getting a divorce, she took a job in a munitions factory at Kiel. There she had an affair with a Dutch forced laborer, an illegal act for both of them. In 1942, she was arrested, condemned by a court for vagrancy (*Herumtreiberei*), and in February 1943 was dropped off at Ravensbrück and categorized as an Asocial.[21]

Another young woman, Mariechen Schneeman, was arrested for "malicious behavior" in 1941. Her crime: wearing a Hitler Youth badge without being a real member. Jailed, then released, in the summer of 1942 she supposedly contracted syphilis, then was jailed again for not visiting a doctor. In January 1943, she was registered as an Asocial prisoner at Ravensbrück, and after two months was never heard from again.[22]

The Asocials at Ravensbrück were an extremely diverse lot. Some, like the women discussed above, were arguably victims of circumstances. Others were women who had trouble keeping jobs or who avoided work (*Arbeitsscheu*) and who apparently lacked any network of family support. Many had had illegitimate children and were dependent upon public or charitable assistance. Some were alcoholics. Many had been prostitutes. Almost all were poor.[23]

The National Socialist state never legally nor clearly defined what was meant by "Asocial," although a decree of 14 October 1937 approached the issue in a general way by noting: "Asocials are those who do not fit into the community, even if they are not criminally inclined...."[24] A circular from the Reich Criminal Police Office of 8 February 1938 approved the incarceration of persons exhibiting a "predilection for criminal behavior," whether or not they had a criminal record. Later decrees established such criteria for detention as "a dissolute lifestyle," "slovenliness," and even "weakness of character."[25] According to Christa Schikorra, a specialist on the topic, "it was a leftover category for all those peculiarities that did not correspond to the Nazi definition of a healthy people."[26] In practice, anybody who violated the "norms" of society could be identified as Asocial. Simply put: the National Socialists wanted to cleanse their society of all the creeps, slackers, whores, bums, troublemakers, and general misfits. And, like the Queen of Hearts in *Alice in Wonderland*, **they** would decide who qualified.

The Asocials were always a large group at Ravensbrück. In 1940, they were the largest single category, comprising about one-third of the camp population. But from that point, the Politicals began to far outnumber them. Once again, however, the numbers must be qualified. Many women were brought to Ravensbrück and categorized as Asocial who were really not. By definition, Gypsies were Asocials, and since, unlike Jews, Gypsies had no separate category, they were issued the black badge. Moreover, since Jews needed to have a second triangle (to complete the six-pointed star), and since the definition of Asocial was so broad, it was often convenient to give them a black badge to fasten over their yellow one.[27]

Once in the camp, the ostracism continued. Unlike many of the other categories of prisoners, particularly the Politicals, who had a well-established common identity and even cameraderie, the Asocials had neither. Moreover, nearly all the other prisoners felt an abhorrence for them and tried to distance themselves from them. In part, what was occurring was that the Nazis' own prejudices were being adopted by the prisoners themselves, as many viewed the Asocials as lazy, corrupt, filthy, and generally despicable.[28]

While on the outside, prostitutes had belonged to a kind of inde-
cent subculture, in the camp they comprised the lowest rung of
camp society. In the absence of men, many reportedly turned to
lesbianism, further degrading themselves in the eyes of fellow
prisoners.[29] This is a sensitive and difficult issue, particularly as
the sources for this information (other prisoners) are overwhelmingly unsympathetic to Asocials in general and prostitutes in particular. There is a stereotype of the "prostitute with a heart of
gold" and another stereotype of the mean, drug-addicted, criminally inclined low-life type of prostitute. It is tempting to say that
the reality lies in between, but it probably doesn't. Many indicators suggest that the average prostitute at Ravensbrück was a
rather tough type who likely had a jail record and who had
learned to survive in the dangerous, back-stabbing, crime-infest-
ed world of sex-for-hire. Nanda Herbermann, who was room senior
and later block senior in the "Whores' Block" (*Dirnenblock*), developed a real distaste for her wards on account of their general can-
tankerousness, which included tattling, stealing, and almost constant fighting.[30] Margarete Buber-Neumann considered the average prostitute at Ravensbrück "something of a cretin,"[31] but then
she had high standards for everyone, herself included.

In the early years of the camp, Asocials and most other prisoner categories were kept separate from each other, each forming
their own blocks. Buber-Neumann, who was a Political with
seniority (No. 4208), was appointed one of the room seniors of the
Asocial Block in 1941. It was a depressing experience for her:

> The Asocials squabbled incessantly, sometimes accusing
> each other of having charged low rates in their former
> careers. Thieving was rampant. They would inform on each
> other for the flimsiest reasons and the smallest advantages.
> They constantly disobeyed rules, even though they knew they
> would be punished. And, in general, they resisted and resent-
> ed all of their room senior's efforts to impose some kind of
> order and discipline on them.[32]

Later, when the camp became overcrowded, the prisoner categories in many of the blocks became more mixed. If Asocials were
in a mixed barracks, they were distrusted and often blamed for
missing items. When Antonia Bruha's toiletry case was stolen
while she showered, another prisoner remarked: "The Asocials,
which we unfortunately have around us here, steal anything they
can get their hands on."[33] An Italian prisoner, Lidia Rolfi, got separated from her fellow Italians and was put in a block with mainly black and green badges. It was a horrible experience for her.
She feared even going to the washroom because she would have to
fight to defend herself. She would wash with one hand and hold on
to her things with the other.[34]

One wonders what accounts for the brutality with which these
women, the Criminals and Asocials, treated their fellow inmates.
Oppressed themselves, they seem to have simply turned things
around and brutalized others. Brian Dunn has suggested another
explanation: No strangers to the world of hard knocks, they did
not suffer the same kind of psychic trauma that other prisoners
did, making it easier for them to adjust and adapt to camp life.[35]

The Youth Camp

Beginning in 1942, a section of Ravensbrück known as Uckermark, located about a kilometer (two-thirds of a mile) from the
main barracks area, was designated as a Youth Camp, a kind of
reform school for wayward girls, most of whom were teenagers. It
was technically not just a camp for Asocials, and indeed the young
women who were assigned there were neither categorized nor
issued badges of any kind. But in practice, nearly all of them fit
the general definition of Asocials, that is of young women who
could not or would not become fully a part of the folkish community.

Like their elder counterparts, they were a diverse group. A few
were offspring of opposition leaders. Eva Rademacher's father was

a dissident politician, and she herself had already offended the authorities by having Jewish friends and belonging to the Swing Youth in Hamburg.[36] Many had reputations for sexual promiscuity, generally involving German soldiers, but in a few cases foreign workers. In fact, of the first 500 girls registered at Uckermark, 220 had venereal disease.[37] One seventeen-year-old was recommended by the Munich Youth Office because she was "a born criminal." Her parents had criminal records, and she now faced her third conviction for theft. Most of the young women sent to Uckermark were referred by welfare authorities, who were given the opportunity of unburdening themselves of their most bothersome cases.[38]

The complicity of welfare and public health authorities in the incarceration of these young women is a delicate and controversial issue that merits some elaboration. Recently, an American historian, Atina Grossmann, has demonstrated that by the late 1920s, the notions of "fit" and "unfit," of "responsible" and "asocial" women had gained widespread acceptance in Germany. This dichotomous thinking, and the ensuing belief that the "unfit" and the "asocial" needed to be dealt with, perhaps by sterilization, certainly by incarceration, had come to permeate not only popular thinking, but also the outlook of social workers and health care professionals, even of the political left.[39] Small wonder that the removal of these young women to a youth camp attracted such little attention, even by opponents of the regime.

In theory, these troubled girls were being sent to Uckermark for re-education and rehabilitation. There were female overseers, but the women who had the closest contact with them were called "educators" or "governesses" (*Erzieherinnen*). However, in practice, there was little emphasis on rehabilitation; almost no effort was made to deal with the psychological problems of the young inmates. The conditions were spartan, the discipline was draconic (any kind of chatting was forbidden, even in the evenings), and the main purpose served by the camp was to isolate these *gemeinschaftsfremd* (literally: "estranged from the community") elements from decent society. A few girls were released to the custody of their parents, but it was a pitifully small cohort. Of some 1,200 girls incarcerated at Uckermark, only 80 (6%) were released. When the Youth Camp was closed in 1944, most of its inhabitants were transferred to the main camp.[40]

Gypsies

When the concentration camp system was created and the categorization of prisoners first envisaged, Gypsies were assigned a brown triangle which was exclusively theirs. However, this lasted only a short while, and by the time Ravensbrück was opened, they were simply registered as Asocials and given a black badge. The daily roll-call reports contained no separate data on Gypsies, making it difficult for later researchers to determine their numbers. But there was, in Nazi terms, a perceived logic in categorizing them as Asocials: They shunned regular jobs. They were frequently in trouble with the police, usually for reported thefts. They resisted or at least ignored the many ways in which the modern state wields authority: They disliked having to get official approval for this or that or obtain licenses. Most important, this small ethnic group of thirty to thirty-five thousand (.05 percent of the German population in 1933) loved the free life, the life of nomads.

Today, in Germany, the polite terms for Gypsies are "Sinti" and "Roma," referring to two distinct groups. Most Gypsies call themselves Roma, although in England and America the term "Traveler" is sometimes preferred.[41] We shall continue to use the name "Gypsy" in this study, mainly because all the quotes and references use this term.

Prejudice against Gypsies was not a new thing in the 1930s. In Europe, the prejudice goes back into the late medieval period when these darker-skinned nomads first arrived, almost certainly from India originally. Many of the Gypsies were brought in as slaves, and in fact the enslavement of Gypsies in certain parts of southeastern Europe lasted into the nineteenth century. This undoubtedly contributed to the marginalization of Gypsies within European life, which continues into the present. Rumors and stories about how Gypsies cheated the locals, but never each other, and how they survived by theft and deceit were, and indeed still are, common.[42]

But the allegations of theft and other illegal activities are only part of the story. Gypsies were craftsmen, they had businesses, they were entertainers, they did many of the things which other people do, but they did not like to settle down, and they maintained a "we versus the world" attitude, particularly in the face of continuing prejudice. Gypsies have always known that they were distrusted and disliked, and their response has been to turn further inward and not to trust the *Gadje* (non-Gypsy).[43] Isabel Fonseca, who achieved considerable success in attempting to examine Gypsy society from the inside, has put the issue directly: "The Gypsy is the quintessential stranger."[44]

In the 1920s and 30s, the same forces pushing for a biological explanation for criminality were also pushing for a biological/ physiological solution to the "Gypsy Question." However, the Third Reich issued almost no legislation specifically aimed at Gypsies. Rather, they were rounded up, arrested, incarcerated, and ghettoized on the basis of existing legislation, particularly that intended for Jews, such as the 1935 Nuremberg Laws. Well before Jews were being confined in the camps simply for being Jewish, Gypsies were being herded into government-run Gypsy camps, partly to get them out of sight, as during the 1936 Berlin Olympics, but also to control what were considered their normal criminal activities.[45] Then, in 1937, Dr. Robert Ritter, a psychiatrist, took over the Research Center for Racial Hygiene and Population Biology in Berlin, which became the main agency to "scientifically" examine the Gypsy question. In 1940, he wrote:

> Further, results of our investigation have allowed us to
> characterize the Gypsies as being a people of entirely primi-
> tive ethnological origins, whose mental backwardness makes
> them incapable of real social adaptation. . . . The Gypsy ques-
> tion can only be solved when the main body of asocial and
> good-for-nothing Gypsy individuals of mixed blood is collected
> together in large labor camps and kept working there, and
> when the further breeding of this population of mixed blood is
> stopped once and for all.[46]

SS chief Heinrich Himmler seized on Ritter's pronouncements, particularly its distinction between "pure" Gypsies and those of mixed blood. As late as 1942, Himmler was still trying to secure exemptions for pure Gypsies as well as for those who had become assimilated. But some party leaders, Joseph Goebbels and Martin Bormann in particular, opposed these exemptions, and eventually all but ignored them. Local police did not like making fine distinctions.[47] However, one of the many peculiarities of life in the Third Reich is that sedentary and assimilated German Gypsies, especially those who held regular jobs, were generally left alone; many survived the war.[48]

Gypsies were in Ravensbrück almost from the beginning. In late 1939, a group of 440 Austrian Gypsies, mainly from the Burgenland area, were sent to Ravensbrück. By early 1940, there were more than five hundred Gypsy prisoners there.[49] At that time they were in Block 22 by themselves, and relations between Gypsies and other prisoners do not appear to have been particularly problematic. Most of these women worked in one of the SS textile factories.

In 1942–1943, Ravensbrück's Gypsy population, along with other Gypsies remaining in the Reich, were deported east, to the new Gypsy camp at Auschwitz-Birkenau. This was the result of further studies by Ritter and his assistant, Eva Justin, which showed that the Sinti (German Gypsies) were virtually all *Mischlinge* anyhow.[50] The study by Ritter and Justin, along with Himmler's concurrence, cleared the way, not only for the deportation of Gypsies from the Reich, but also for their extermination.[51] Unlike other groups, the Gypsies were allowed to stay together as families in their camp at Auschwitz-Birkenau, but this was only a prelude to tragedy. Of the roughly twenty-three thousand inmates of the Auschwitz "Gypsy Camp," about twenty thousand either died of disease and malnutrition or were murdered.[52]

In 1944, with the war in the east closing in on them, the SS stepped up their "selections" at Auschwitz, condemning many prisoners to the gas chambers, but sending other work-capable prisoners to camps in the west. On three occasions in 1944, there were transports of Gypsies to Ravensbrück, totaling 1,107 women, mostly between the ages of eighteen and twenty-five.[53]

The Gypsies traveled to Ravensbrück still in family groups, but upon arrival they were split up—the women and children staying in the main camp, the men and older boys going to the men's camp, at least temporarily. Ravensbrück was a different camp in 1944 than it had been two or three years earlier, and the introduction of over a thousand Gypsy women intensified this difference. For one thing, the overcrowding had already reached horrible dimensions. For another, now Gypsies would not have a barracks all to themselves, as they had earlier. There would be one predominantly Gypsy block, but the other Gypsies would be parceled out among five different blocks. Compounding the problems, some boys of thirteen and fourteen had been allowed to stay with their mothers. They now had to sleep between the women and even shower with them, a hard pill for Gypsy women to swallow, given their traditional modesty.[54] But what choice was there?

The re-admission of hundreds of Gypsy women into Ravensbrück, particularly since many were scattered among different blocks, awakened prejudices and caused considerable unrest. Many prisoners later mentioned the Gypsies' reputed inclination toward theft: "They stole like ravens and taught their children to do the same,"[55] one woman noted. Women who were assigned to the predominantly Gypsy block complained that they had to sleep with their bread rations under their heads to keep them from being stolen.[56] Some prisoners voiced the old prejudice that Gypsies were by nature dirty and didn't mind living in filth.[57] For example, a Polish prisoner, Maria Plater-Skassa, expressed temporary relief at being sent to the Infirmary for experimental operations because there were "no shouting overseers and no dirty Gypsies there."[58]

Only one Gypsy, as far as we know, has written an account of her experiences in the concentration camps. Ceija Stojka was twelve years old when the Gestapo took away her father in 1941 (he died soon after in Dachau), and later that year (or perhaps 1942—she is vague on dates), the rest of the family was sent to Auschwitz. Ceija had her prison number, Z6399 (Z stood for *Zigeuner*, the German word for Gypsy), tattooed on her arm. (At Ravensbrück, prisoners were never tattooed.) At a selection, Ceija followed her mother's advice, telling the camp authorities: "I'm a good worker and I'm sixteen years old." It worked. She and her family were sent to Ravensbrück, categorized as Asocial-Workshy. "But," she asked, "how could I be work-shy? I was just a kid."[59]

At Ravensbrück, the older boys were sent to other camps, and the girls were put to work in the SS textile factories. Ceija worked in the sewing room, alongside a girl her own age named Resi. They became friends, and since Resi had no family, the Stojkas adopted her, unofficially, but substantively. Making room for another family member never bothered Gypsies.

Their block-senior was a green-badge named Ria, about thirty years old. She was kind to Ceija, particularly when the young girl began to help her by cleaning the toilets and scrubbing the floor. Soon Ceija had "a dear Auntie" who gave her leftover food, a good potato, and an extra blanket.[60] So much for stereotypes.

One day, shortly before New Year's 1945, the overseers came to the Gypsies and told them that the authorities in Berlin had agreed to release any of them who would "volunteer" to be sterilized. Almost all agreed to this and signed the consent form. One day they came for Ceija and her sisters. They were taken to the infirmary, but nothing could be done because of an electrical failure. Her mother attributed this to divine intervention.[61]

The forced sterilization of Gypsy girls must rank as one of the most insidious of Nazi programs, and followed logically from the "research" and conclusions drawn by Ritter and Justin. In theory, the women were volunteers, although none of them were ever released, as promised. Moreover, many of the young women (or their mothers, who had to sign for them) didn't truly understand the procedure. Wanda P. was told it was "just an examination" using an X-ray machine. The twenty-two year-old agreed to it.[62] But even when some of the infirmary's prisoner workers explained to them what was really going on, the Gypsies would not listen to them, so desperate were they for their freedom.[63]

Between 120 and 140 Gypsy women were sterilized in Ravensbrück, almost all in January 1945. The procedure was done in one of several ways: by spraying a chemical solution into the uterus,[64] by using a high-powered X-ray machine,[65] or by the use of a "high tension apparatus" in which one electrode was placed inside the vagina and the other over the abdominal wall by the ovaries.[66] It was experimental medicine, to say the least. Prof. Carl Clauberg, from Berlin, convinced the authorities that the X-ray technique was simple and effective, despite the fact that a number of the women got very ill as a result, and some died.[67]

The Gypsy experience under the Nazis has reinforced their old "us versus the world" outlook, and has driven them further inward in their thinking than ever. This has made it difficult for researchers, who have frequently had a hard time penetrating the barriers created by understandable suspiciousness and even hostility to outsiders. In recent years, however, there has been some movement away from this, as some Gypsy spokespersons like Romani Rose have stepped forth and encouraged cooperation, particularly for purposes of historical research and commemmoration. The publication, in 1988, of Ceija Stoika's autobiography was an important step in this direction, and hopefully will be followed by other memoirs and oral histories that will shed more light on what is rightly called "the Gypsy Holocaust."

CHAPTER

Lavender Triangles: Jehovah's Witnesses

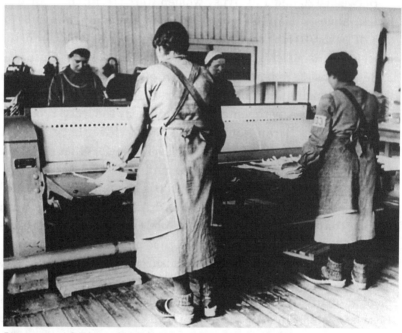

Inmates working in the Camp Laundry. These women are probably
Jehovah's Witnesses, since that group held a virtual monopoly on jobs
there. (SS Photo.) *Sammlungen Mahn- und Gedenkstätte Ravensbrück.*
Courtesy U.S. Holocaust Memorial Museum Photo Archives.

Intransigence and Persecution

In January 1942, there occurred the first incident in the history of the Ravensbrück concentration camp that was called a revolt, at least by other prisoners. It was not an armed uprising, nor even close to it. Rather, it was an organized act of passive resistance by the Jehovah's Witnesses women, usually called *Bifos*, a shortened form of *Bibelforscher* or "Bible Students." They had always refused to do anything having direct military value, but now they refused even to sew buttons on SS uniforms or to load straw intended for SS horses. In addition, they refused to stand at the command "Attention" at roll call or even during a visit from Himmler. Their reasoning was that they did not stand up in awe and reverence for man, but only for Jehovah.

The women were severely disciplined for their defiance. They were put in the Bunker, then in the Punishment Block. Food was withheld from them. They were made to stand long hours in the snow. Some were beaten. Some died. Still, they persevered in their revolt.[1]

The Jehovah's Witnesses became an outlawed organization in Germany in April 1933. Only two years earlier they had changed the name of their organization from "The International Bible Researchers Association" (*International Bibelforscher-Vereinigung*), to Jehovah's Witnesses (*Zeugen Jehovahs*), but many people continued to call them Bible Students or Bible Readers. The Nazis never called them Jehovah's Witnesses. Their records always referred to them by their original initials, IBV, considered, perhaps, an innocuous and unattractive designation.

There were about twenty thousand Jehovah's Witnesses in Germany in early 1933. They were politically neutral, but in their refusal to give the "German Greeting" ("Heil Hitler"), to take the oath to Hitler (or any other secular authority), to join National Socialist organizations, or (after 1935) even the army, they were considered by the new regime to be a subversive force. Outlawing the organization made it easy to arrest those who still belonged to it.[2]

And arrested they were, in huge numbers relative to the size of the organization. Probably half of their members were imprisoned by the Nazis. The Jehovah's Witnesses responded by creating an underground organization to continue publishing and distributing their religious material, but this underground effort appears not to have been very subtle, and many of its adherents were found out. By 1936–1937, the state was taking away the children of Jehovah's Witnesses, assigning them to foster homes or orphanages where they would be better taught Nazi ideals.[3]

Jehovah's Witnesses women were well represented in Moringen and Lichtenburg, the precursor camps to Ravensbrück. Actually, the majority of concentration camp inmates who were incarcerated in the period between 1933 and 1937 were released. After a period of re-education, they could go home, subject, of course, to surveillance. The Jehovah's Witnesses could have gone home, too. All they had to do was sign a statement renouncing their beliefs. A few did this, but the great majority did not, and by the time Ravensbrück opened in May 1939, the slightly over four hundred Jehovah's Witnesses formed a hard core of true believers from which there would be almost no defections.

The Jehovah's Witnesses' mind-set is not an easy one for modernists or secular humanists to fathom, nor was it particularly easy for fellow inmates who did not share their views. They were often admired for their steadfastness, but considered "religious fanatics,"[4] or even mentally sick.[5] But there is a basis for their position, and it is worth considering.

Jehovah's Witnesses believe that this world is essentially a struggle between the forces of Satan and those of Jehovah. Humans must prove their dedication to Jehovah through living a life of integrity and good works. Only those who refuse to compromise with Satan and his forces will gain immortality.

In the 1930s, the Jehovah's Witnesses looked upon the Nazi state as the work of Satan. There could be no accommodation, no compromise with this Anti-Christ. When this state began to persecute them, another of their principles came into action: Humans must prove their faith under pressure. Martyrdom was not just preferable to surrender; it was expected of them. Gertrud Pötzinger acknowledged: "We have accepted this burden as a trust from God."[6]

Jehovah's Witnesses women not only accepted their role as martyrs, they exulted in it. In one of the first acts of defiance inside a concentration camp, the Jehovah's Witnesses women at Moringen refused to turn out to listen to a speech by Hitler. When the authorities threatened to punish them, other inmates attempted to "reason" with the women. Nothing doing. The Jehovah's Witnesses' response: "[We] can have only one *Führer* and that is Jehovah. Listening to a speech by another *Führer* would be a betrayal." They were punished severely for their non-compliance.[7] Late in the war, Margarete Buber-Neumann, the former block senior of the Jehovah's Witnesses, learned that Anna Lück, a Jehovah's Witness, was on a selection list to be sent away for extermination. Buber-Neumann went to her and encouraged her for the sake of her family to go to the authorities and sign the required statement. When Lück did this, the other Witnesses were outraged at Buber-Neumann and refused to cooperate any further with her.[8]

When the Ravensbrück camp opened in May 1939, Jehovah's Witnesses were the largest single category. However, their numbers were soon outdistanced, first by Asocials, and then by Politicals. In the early stages of the camp's history, they were assigned jobs much like those of other prisoners: unloading coal from barges, hauling sand for construction purposes, and working in agriculture. But by 1941, a trend was already observable of assigning them as house maids and cleaning women, particularly in the homes of SS officers. After all, they spoke German (fewer than one percent of Jehovah's Witnesses were non-Germans). There was no need to worry about theft by any of them, given their religious scruples, and they were clean and orderly.

Their barracks was always considered a model of order, cleanliness, peace, and quiet, although lacking some of the luxuries and refinements of the elite blocks. Their longtime block senior, Buber-Neumann, a Political, wrote: "And now I was in charge of this complicated purgatory of cleanliness and order." But, as she admitted, running this block went "like clockwork." Her decisions were accepted without argument. There was no stealing among the Jehovah's Witnesses or betraying each other. Most of them, she noted, were of peasant background: "simple-minded women of little or no education," but absolutely trustworthy.[9]

Under Commandant Koegel, there had been some nasty incidents involving Jehovah's Witnesses, including the January 1942 "revolt." Shortly after the start of the war, in late 1939, Commandant Koegel held a special roll call just for the *Bifos*. He then ordered all those who refused to sew for "our soldiers" to go to the other side of a line. Everyone went, with no exceptions. Everyone was punished. That winter, the Jehovah's Witnesses were only issued summer dresses, and their food rations were cut as well.[10]

On another occasion, during a particularly long roll call, the Jehovah's Witnesses women all lay down on the ground. At this, the overseer ordered other prisoners to fetch pails and pour cold water on them, but the Jehovah's Witnesses would not budge. Again, they were punished severely, being placed in the Bunker, with deaths resulting.[11] Still, there was no movement to compromise, let alone give in.

The "Volunteer" Prisoners

In mid-1942, *SS-Obersturmführer* Fritz Suhren replaced Koegel as camp commandant. Under Suhren, different arrangements were made to deal with the Jehovah's Witnesses. They now were given, almost exclusively, assignments that took them outside the main camp, particularly as service personnel in the homes of SS officers and their families, but also in gardens and other facilities near the camp. They were even allowed to come and go without supervision, the envy of all other inmates. Camp officials referred to them now as "volunteers," since they could return home by signing a piece of paper.[12] They were also allowed, within limits, to select their own block and room seniors.[13] What we do not know is why, when, and how these specific arrangements came about. Almost all of the SS administrative records are missing, destroyed in the closing stages of the war. It seems clear that Suhren recognized the futility of trying to break the will of the Jehovah's Witnesses and simply made an agreement with them: We will put you in positions where trust is required and you must promise not to take advantage of this.

In general, this accommodation worked for both sides, but it did not head off all problems. In 1943, the Jehovah's Witnesses objected, on religious grounds, to the inclusion of blood sausage in their meals. But now there was no Bunker, no Punishment Block, and there were no beatings. Instead, the SS punished the *Bifos* by putting one hundred Asocials in their block. The Asocials stole from them, cheated them, and even denounced them, but the Jehovah's Witnesses responded by being kind to them, even converting a few, until the SS reassigned the Asocials.[14]

If the SS could punish the Jehovah's Witnesses by putting problem prisoners with them, they could reward favored prisoners by putting them with the Jehovah's Witnesses. When a group of thirty Norwegian women was sent to Ravensbrück in 1943, they were put in Block 12, one of the Jehovah's Witnesses' blocks. The Norwegians objected, moderately, to the hymn-singing and Bible-reading, but they appreciated Block 12's other qualities: plenty of order and cleanliness, and no stealing.[15] In fact, on those occasions when outside inspectors, such as officials from the Red Cross, would come into the camp, they were nearly always shown a Jehovah's Witnesses' barracks, "free of even a speck of dust."[16]

After 1943, the Jehovah's Witnesses became a kind of privileged element at Ravensbrück. Certain jobs in the camp became virtually *Bifo* monopolies: checking incoming prisoners for lice, working in the camp laundry, and, most important, working in the homes of SS officers. They worked as cleaners, nannies, and general servants for the SS officers and their families. "In their dedication, industriousness, absolute honesty, and in their strict obedience to SS commands, the camp authorities could not have dreamed up more ideal slaves," noted Buber-Neumann.[17]

The camp administration appears to have appreciated the Jehovah's Witnesses women. One telling piece of evidence is this: while other categories of prisoners were frequently shuttled from main camp to subcamp and even to other major camps, the Jehovah's Witnesses were not. They were kept at the main camp at Ravensbrück.

Gertrud Pötzinger's life story is a testimony to the Jehovah's Witnesses' spirit. Once the Nazis came to power in 1933, she became active in the Jehovah's Witnesses' underground organization. In 1935, she was arrested, only three months after marrying, but she refused to sign anything renouncing her beliefs, and so was imprisoned. In 1941, she was brought to Ravensbrück and was held there until 1945. One day, probably in late 1943, she had to report to Commandant Suhren, who interviewed her, then assigned her to the household of SS *Sturmbahnführer* Kiener. There she worked for many months, primarily as a nanny for his children. One day Kiener lectured her on the *Führer's* ideals: "Strength through joy," "Work makes you free," "My honor is my loyalty." Then he noted that these were also her ideals as a Jehovah's Witness. When he asked her what she would do with the children if the Russians broke through, she answered: "The same as I do now." He thanked her, knowing he could count on her. About a week before the Russians did break through, Frau Pötzinger agreed to accompany the Kiener family to Munich, continuing to care for the children. There, in May 1945, she was liberated and allowed to rejoin her husband, just released from the Mauthausen Concentration Camp.[18]

CHAPTER 5

Yellow Triangles: The Jews

Badge worn by a Jewish inmate. *Sammlungen Ravensbrück.*
Courtesy *Mahn- und Gedenkstätte Ravensbrück.*

German Anti-Semitism

The long and torturous journey of the Jews to Ravensbrück and other concentration camps of the Nazi system began, like that of the Gypsies, many centuries earlier. In medieval Europe, the exclusion of the Jews from certain occupations and their forced settlement into the various Jewish quarters (*Judenviertel*) were primarily aspects of the more general compartmentalization of society. Each component had its place, and the Jews had theirs. But unlike the other components, the Jews were seen as "outsiders," people who were perceived to have separated themselves from Christianity and Christian living. In times of crisis, of which the most spectacular example is the Black Death of the fourteenth century, the wrath of peasant as well as noble was focused on these outsiders, for whom no crime was too outrageous not to be believed.

Following the French Revolution, the emancipation of Jews was a part of the general restructuring of society that was meant to free Europe from the artificial divisions and constraints of the *ancien régime*. Not only were the privileges of the hereditary elite removed, but the other groups and classes, including Jews, were allowed to live wherever they wanted (or could afford) to and to pursue any vocations for which they qualified. Although the removal of anti-Jewish sentiments was hardly a priority for the reformers, the general feeling was that these sentiments would disappear as society moved inexorably in the direction of secularism and social assimilation.

In fact, in the nineteenth and twentieth centuries, European and other western societies did move in these directions. Society became more secular, and some groups which under the old regime had been discrete components of society melted away. Jews were certainly affected by these trends, particularly the drift toward social assimilation. By the turn of the twentieth century, in Western Europe, many Jews had intermarried, converted, or dropped out of the Jewish community, and were living lives identical to those of their non-Jewish neighbors.

By the 1920s, Germany's small (less than one percent of the total population) Jewish minority was overwhelmingly assimilated into German life. Intermarriage between Jews and non-Jews had become so common that some Jewish leaders were raising concerns about the future of the Jewish community.[1] Politically and in other ways, too, Germany's Jews had become largely mainstreamed. Zionism was not the significant issue that it was in Eastern Europe; few German Jews belonged to the movement. The largest Jewish organization was the Central Association for German Citizens of the Jewish Faith (*Zentralverein deutscher Staatsbürger jüdischen Glaubens*), a middle-of-the-road organization that attempted to maintain some degree of Jewish tradition while not rejecting assimilation.[2] But Jews could not escape from the dilemma imposed on them by anti-Semites: If they did not assimilate, they were suspect for being clannish and standoffish; if they did assimilate, especially if they were successful, they were accused of being pushy and trying to take over. Some anti-Semites saw intermarriage as part of a Jewish conspiracy to defile German blood and weaken the race.[3]

Probably the most powerful intellectual trends of the late nineteenth century, and certainly the most popularized, were Darwinism and its illegitimate (seeing as how Darwin rejected it) offspring, Social Darwinism. These had far-reaching impacts and permeated a great deal of Western thinking for at least two generations. Social Darwinism appeared to give a scientific basis, not only for racism, but also for attributing fixed characteristics, including physical properties and psychological behavior, to biological inheritance. In other words, humans were like they were because of their natures, and no amount of assimilating or educating could ever change this.[4] The notion held terrible implications, for in the hands of Social Darwinists it could be applied to any number of groups (criminals, the handicapped, vagrants, drunkards, Gypsies, Jews) both to explain their "natures" (and/or reasons for their marginality) and to offer remedies, which generally meant exclusion, one way or another.[5]

In the Germany of the 1920s, these currents combined with peculiar historical conditions (Germany's loss in the world war, the imposition of a harsh peace settlement, the instability of a new republican government, runaway inflation, to name just a few factors), and the mixture was extremely volatile.[6] In the circumstances of this polarized society, anti-Semitism flourished. It was far more than scapegoat-hunting. In the turmoil of the times, it was part of an ongoing effort to redefine who the Germans were and what kind of society was most appropriate for them. Nazi leaders understood that an anti-Jewish program was unlikely to bring forth significant public opposition.

Nazi Anti-Jewish Programs, 1933–1939

Once in power, the Nazis lost no time in assuring their followers that their anti-Semitic agenda was not just empty rhetoric. After the immediate enemies—Communists and Socialists—were brought under control, some of them being placed in the early makeshift concentration camps, the Nazis turned their attention to Germany's Jews.

These initial Nazi efforts to deal with the "Jewish Question" proceeded on two levels. On one level, that of hooliganism, Nazi thugs in the form of SA units harassed, humiliated, and beat up Jews. Some of this was spontaneous, or at least not directed by Hitler and the inner leadership, as a wave of gratuitous violence swept the country. A key component of this approach was the nationwide boycott of Jewish businesses and professions, which began on 1 April 1933. Again, the overzealous SA was the chief enforcer of this program, physically preventing non-Jews from entering Jewish places of business.[7] But, from the Nazis' point of view, the response of the public was disappointing, as many Germans showed minimal enthusiasm for the boycott or even ignored it altogether.[8]

The other level was that of legislation, allowing Hitler to achieve his goal of effecting a "legal revolution," or at least its appearance. Between April and October 1933, laws had been passed excluding any "non-Aryan" (initially, a person with at least one Jewish grandparent) from the civil service, certain legal positions, cultural and entertainment institutions, and the press. Further, a quota system (*Numerus clausus*) was imposed on Jewish students in institutions of higher education, limiting them to 1.5 percent of new admissions.[9]

The 1933 laws were but a prelude to what became known as the Nuremberg Laws, a series of laws passed in September 1935 that effectively removed the rights of citizenship from Germany's Jews. The most notorious of these laws was the "Law for the Protection of German Blood and Honor." This made marriages and even sexual relations between Jews and Aryans punishable offenses.[10] The Nuremberg Laws targeted Jews in particular, but they were also applied to other groups which did not have "German Blood," such as Gypsies and Negroes. The latter group, statistically miniscule, was mainly the result of relations between German women and black French soldiers from North Africa following World War One. In the mid-1930s, these "Rhineland Bastards," as the Nazis called them, were rounded up and sterilized almost without notice.[11]

Following the Nuremberg Laws, a whole range of laws and edicts were put into effect that very simply made it nearly impossible for Jews to live in Germany. They were not permitted to use public transportation. They were forbidden to enter public buildings. They could not own radios or woolen clothing. They were not allowed to own telephones or to use public phones. Eventually, Jews were forced to sell their businesses and property, often far below value (an action known as Aryanization). All of these methods were designed to pressure the Jews to emigrate, and many did. About 60,000 Jews left Germany in the first two years of Nazi rule. But about 10,000 of these returned in 1935, as the government appeared to moderate its stance against Jews. Then, following the Nuremberg Laws, emigration picked up again. By 1938, approximately one-third of Germany's Jews (150–170,000) had left the country.[12]

Nazi programs had a particular impact on Jewish women. In theory, all Jewish civil servants and medical doctors were dismissed, but in practice there were many exceptions granted initially, for veterans, for example. Thus, only 40 percent of Jewish men actually lost their positions, compared to nearly 100 percent of Jewish women. (Before 1933, about 13 percent of women doctors in Germany were Jews.) Moreover, as increasing numbers of Jewish men lost their positions (and their livelihoods), their wives had to take up much of the slack, often taking menial jobs and performing tasks formerly held by men. This role reversal only went so far—German men, including Jews, were not accustomed to making major contributions inside the household, still considered the domain of women.[13]

Nazi fixation on racial distinctions led to their establishing four categories of Germans:

1. Aryan
2. *Mischlinge* (Mixed race) 2nd Degree: one Jewish (or other non-Aryan) grandparent
3. *Mischlinge* 1st Degree: two non-Aryan grandparents
4. Full Jew (or other non-Aryan): three or more non-Aryan grandparents

In keeping with their notion that women were the weaker sex, and therefore could not be held to the same standards as men, the Nazis did not persecute Jewish women as fully as they did Jewish men, and the same held true for *Mischlinge*. Mixed marriages of Aryan men and either Jewish or *Mischlinge* wives were given favored treatment ("privileged marriages") over mixed marriages of Jewish men and Aryan women. In the early stages of the National Socialist period, couples in "privileged marriages" were subjected to very little of the persecution suffered by Full Jews, although this would later change.[14]

Before 1938, Jews were technically being sent to concentration camps not because of their race, but for political reasons and for minor infractions of any of those rules that governed their behavior. Given the large number and complexity of these laws, it must have taken a supreme effort *not* to violate any of them. Still, the evidence indicates that until 1938, the concentration camps were used to detain political enemies of the Nazis; few Jews were being held there.

All of this changed in 1938 as the regime prepared for war and adopted an even more get-tough policy toward Jews. In that year, further supplements to the Nuremberg Laws were enacted, preventing Jewish lawyers from practicing law or Jewish doctors from treating non-Jewish patients. In the summer, synagogues in Munich and Nuremberg were torched, and the first large-scale incarcerations of Jews in the concentration camps occurred.[15] More than two thousand "Asocial Jews" were arrested for everything from parking violations to being "work-shy" and were sent to the concentration camps at Dachau, Buchenwald, and Sachsenhausen. They were promised release if they would immediately emigrate.[16] In addition, the German government deported large numbers (about 17,000) of Polish Jews in late October. The Polish government did not want them, but Germany forced the issue, and the refugees were made to camp just across the border, under miserable conditions, in the towns of Zbaszyr and Chojnice.[17]

The effort to make Germany "free of Jews" *(Judenfrei)* was proceeding steadily, but for the SS, steadily was not fast enough. In November 1938, an incident occurred that played into the hands of the Nazis and which they used to unleash the most severe anti-Jewish measures to that point. A young Jew, Herschel Grynszpan, whose family was among those deported to Poland and living in squalor in a refugee camp, took matters into his own hands by going into the German embassy in Paris and shooting an official. Apparently, he wanted to kill the ambassador, but he found only an undersecretary, Ernst von Rath, who died the following day, 9 November.

The result was *Kristallnacht* (Crystal Night = Night of Broken Glass), a pogrom ordered by Goebbels, with Hitler's approval, and directed by SS leaders Himmler and Heydrich. The pogrom was to appear spontaneous, but in fact it was orchestrated from the top. Steps were taken to prevent plundering, and fires were to be started only when it was certain that fire brigades could protect adjacent buildings.[18] All over Germany, synagogues were burned and Jewish businesses were broken into, leaving streets littered with glass and discarded plunder. Over 7,000 shops and businesses were demolished, and nearly all of Germany's 275 synagogues were destroyed. Following the two nights of terror, Jews were made to pay for the clean-up, estimated at RM 25 million, and some 30,000 Jewish men were arrested and whisked into concentration camps. Most were released shortly, after giving proof of their plans for imminent emigration.[19] According to the Nazis' own internal reports, most Germans, even those who were considered "moderately anti-Semitic," were appalled by the violence and the treatment of Jews.[20] But this reaction was private rather than public, as by this time the population had learned to play it safe.

Kristallnacht stands as a watershed in German-Jewish relations. After November 1938, no Jews could harbor hopes that there was any future for them in Germany. All remaining Jewish firms now became Aryanized. In December 1938, any Jews not registered as employed could be conscripted for forced labor. In 1939, Jews were removed from welfare rolls, they had to observe a curfew, and when rationing was introduced in April, they were allowed less than other Germans.[21] The urge to emigrate now became a panic to emigrate. But where? Many countries, including the United States, were not suddenly opening their doors to this potential flood of Jewish refugees.

Kristallnacht also marks a turning point in the evolution of Germany's concentration camp system. Before 1938, the camps were small and held only a few thousand prisoners, most of them political dissidents. It is estimated that by early 1938, the total concentration camp population was between seven and ten thousand, but by the end of the year their numbers had increased significantly.[22] It is hardly a coincidence that in November 1938 the first contingent of male prisoners was brought from Sachsenhausen to Ravensbrück to begin construction on the camp for women.

Jewish Women at Ravensbrück

Following *Kristallnacht*, when Jews were rounded up in sizable numbers and sent to concentration camps, it was primarily men who were incarcerated. There seems to have been little effort on the part of the SS to include Jewish women in the large-scale arrests of 10 and 11 November 1938.[23] Nevertheless, some Jewish women had already been arrested and were being detained at Lichtenburg,[24] and a small minority of Jewish prisoners was admitted to Ravensbrück when it opened in the spring of 1939. A Prisoner-Strength Report of 24 June 1939 showed 127 Jews out of a total camp population of 1,048. This number would rise slowly in the coming months, until February 1942, but was generally just under ten percent of the camp's composition.[25]

The history of the Jewish women of Ravensbrück can be divided into three main periods.[26] In the first stage, from the opening of the camp to early 1942, Jewish women were handled much the same as other prisoners, and almost all the Jews at Ravensbrück were from the *Reich* (roughly, German-speaking Central Europe). The German conquest of Poland in the fall of 1939 had brought three million more Jews under German control, but they were not sent to camps in Germany at that time. Rather, they were crammed into the newly created ghetto system, vastly overpopulated holding pens. The invasion of Russia in 1941 added perhaps another three million, some of whom were killed on the spot by the most notorious of SS groups, the *Einsatzgruppen*.

The second stage of Jewish history at Ravensbrück began in 1942 when Himmler enacted measures designed to make

Germany *Judenrein* (cleansed of Jews). From this point, there were transports of Jews to killing centers or to ghettos and camps in Poland. In 1941–1942, the directors of the Adult Euthanasia Program, known simply as T4 (on account of their address, Tiergartenstrasse 4 in Berlin), were involved in a killing operation known cryptically as Special Handling 14f13. The operation was aimed primarily at handicapped adults, but in fact the major criterion for selection was a prisoner's ability to perform physical labor. Handicapped and work-incapable Jews were particularly liable.[27] In May 1942, Rosa Menzer, an elderly Jewish woman who had been brought to Ravensbrück in early 1940, was selected for a transport, then sent to a euthanasia center at Bernburg and killed, very likely by gassing.[28]

By the end of 1940, there were four euthanasia centers operating in Germany, and the regime's preferred method of killing — gas chambers designed as shower rooms — had proven its effectiveness.[29] In the case of the 14f13 operation mentioned above, T4 physicians visited Ravensbrück and made decisions based on infirmary records and physical examinations, including analysis of "poor behavior." (Bad behavior was considered an indication of genetic disease.)[30] Recently, Henry Friedlander has demonstrated how fully the Final Solution evolved out of the euthanasia program: "The success of the euthanasia policy convinced the Nazi leadership that mass murder was technically feasible, that ordinary men and women were willing to kill large numbers of innocent human beings, and that the bureaucracy would cooperate in such an unprecedented enterprise."[31] The result was that by late 1941–early 1942, the system was committing itself to large-scale extermination of Jews and other "undesirables," and the bureaucratic machinery created by the SS had its own dynamic and momentum for carrying this out.

In August 1942, a transport of six hundred Jews was sent from Ravensbrück to Auschwitz.[32] These transports continued until 21 June 1943, when according to Nazi plans, the last Jews were removed from Ravensbrück.[33] In practice, however, Ravensbrück never became *Judenfrei*. As the supposedly "last Jews" were being taken out, others were being brought in.[34] However, only a few Jewish women remained at Ravensbrück between early 1943 and mid-1944.

In the late summer of 1944, as the third and final stage commenced, the trend was reversed. Work-capable Jews from camps and ghettos in the east were dispatched to camps in the west, in advance of approaching Soviet armies. In the winter of 1944–1945, Ravensbrück took on the character of a human distribution center as thousands of newcomers were brought into a camp already overcrowded beyond belief. Many of these newcomers were whisked as quickly as possible to subcamps, and their experience at Ravensbrück was limited to a stay of only a few days. In fact, some Jewish women thought that Ravensbrück was only a transient camp, that nobody stayed there permanently.[35] In retrospect, those women whose residency at Ravensbrück in the winter of 1944–1945 was limited to a fortnight or less were the lucky ones. Those who stayed longer, probably domiciled in "the tent," had a greatly diminished chance of surviving.

Many of the German-Jewish women were from the middle class, often from small, tightly knit communities. The whole process of separating them from their families, shaving their heads, parading them naked in front of strangers, and placing them in noisy and overcrowded barracks was a particularly traumatizing experience.[36] The SS seemed to delight in exacerbating their condition by assigning bourgeois Jewish women to work that was physically very demanding, such as the road building crew, then ridiculing and punishing them if they proved unable to perform these manual tasks.[37] Not surprisingly, some Jewish women who were classified as Politicals took special precautions to prevent having their Jewishness discovered. One such inmate went so far as to avoid all contact with other Jews.[38]

There was a widespread belief among non-Jewish prisoners that the SS's treatment of Jewish women was more discriminatory and more brutal than their treatment of other inmates,[39]

although not all Jewish prisoners shared this opinion.[40] Some of
the SS personnel who were thought to be relatively decent in their
conduct toward most prisoners were frequently quite unsympathetic and harsh in their dealings with Jews.[41] Some SS personnel
absolutely refused to work in close proximity, such as in the same
office, with Jews.[42] Certain SS doctors had a reputation for being
so prejudiced against Jews that other staff members avoided sending Jews to them.[43] All of this was reflected in the reality that Jews
were rarely given desirable work assignments, they were almost
never appointed to positions as prisoner officials, and their barracks were the first to become overcrowded. They were, in short,
prevented from becoming part of the camp's power structure, and
as such, they lacked the wherewithal to trade favors and "scratch
backs" which might have improved their status.

In contrast to the blatant anti-Semitism displayed by so many
of the SS, however, there is astonishingly little evidence of anti-
Semitic attitudes or behavior among the female prisoners. The
recurrent expressions of anti-Gypsy sentiment by women inmates
are not paralleled by anti-Jewish biases. On the contrary, many
women felt sympathy for the Jews. Many prisoners felt particular
empathy toward Jews from their own countries.[44] Dagmar
Hajkova became frustrated because Czech Jews were kept isolated from the rest of the Czechs, and therefore it was difficult to
help them.[45] In 1942, however, when the entire Jewish Block was
punished by receiving food rations only every fourth day, the
Czechs were successful in organizing an effort to gather food and
smuggle it into the Jewish Block every other day.[46]

In discussing the Jewish society of Ravensbrück and the daily
life of Jewish women in the camp, it is necessary to make a distinction between the two periods during which there was a significant Jewish presence there: 1939–1942, and late 1944–April
1945. In treating the earlier period, we are considerably disadvantaged by the almost complete lack of firsthand accounts or
oral histories. Many of the Jewish women who were in the camp
then were transported to points east in 1942 and 1943, and pre-

sumably were killed. But from other sources, it is possible to piece together some of the key ingredients.

Until their expulsions in 1942–1943, Jews had their own block, always presided over by a non-Jewish block senior. It was one of the first blocks to experience significant overcrowding. As the number of Jewish women in the camp rose to over four hundred in 1941, and over six hundred in 1942, the inhabitants of the one Jewish block had to make room for the newcomers, however uncomfortably.[47] In those years, Jews were mostly assigned to outside work, hard physical labor. The road-building crew, which pushed the monster concrete rollers, was almost exclusively Jewish, as was the crew that loaded stones and gravel for construction.[48]

However disadvantaged Jewish women were in the early stage (1939–1942) of their stay at Ravensbrück, their conditions were clearly worse in the later stage, from mid-1944. Now there was no Jewish barracks, but only a tent and some makeshift sheds. Those who were put in the tent for any length of time were virtually condemned. Most of the Jewish women who were sent to Ravensbrück in the winter of 1944–1945 spent only a short time there before being sent elsewhere, generally to one of the subcamps. Under these conditions, it was extremely difficult to create any kind of social organization. Rosi Mauskopf, who arrived in late 1944 as a sixteen-year-old, remembered the circumstances with no hint of nostalgia: "It was chaos in the block. They beat each other for a piece of bread. In this hell it was impossible to remain human. I experienced neither friendship nor solidarity with fellow prisoners."[49]

Jewish prisoners who were sent to a regular block at this time, rather than being sent to a subcamp, were not given work assignments. This was because there were simply not enough jobs for all the new arrivals, but it did cause animosity between them and the other prisoners who had to work every day. Even among the Jews, there was some contentiousness, as Alexandra Gorko, recently arrived from Auschwitz, remembered:

Mostly the girls I was in the barracks with spoke Jewish [Yiddish]. I didn't, so I couldn't communicate. I understood them, but I couldn't speak to them. I answered them in Polish, and they didn't like it. They said, "Oh, this is one of those intelligentsia." Even the Jews were ridiculing each other: "You don't know how to speak Jewish, what?" And it was very unpleasant.[50]

Faye Eckhaus rhetorically asked: "You know when a Jew sings? When he's hungry." And she describes how in the evenings they would gather in their barracks and sing Jewish songs. Other prisoners found this peculiar; conditions were about as disagreeable as they could become, and yet the Jews appeared to be having a grand time.[51] What made this so perplexing to other prisoners was that deep down many of them sensed that the suffering of the Jews went beyond that of other groups. In March 1945, when the SS was relaxing its grip in the camp, they still had chicanery in reserve for Jews. For some minor infraction of regulations, Tanja, a *Mischling*, was required to stand outside in a snowstorm for an entire evening in the glare of spotlights wearing a sign which read: "JEWISH SOW AND WORK-SHY. THAT'S WHY I'M STANDING HERE."[52]

Red Triangles: Politicals

Aat Breur, "The Dutch Table in Block 32." (Damaged)
From *Een verborgen herinnering*. Courtesy Dunya Breur.

The Politicals, or red badges, as most prisoners called them, became eventually the largest inmate category, comprising over eighty percent of the total prisoner population.[1] They were also the most diverse, composed of a dozen different nationalities and several quite distinct political groups.

In a general sense, a political prisoner was simply someone who was thought to be an opponent of the National Socialist regime, and who, like the Jehovah's Witnesses, did not fit into one of the other categories. As a beginning teacher, Theolinda Katzenmaier had been outspoken in her criticism of the euthanasia program, characterizing it as "purely murder." In 1943, she was arrested, brought to Ravensbrück, and assigned a red badge.[2] In early 1944, Ilse Stephan refused to report for mandatory labor service, arguing that she needed to continue working her three jobs to help support her family. She was arrested by the Gestapo, and after a period of interrogation, was sent to Ravensbrück.[3] (Had she not been working, she might have been classified as an Asocial.) Some women had been arrested for making anti-Nazi or anti-Hitler statements. One woman had been denounced for suggesting that Hitler was having a sexual relationship with Rudolph Hess.[4] An elderly woman was denounced and arrested because in a momentary lapse of good judgment, while queuing in a store, she yelled out: "It's impossible to do everything HERR HITLER demands of us. HE, after all, doesn't have to stand in line at the grocery store!"[5]

Communists

From the beginning, the core of the Politicals and the component that gave them their essential identity and reason for being were activists of the political left, Communists and Socialists, particularly the former. The two groups had not gotten on well in the pre-Nazi era, but at Ravensbrück these women realized they had a common enemy that required their cooperation. They also tried to bring other women, even anti-Fascist bourgeoise groups, into a kind of popular front.[6] But there was a condition, generally understood, and it was that the Communists would direct the coalition. Erika Buchmann, a German Communist, justified it this way:

> They had long years of political struggle behind them, and many experiences from which they could draw. They saw more clearly than anyone the true political situation and they were the most conscious anti-Fascists. They knew best that, not the individual, but only the prisoners fighting together, could be a force to resist the SS. They had gained expertise in the organization of this struggle. They were accustomed to the fight and ready for action.[7]

The first political inmates at Ravensbrück were, naturally, women from Germany and Austria. In the initial stages of the Third Reich, many KPD (Communist Party of Germany) women had been arrested and imprisoned. Most were placed in regular prisons, but a few were put in the women's camp at Moringen. Many were held only a few weeks, ostensibly for re-education, and then released.[8] But others were held longer. Lisa Ullbrich was a KPD Reichstag delegate who was arrested in 1933, sent to Moringen, then Lichtenburg, and in May 1939, became one of the first female prisoners at Ravensbrück.[9] Another KPD Reichstag delegate, Olga Körner, arrested in 1933, was released after a year and a half, then was rearrested in 1939 and sent to Ravensbrück.[10] Once the Nazis established their "right" to rule without reference to established legal procedures, a common tactic was simply to prolong sentences. Margarete Jung and her husband were KPD members who continued to distribute anti-Fascist literature after Hitler came to power. They were arrested. She was given a prison sentence that should have ended in 1941, but she was then further detained and transferred to Ravensbrück.[11]

Initially, the camp leadership regularly harassed German Politicals, whom they considered "traitors to their folk." This was among the reasons the SS gave preference to Criminals and

Asocials in handing out positions in the prisoner hierarchy. "Better a murderer with patriotism than a treacherous Communist" seems to have been their way of thinking.

However, the German Communists and their allies were persistent in their efforts to build bridges, to foster prisoner solidarity, to create an organization that would end the brutal tyranny of the green and black badges. As newly arrived inmates were processed, "old Politicals" like Charlotte Müller would make contact, find out if there were any Communists or sympathizers among them, and then use already existing connections to place them in a favorable block and in strategic work assignments.[12] Madeleine Thonnart, a Belgian Communist, was contacted by German "comrades" as soon as she arrived, and she immediately was accepted into the Communist network of the camp. This was helpful in getting her assigned to the Siemens camp, a relatively favorable workplace.[13]

Once this network was in place, it could be used not only to place people in good positions, but also to help those who were in need. Twice a week, Charlotte Müller met with her friend and fellow Communist, Erika Buchmann, the block senior of the Punishment Block. Besides exchanging information, Müller would give Buchmann food packages for their *Kameradinnen* (female comrades).[14] When Olga Körner became distraught upon learning that her husband had died and her son had been killed, her Communist comrades rallied to her support, and maintained a nightly watch at her bedside.[15]

Once the Communists had brought a number of key positions into "reliable hands," as they liked to say, they could use this to do the kind of pushing and shoving that would really achieve results. In 1943, when Lucie, a former dancer and the wife of a wealthy factory owner, was appointed the new block senior of Block 2, the main Political block, their organization went into action. A conspiracy was unleashed to undermine her, chiefly by informing the other block seniors that she could not be trusted. It worked; after a short time she was replaced.[16]

The Communists at Ravensbrück were quick to help each other, but like other groups they were clannish, and they were not blind to the personal and group advantages that came with wielding power. They were also hostile toward those who broke ranks. This is illustrated in the case of Margarete Buber-Neumann, whose husband, Heinz Neumann, had been an important member of the KPD Politburo. In 1933, they emigrated, eventually seeking haven in Moscow. In the upside-down world of Stalinist politics, they were arrested in 1937 by the NKVD, the Soviet secret police. He was killed, and she was sent to a camp in Kazakhstan. But in 1940, as a result of an exchange between the Russians and the Gestapo, she was sent to Ravensbrück. Almost as soon as she arrived, the Communist organization contacted her and arranged an "interview." She told them and other Communists that "compared to Soviet camps, Ravensbrück was a sanatarium, and they should be thankful to be there and not in one of Stalin's prisons."[17] They concluded that Buber-Neumann was a Trotskyite, a "counter-revolutionary and an enemy of the people." Buber-Neumann was ambitious, and had already won the approval of the Polish Block to be their block senior. Instead, she was now appointed to be a room senior to the Asocials, not a choice assignment.[18] She continued to be ostracized by the Communists, whose "hard-liners had sworn to tie [her] to the stake if and when the Russians liberated the camp."[19]

By 1942, the Politicals had supplanted the Criminals and Asocials as the most powerful prisoner component in the camp. From this point most (but not all—the Poles were an important exception) of the key positions in the prisoner hierarchy would be either in their hands or in those of sympathizers. This change in power relationships was likely the result of two factors. First, in that Hobbesian world of internal concentration camp politics, the Communists played the game with measures of determination, skill, and ruthlessness that simply outclassed the competition. In this they were aided not only by their sense of purpose and international solidarity, but also by the remnants of an organization which could be reassembled and redirected.

There was yet another factor in this power shift. About this time, Ravensbrück was undergoing a transformation from a protective custody type of camp to one in which economic productivity played an increasingly greater role. From 1942 until the end of the war, Ravensbrück was the center of a massive slave-labor system in which productivity, measured in terms of output, income, and expenditures, mattered a great deal. This system still contained many ingredients of a protective custody camp, and it was anything but genuinely efficient. Still, it had to produce.

Military setbacks by the winter of 1941–1942 had prompted Himmler to make certain decisions leading to greater utilization of concentration camp labor, and in 1942, the machinery was being set in motion to bring this about. The WVHA (Economic and Administrative Office of the SS) under *SS Obergruppenführer* Oswald Pohl was in charge of this.[20] Again, the matter of the missing or destroyed SS records at Ravensbrück is problematic. It is simply not known whether the camp leadership accompanied these economic changes with corresponding decisions to allow the Politicals greater authority inside the camp. It seems likely they did. They could not have been blind to the reality that in comparison with the Criminals and Asocials, the Politicals ran their barracks and their work crews with considerable attention to order and discipline, thus potentially improving productivity.

Growing importance in the prisoner administration brought with it other privileges, not the least of which was the power to help their friends in a multitude of ways. When the camp was expanded and reorganized in early 1943, the Politicals were placed in blocks that other prisoners considered privileged.[21] This meant clean uniforms and linen, better sanitary facilities, and, best of all, none of the overcrowding that was soon to envelope most of the camp.

Indeed, what had already arisen at Ravensbrück was a system of haves and have-nots in which, according to Micheline Maurel, a French prisoner, the privileged were well fed and "strode around purposefully," while the others were "weak, sick and undernourished."[22] This was maybe an oversimplification and it would be even more oversimplifying to suggest that only the Politicals had power and privilege. But they undeniably had much of it; later many would admit that they had it much better than the great mass of prisoners.[23] After the war there were recriminations by some former inmates, charging that those who lived in the "Big Shot Barracks" (*Bonzen Blocks*) were far removed from the miserable reality of the rest of the camp.[24]

Members of Foreign Resistance Groups

As the war progressed and Nazi rule in Europe brought forth its inevitable reaction in the form of resistance movements, increasing numbers of foreign women were arrested and brought to Ravensbrück. Spanish women who had fled to France after the Civil War were now rounded up and brought to Mecklenburg, a place they called "Little Siberia."[25] After the occupation of Norway, Inger Gulbrandsen worked with the Norwegian underground, encouraging German soldiers to desert, and then smuggling deserters to Sweden. She was arrested in December 1942 at age nineteen, and taken to Ravensbrück the following year.[26] French women like Fanny Marette, Micheline Maurel, and Catherine Roux had all been involved in the French Resistance, and were incarcerated at Ravensbrück.[27] Some of the French women who had worked against the German occupation of their *Patrie* (country) were given a special designation, *NN*, which stood for "Night and Fog" (*Nacht und Nebel*), supposedly because they were just to vanish into the darkness and mist, and never be heard from again. They were housed in a special barracks, isolated from all the other barracks, apparently pending further investigations and their likely disappearance. They were not allowed to receive mail or packages, they were never allowed to work outside the camp, and they had virtually no contact with other prisoners.[28] All of these women were categorized as Politicals, and a number were Communists. But, as will be seen, considerations of nationality complicated prisoner classifications and often overrode other factors in determining group identity and solidarity.

Soviet Army Women and "Special Prisoners"

It was quite a spectacle, and none of the women who were at Ravensbrück on the night of 27 February 1943 would ever forget it. Five hundred Soviet army women, all wearing uniforms, were marched into the camp. At first they refused to cooperate with the SS on the grounds that as POWs they should be dealt with by the Red Cross. As punishment, they were made to march around the camp streets for an entire morning. In defiance, they sang as they marched. The Politicals applauded "this demonstration against Fascism"[29] as they marched by their barracks, and later sent them their lunch bread as a display of solidarity.[30]

In the following months, other Soviet women, both soldiers and civilians, were brought to Ravensbrück. Most were sent to subcamps, but a noticeable contingent remained at the main camp. In general, the other prisoners, and not just the Politicals, respected them for their unity and their willingness to stand up to camp authorities. On one occasion, the Soviet women were punished by confinement to their barracks without food. They decided to defy the camp authorities by singing. So they sang Soviet and Russian folk songs at the top of their lungs. When the SS came, they kept singing, doing this off and on for three days. Finally, the authorities gave them food, and the other prisoners gave them admiration.[31]

The Soviet women had their own barracks, isolated from the rest of the camp, but they lived in reasonably good conditions. Communists from the better blocks would sometimes visit them and bring them provisions, or in one case, a picture of Stalin.[32] Some prisoners thought the Soviet women were privileged.

During work they were allowed to talk with each other and sing songs. The inmates said to each other: "The SS is afraid of Stalin."[33]

There are two other subgroups of Politicals, certainly less prominent than the ones already discussed, but still deserving of mention. First, there was a group of German women who had been accused of having sex with foreigners. The regime, peculiarly, labeled this a political act and designated those prisoners as Politicals. They were quite proud to wear the red badge, but the more genuine Politicals despised them and called them "bed Politicals" (*Bettpolitisch*).[34] The regime also classified some as Politicals who had been involved in the black market. Most prisoners considered these groups as low-lifes who really belonged with the Criminals and Asocials.[35] Clearly they did, but the regime may have had its own reasons for putting them with the red badges, perhaps preventing too much cohesiveness or camaraderie from forming in their blocks.

The other subgroup was the Special Prisoners (*Sonder-Häftlinge*). This was a diverse group. Some of them were Nazi women or wives of Nazis who were found guilty of fraud or embezzlement. Most of these women were at Ravensbrück only a short time and did no work at all. Like other Special Prisoners, they were not just privileged; they were pampered.[36] There were also prisoners who because of their fame and/or connections were given special consideration. Silvia Salvesen, a friend of the King of Norway, got special treatment.[37] Emma La Guardia Gluck, sister of the mayor of New York City, and one of only two known native-born Americans at Ravensbrück, was likewise shown favoritism in spite of her later statement that at Ravensbrück "we [prisoners] were all equals. There was no wealth, no titles, and no envy to divide us."[38] The other American, Virginia D'Albert Lake, was married to a French aristocrat with whom she had joined the resistance. Sent to the Torgau subcamp, she acknowledged that, as an American, she was given preferential treatment. In February 1945, her mother was instrumental in getting U.S.

Secretary of State Cordell Hull to negotiate her transfer to a Red
Cross camp at Lake Constance, where she spent the remainder of
the war in relative comfort.[39] Charlotte Schuppe was the sister of
the man who had saved Hitler's life in the 1923 assassination
attempt. Hitler had reportedly put the whole family under his protection, but she was arrested for having an affair with a Polish
minister. At Ravensbrück, however, she was thought to be a Nazi
agent. Hildegard Brandt, an infirmary worker, noted that
Schuppe often received packages from the local Gestapo chief,
Ludwig Ramdohr, but would tell the other prisoners they were
from her mother.[40] There were other special prisoners: Genevieve
de Gaulle, granddaughter of the French leader,[41] and Olga Himmler, sister of the SS chief, incarcerated because of her affair with
a Polish officer.[42] Following the 20 July 1944 plot to kill Hitler, several notable male suspects were brought to Ravensbrück for interrogation: Karl Seitz (former lord mayor of Vienna), Helmuth von
Moltke (leader of the Kreisau Circle of anti-Nazis), and Julius
Leber (SPD Reichstag delegate and active conspirator).[43]

Most of the inmates heard of little or nothing about most of
these Special Prisoners, but they did know about one of them:
Rosa Thälmann. The wife of long time KPD head, Ernst
Thälmann, she was brought to Ravensbrück in September 1944.
Although she was isolated from other Politicals at first, the
Communists soon learned of her arrival and spared no effort to
ensure her safety and her comfort, first getting her sent to the
infirmary, then to one of the elite blocks, where she spent the
remainder of the war.[44] Thus, Frau Thälmann's position as a
Special Prisoner, unlike the other Sonderhäftlinge, had little to do
with the SS's decisions and much to do with the cameraderie and
organizational strengths of the camp's Communists.

Nationalities

France Audoul, untitled drawing.
From *Ravensbrück: 15,000 Femmes en Enfer.*

Nationality Conflicts

Although each newly arriving prisoner was assigned to one of the badge classifications preconceived by the Nazis, for many prisoners this was not at all the most important designation. This was particularly true after 1941, when large numbers of foreign women were brought to Ravensbrück, and, except for Jews, nearly all were classified as Politicals. The observation is inescapable that for most of these other prisoners, including Belgians, Poles, Czechs, and so on, the red badge meant far less to them than the initial inside it (B, P, T) that indicated their respective country.

More than twenty nationalities were represented at Ravensbrück, but four groups comprised three-fourths of the total. This table is from the study by a Polish survivor, Wanda Kiedrzynska:

Nationality	Number	Percent
Poles	6,135	24.9
Germans	4,990	19.9
Jews	3,801	15.1
Russians	3,758	15.0
French	1,828	7.3
Gypsies	1,356	5.4
Ukrainians	1,040	4.1
Belgians	729	2.9
Czechs	478	1.9
Yugoslavs	338	1.3
Dutch	121	0.4
Italians	90	0.35
Spanish	15	0.05
English	15	0.05
Norwegians	12	0.04
Others	322	1.28

Aat Breur, "Russian Women." From *Een verborgen herinnering.*
Courtesy Dunya Breur.

Kiedrzynska based her study on the surviving entrance lists
(*Zugangslisten*) which, like most of the archival records, are
incomplete.[1] Nevertheless, this tally of 25,028 prisoners is a
broad-based survey, and in any case it represents the best estimate we have of the camp's composition.

The memoirs and reports of experiences (*Erlebnisberichte*) of
survivors sometimes give the impression that none of the groups
liked any of the others. Two sisters noted: "At Ravensbrück there
was little comradeship, but rather, a strong hatred based on
nationality."[2] Not all the survivors would go this far, but it seems
true that in the concentration camp one's own national identity
was confirmed and strengthened in relation to almost all others,
which is to say that national animosities abounded.

It was natural that Germans would be on the receiving end of national hatreds: "The Germans, a shameful breed who knew only how to kill the defenseless."[3] And this: "Every German is a *Boche* [Hun] we say, a born thug. Every German, man or woman, is at heart a 'Hitler'."[4] Strong statements, but consider that virtually all the SS personnel, all the overseers, and many of the prisoner officials were German. Moreover, the feeling ran very deeply that German prisoners enjoyed great privileges.[5] Some of the German prisoners acknowledged the truth of this, at least in retrospect.[6] German prisoners assigned to barracks outside of the elite blocks often noted that non-Germans were openly hostile to them and would have little to do with them.[7] At the subcamp at Barth, the Gypsy block senior would address her German prisoners as "Ihr deutschen Schweine." (You German pigs!)[8] These anti-German sentiments became even more pronounced in the closing months of the war, as many prisoners displayed a hatred of everything German. Even foreign Communists who had earlier cooperated with German comrades now showed them nothing but scorn.[9]

But Germans were not alone in being targeted in this cauldron of nationalistic furor. Everyone, it seems, had favorites and pariahs. Wanda Poltawska, a Pole, thought the Norwegians were nice, but the Dutch, particularly the older women, were difficult: "spiteful and boring."[10] The French anthropologist Germaine Tillion admired the Czechs for their sophistication and high cultural level, but feared "the Ukrainians' indescribable savagery that easily made them the least desirable neighbors in the camp."[11] The antagonisms were generally intensified in mixed blocks when there were clear majorities and minorities. At the Neubrandenburg subcamp, a handful of French women shared a barracks with Poles and Russians, who despised the French for being weak and effete.[12] A French prisoner's response: "Among the Slavs, who outnumbered us 15 or 20 to one, were many strange creatures, brutes with gorilla faces who were impervious to reason."[13] A Jewish woman from Poland, Alexandra Gorko, described her group's relations with Catholic Poles: "They had hair, we didn't. . . . We were laughed at, ridiculed, cursed. They said that because of us they are in the camp."[14] Even among Jews there was discord. When a group of Hungarian Jews had to find space for themselves in an overcrowded tent inhabited mainly by Polish Jews, the latter kicked at and pushed the former, chiding them: "What kind of Jews are you that you don't speak Yiddish?"[15]

All of these expressions of prejudice and hatreds based on nationality differences would deserve to be only footnotes except for the fact that they were often translated into action. Not only were there "frequent fights between prisoners of different nationalities,"[16] but also by ridiculing and even dehumanizing those "others," all sorts of chicanery and even brutality became justified. On the whole, prisoners did not steal from their own group, but liberating a blanket or pair of shoes from outsiders was not considered so bad. In a mixed barracks at the Holleischen subcamp, Russians and Poles regularly stole the light bulbs from the French area, which the French had dubbed their "Bel-Masure" (Beautiful Hovel).[17] Not only did each nationality group hang out by itself—language barriers alone conditioned this practice—but if prisoners extended a helping hand to anybody, it was almost certain to be one of their own. A Norwegian woman echoed a common lament when she said "ninety percent of the German prisoners would only lend a hand to each other."[18] Buber-Neumann observed that many of the prisoner doctors in the Infirmary "shamelessly favored the sick of their own nationality."[19] The literature almost overflows with testimonies of how Austrian prisoners rescued a fellow Austrian,[20] or how the Norwegians might squabble among themselves, but had great solidarity in relation to outsiders.[21] A Belgian survivor claimed that the spirit of camaraderie among the Belgian women fostered a sense of honesty and fairness that was the envy of outsiders, including the Czechs, who didn't have such a system.[22] But a Czech survivor, Dagmar Hajkova, described what was undoubtedly a similar system: orderly, clean, fair—and the Czechs were determined to keep it that way. "It was a question of national honor." And she, too, believed that non-Czechs all admired them.[23] Actually, many of them did. Most of these national groupings were so self-contained, particularly if they had their own barracks—which both the Czechs and Belgians did (the latter in the Siemens Camp)—that they really did not know much about life in the other blocks.

Most people who have traveled abroad understand this phenomenon: You meet somebody from your own country on a train or in any unexpected locale while in a foreign land, and immediately you become friends. In the conditions of a women's concentration camp, this is even more understandable. One night, in a terribly overcrowded barracks, Lidia Rolfi was picking her way through the new arrivals who were sleeping on the floor. (Lidia was one of the lucky ones who shared a cot with only two other women.) As she did this, she accidentally fell on one of the unfortunate women, whose first reaction was to hit her, then curse at her. But her curses were in Italian, Lidia's own tongue! At once they became comrades, got acquainted, and from that point on, Lidia did all she could to help Maria, her new friend.[24]

When Sunneva Sandoe, a Dane, learned that a group of Danish women had just been brought into Ravensbrück, she immediately went to them and greeted them: "If you are Danes, you are welcome in this hell-hole."[25] Pretending to be an official, she took their coats from them, knowing the SS would do this anyway, and she hid them so she could give them back later. Then on Christmas night, 1944, she went to them. The eleven newcomers and Sunneva huddled together on three beds in an unheated, overcrowded barracks, surrounded by Poles, Jews, and others. There they shared the little breads she had brought with her, as well as a feeling of solidarity.[26]

To their credit, the Communists, more than any other group, had worked to build a system that went beyond ties of nationalism. But even here there were limitations, conditioned largely by language, culture, and group identity. German Communists seem to have been more willing than others to reach across national lines, both to build an organization and to help people. But in most of the other cases (the Czechs, the French, the Yugoslavs, even the

Russians—there were practically no Polish Communists at Ravensbrück), it is clear that their national identity was much stronger than their feelings of ideological solidarity.

The Poles

With the outbreak of war in the fall of 1939, the first Polish women were brought to Ravensbrück. Their numbers were initially quite small, a few hundred women, mostly from the newly incorporated territories of Pomerania and Poznan. Like most other inmates there, they were assigned to blocks headed by Criminals and Asocials (green and black badges). The Poles were all Politicals (red badges). In the next few years their numbers would swell, principally because of involvement in illegal activities during the occupation of their homeland.[27] By 1942, they had become the largest national component at the camp, and had already supplanted the Criminals and Asocials, taking over many of the leadership functions in their own blocks and elsewhere in the camp.

The Polish women were perhaps the most heterogenous of all the national groups at Ravensbrück, and came pretty close to reflecting a cross-section of their own society. Most were simple women from villages and small towns, without strong political views. Many were from the bourgeoisie: students, teachers, and professionals. And there were some aristocrats.[28]

There is a place where my "cross-section of Polish society" argument falls apart, and I need to point it out right away. In the spring of 1940, a transport of about eighty Polish women was brought to Ravensbrück. They were mostly teachers and professors, and their addition raised the cultural-intellectual profile of the Poles considerably.[29] In the next years they were to play an extremely important role in the educational programs of the Polish contingent, making it the envy of other nationalities.[30]

Polish women did not oppose the effort of the Communists to create camp wide solidarity, but they did not wholeheartedly endorse it either. Among the Poles there were few Marxists, but there were many fervent Catholics. And almost all the Polish women shared a deep sense of nationalism,[31] "patriotic to the point of chauvinism," according to Hajkova, a Czech Communist.[32] Efforts to bring the Poles into the solidarity movement were only partially successful, and Hajkova blamed this on their general backwardness, particularly their low level of class consciousness. She was particularly exasperated by the willingness of the simple village women to serve the Polish aristocrats. As they had done at home, they made their beds, washed their clothes, and waited on them.[33]

Outsiders might criticize the Poles for their "shocking attitude of submission,"[34] but their leadership apparently calculated that the Polish women would best be served by re-creating a microcosm of Polish society in the camp and getting as much power as possible in their own hands. This would require considerable cooperation with the German authorities, a task facilitated by the fact that many of the Polish women from the annexed territories were fluent in German when they arrived. An example of this cooperation occurred when Marta Baranowska was appointed block senior of Block 13, one of the Polish blocks. She went to her block leader, the Overseer Erika Boedeker, and simply "made a deal." Baranowska promised to maintain order and discipline in the block and cause Boedeker no problems if the overseer promised in turn not to bother them. It worked. Boedeker was protective of "her" Poles, often arranging favorable work assignments for them. Baranowska, for her part, was given a free hand in running her block, and she ran it with discipline and humanity. There was no resistance to authority, and Boedeker had no reason to regret the arrangement. When Boedeker was transferred to the Mauthausen Concentration Camp, she went to Baranowska, shook her hand, and wished her "a prompt return home to a free Poland."[35]

By 1942–1943, the Polish women at Ravensbrück had achieved an eniviable level of power and importance in the camp.[36] Perhaps they really were, "after the SS, the bosses of Ravensbrück,"[37] although Tillion's assertion seems to be a bit of an overstatement. However, there were by now so many Polish block and room seniors and work crew chiefs that the Polish terms of *Blockova*, *Stubova*, and *Kolonkova* came to be generally used by everyone.

From this power base, the Polish contingent in the camp was able to create an amazing and efficient system of mutual aid. Since Poles were a majority in the kitchen crew (most of the rest were Czechs),[38] they could nearly always bring home a little extra bread or kitchen scraps for their mates or the needy. A sympathetic block senior was indispensable in so many ways, from arranging tolerable work assignments to securing approval to go on sick call. After the war, many Polish women testified that without their particular Polish block senior, they would never have survived. But it was not just raw survival; having sympathetic and effective prisoner leaders made it possible to hold masses in the barracks, to organize a wide-ranging educational program with lectures and discussions, and to create a network of "families" which protected and gave comfort to their members. The Poles were sometimes accused of selfishness,[39] but they viewed their actions as merely turning inward, not only to protect each other and those things, such as their religion, which were crucial to them, but also to live a life inside the camp with some semblance of order and dignity.[40]

All of this took discipline and power, not only in relation to outside power brokers, but also to each other. The Poles had their own judicial system. If a Polish prisoner, particularly one in authority, "forgot her dignity as a Pole" (that is, behaved illegally or mishandled other Polish prisoners) she would be reminded of her duties and, if necessary, warned that this matter would be brought before a Polish court when they returned home.[41]

The French

The experience of most French women at Ravensbrück was fundamentally different from that of their Polish counterparts. For one thing, the French did not arrive in significant numbers until late 1943–early 1944. By then the Communists and Poles had already established themselves as the primary leaders among the prisoners, and they would not have been easily dislodged. Not that the French tried; the fact that French women were almost never appointed to leadership positions was a source of national pride. One French woman almost gloated: "These red arm bands [the badges of prisoner officials], no French woman has ever wanted or accepted one, because none of us wants to be a hangman for our compatriots or serve the will of the *Boches*."[42] Also, the timing of the French arrival coincided with the arrival of other groups and helped to cause the massive overcrowding that made Ravensbrück such a hellish place in the last year of its existence. Where were the French to be put? Except for the elite blocks, there was nothing but overcrowded barracks.

The largest transport of French women arrived at Ravensbrück in February 1944. This was a group of 958 prisoners who became known as the "twenty-seven thousands" since they were allotted numbers between 27030 and 27988. In August of that year, another 800 French women arrived.[43] All of these women were categorized as Politicals and assigned the red triangle. However, unlike other Politicals, French prisoners were not permitted to place an "F" inside their triangle to indicate their country of origin. Fearing (and resenting) that they would be confused with German Politicals, who also had no letter,[44] many French women initially defied the rules and made themselves a distinctive black "F," which they proudly displayed. But, not unexpectedly, a price was paid for this small act of defiance,[45] and the practice appears to have been soon discontinued.

Although there were a few French criminals (black marketeers, thieves who stole from Germans) and prostitutes (arrested because they had infected German soldiers), the majority of the French women were genuine Politicals, confined because of their involvement with the French Resistance.[46] They were quite a diverse group, but unlike most of the other national components at Ravensbrück, including the Poles, there was a relative over representation by the upper social classes. This reflected the way in which the professional and liberal *bourgeoisie* joined forces with old aristocratic families as well as workers to provide leadership in the Resistance.[47] Many were young intellectuals, and since they had traveled the same route—through the Gestapo jails of Paris and the prison camp at Romainville, many of them making the journey together[48]—they arrived with an *esprit de corps* that months of brutal treatment at the hands of the SS could not subdue. The French contingent at Ravensbrück were more than patriotic; they were politicized and resistance-oriented beyond that of any other group, with the possible exception of the Russian Red Army women.

It is clear that the SS singled out the French for special measures. Perhaps it was because so many of the French prisoners had been engaged in active resistance against German forces occupying their homeland. Many French women were consigned to the isolation of the NN Block, and a number of these unfortunates "disappeared."[49] Even French women who were placed in regular blocks had to endure special discrimination, such as not being allowed letters or packages for the first months of their imprisonment.

The principle underlying SS policies toward the French was apparently to minimize their influence and prevent an organized resistance from forming by keeping the French women divided and powerless. There was no French Block, although one block (Block 27) was predominantly French. The pattern seemed to be to assign small groups of French prisoners to overcrowded barracks where one group or another had already established dominance. Resentment against the French was no doubt helped along by the often observed habit of many French people to stick togeth-

er, form cliques, and avoid speaking any language but their own.
Some French women were resolute in their insistence that speaking German or even learning the language was a form of collaboration.[50] But eventually the French, like all other national groups,
learned and spoke a kind of camp Esperanto in which many key
German words like *Appelplatz* (roll-call grounds), *Nachtschicht*
(night shift), *organisieren* (wheel and deal), and of course *kaput*
were used freely.[51]

The arrival of the French women stirred up some strong emo-
tions among other groups. Women in blocks controlled by Poles or
Czechs sometimes felt antagonistic toward the French women
because those in charge held it against France for not honoring its
commitments to their countries in 1938–1939.[52] But this resentment was not universal. Eugenia Kocwa, a Pole, had a quite different reaction:

> One of these transports contained the flower of the French
> intelligentsia. Women who had studied several disciplines
> were no rarity among them. These overdelicate creatures,
> who had been torn from the *milieu* of a higher civilization and
> were not accustomed to hard physical work, had no chance of
> survival. . . . But to their last moments, they maintained a
> smile or even a song on their lips. . . . Of all the nations rep-
> resented in the camp, they were to me the dearest.[53]

By the time the French arrived at Ravensbrück, the key positions in the prisoner hierarchy were already held by Communists
and Poles, and the really good jobs in the kitchens, the infirmary,
and the gardens were firmly in the hands of others. Some positions at the Siemens factory were available, and since many of the
French women were intellectuals, they easily passed the tests to
gain work there. But most of the French women did not like taking work that so directly benefited the German war machine, and
thus they generally turned down these opportunities. At least they
did so initially, and after that it was too late. With few exceptions—there were, for example, three French doctors and ten

French nurses in the infirmary—French women were assigned to some of the worst jobs, most often as Availables. In short, "They formed the sub-proletariat of the camp."[54]

Having been part of resistance movements on the outside, many French women attempted to continue such activities inside the camp. However, the divide-and-rule tactics of the SS were overwhelmingly successful in preventing a genuinely organized resistance from being founded. What arose instead was a loose organiza-

Aat Breur, "Marie-Jeanne from France." From *Een verborgen herinnering*. Courtesy Dunya Breur.

tion based mainly on personal connections between members of smaller groups.[55] The French did have a well-developed grapevine, capable of circulating news and rumors quickly through their ranks.[56]

The German emphasis on order (*Ordnung*) was repugnant to many French prisoners. "The natural inability of the French to follow regulations is one of their great virtues," emphasized Micheline Maurel.[57] The French gained some notoriety for impeding production and slowing things down by pretending to make mistakes.[58] In addition, there was some sabotage of machinery.[59] But, for the most part, French resistance to their German captors was played out in countless little ways that were more morale-

boosting to the French than damaging to the Germans. They held
Bastille Day celebrations on July 14 and enthusiastically sang the
"Marseillaise," accepting the inevitable punishments.[60] For a time,
a little newsletter, *Le Verfügbar* (*The Available*) containing poems,
stories, and humor, was "published" and circulated among the
French.[61]

Humor was an essential tool in the French strategy for survival. As a veteran Available, Germaine Tillion wrote a comic
operetta in the fall of 1944 called *Le Verfügbar aux enfers* (*The
Available in the Underworld*). It was a take-off on Jacques
Offenbach's opera *Orpheus in the Underworld*. In the closing lines
of the operetta, the heroine, protesting that she is not pretending
to be sick, says: "I want to be sent to a model camp, with all the
comforts: water, gas, electricity." To which the chorus responds:
"Gas, above all."[62] They kept their sense of humor through every
ordeal. A Danish inmate, Sunneva Sandoe, who was arrested with
the French in 1944 and was kept with them throughout their stay,
later described how her companions were always joking about
their comical clothes and never tired of giving themselves funny
nicknames. "To me, they were like a breath of free France, which
always has and always will, fight for the idea of freedom."[63]

The death rate of the French women far exceeded that of most
other groups in the camp. Other prisoners were aware of this and
many had explanations for it, including some Czechs, who once
told Germaine Tillion it was because of "the intrinsic weakness of
[her] people."[64] Tillion, a French anthropologist, could not accept
this explanation, of course. Nor can we. Without even any pretense of political power, without the mechanisms to acquire favorable work assignments or gain a little extra food, if only for bar-
gaining purposes, the French women were condemned to remain
in their overcrowded barracks and be subjected to continued
oppression, not only by the SS, but also by their fellow prisoners.

CHAPTER

The Prisoner Administration

Violette LeCoq, "Roll call of the NN Prisoners," from *Témoignages*...
Courtesy Mme. Violette Rougier-LeCoq.

The system of "prisoner officials" or "prisoner functionaries" (*Funktionshäftlinge*) which played such an important role at Ravensbrück was inherited from the concentration camps that were already in existence when the women's concentration camp was created. And, at Ravensbrück, this system was modified, partly to fit the special needs of a women's camp, and, over time, by prevailing practices. Eugen Kogon, himself a survivor of Buchenwald, whose work on concentration camps is a pioneering (and still useful) study, even speaks of a system of "prisoner self-government."[1] One must be wary of this phrase, particularly in applying it to Ravensbrück, but there are ways in which it is partially applicable.

Block and Room Seniors

In theory, at the top of the prisoner administration there was the position of camp senior (*Lager-Älteste*). This was certainly one of those positions for which camps like Buchenwald served as a model. But whereas at Buchenwald this position carried tremendous authority—nominating block seniors and representing the prisoners to the SS[2]—at Ravensbrück the position appears to have been largely that of a figurehead. Here power was more diffused; each block senior (*Blockälteste*), or *Blockova* as they were called, reported to her block overseer (*Blockleiterin* or *Blockführerin*), and this relationship, more than any other, defined the scope and nature of prisoner power in the women's camp. Collectively, block seniors could and did wield considerable influence, but even so, they were never the focal point of authority that a strong camp senior was at Buchenwald.

Block seniors were, without exception, appointed by the SS. The head female overseer (*Oberaufseherin*) made the actual appointment, but she did this in consultation with other SS camp leaders, most importantly the camp leader for protective custody. It was possible for prisoner officials to provide input into the decision-making process, but, of course, decisions were made by the SS. Expecting a transport of Polish prisoners momentarily, Head Overseer Langefeld called two Poles, Cetkowska and Baranowska, to her office. There was an exchange of views, and the two were then appointed block senior and room senior (*Stuben-Älteste*, also called *Stubova*) respectively.[3] This was not democracy, but it did indicate a degree of prisoner input. After 1942, the Jehovah's Witnesses "elected" their own block and room seniors,[4] but apparently they could only choose from among women who had already distinguished themselves in positions of leadership and were therefore acceptable to the SS.

All prisoner officials, and block seniors in particular, constantly had to perform a delicate balancing act if they were to survive and be successful. On the one hand, they could not forget that their authority emanated from the SS, and that to maintain their positions the policy and will of the SS needed to be carried out. On the other hand, for them to be effective in maintaining order in their blocks and getting things done, the cooperation of at least an important element of the prisoners was essential. Overwhelmingly, this was handled through a patronage system whereby in exchange for support and collaboration, block seniors distributed rewards to a select few, generally (but not necessarily) members of their own group. These favorites, or clients, thus became *de facto* part of the prisoner administration. It was often in the interest of a block senior to choose some of her inner circle on the basis of useful skills, such as a talent for organizing or interpreting.[5] In the elite blocks, where there were more rewards to be passed around, this system was implemented with less contentiousness than elsewhere in the camp. But everywhere, the system encouraged a kind of jockeying for position on the part of the women prisoners who understood that their very survival was at stake.

The Third Reich, as a system, did not believe in job descriptions. Power in any position was what you could make of it, whether party province chief (*Gauleiter*), head overseer, or block senior. The block seniors had certain responsibilities, chief among them maintaining order and discipline in their blocks, but how this was to be done was never stipulated. Nor were the parameters of their power defined. Depending on many variables, most importantly connections, that is, relations with other power brokers in the camp—overseers, work crew leaders, infirmary workers, and other block seniors—a particular block senior could potentially wield enormous influence, and some of them did just that. Others, chiefly Asocials and Criminals, might rule their own blocks as dictators,[6] but outside those blocks their influence was minimal. This certainly was a factor in their gradual replacement as prisoner leaders by the Politicals as well as the Poles.

It was the responsibility of the block senior, aided by her room seniors, to wake the inmates in the morning and get them out of the barracks for roll call. Many prisoners remembered with much distaste how their *Stubovas* would run around the barracks wildly, yelling "Aufstehen!" (Get up!).[7] Once they were assembled, the block seniors took the roll call and recorded this in their Block Book, which contained a record of the prisoners in the block, where they worked, whether they were in the infirmary, and what their present status was.[8] This gave them the opportunity, if they were willing to take risks, to cover up for a missing inmate.[9] Then, at the required moment, they would report to their overseer.

Block seniors had other responsibilities as well. They decided whether a prisoner was sufficiently ill to be sent on sick call. (After 1943, in some of the blocks, this was done in collaboration with a health official, called a block nurse.)[10] As part of their general obligation to maintain order in their block, they were expected to make Reports concerning misbehavior of inmates. Prisoners feared this, as it would lead to punishment, including being sent to the Punishment Block or the Bunker. However, a kindly block senior could find ways to avoid this.

Each block senior chose her room seniors and camp runners (*Lagerläuferinnen*), subject again to the approval of the overseer. The room seniors, one for each wing of the barracks, were her chief aides, but they were also specifically in charge of food distribution. They were responsible for getting the food from the kitchens to the dining areas of the barracks. Once there, each wing was divided into groups of about forty women (in the more overcrowded barracks, women had to eat in shifts), each headed by a table senior (*Tischälteste*), the only genuinely elected prisoner official.[11] The camp runners delivered messages and orders around the camp. Regular inmates would be arrested for being away from their own barracks except at certain designated periods. Thus, if they needed to go anywhere, they had to be accompanied by a camp runner or another prisoner official.[12]

There were, naturally, privileges which went with these positions. Block seniors got their own rooms, or at least they had the use of the room of the overseer, who was rarely there.[13] Room seniors and camp runners got their own lockers. Each of them got first place in the food line, as well as extra rations.[14] Further, these positions entitled them to be issued dresses that actually fit, and most importantly, they were issued green arm bands (not to be confused with green triangles). These arm bands distinguished the wearers as prisoner officials and allowed them to go almost anywhere in the camp at any time.[15] Finally, it was not a right, but it was customary to share the contents of packages with one's *Blockova* and *Stubova*.[16]

Few prisoners would have disagreed with the observation made by Charlotte Müller: "Much about the life of the prisoners depended on the personalities of their block seniors."[17] An unsympathetic block senior made one's very existence a nightmare, and there were many examples of this, particularly in blocks headed by Criminals and Asocials.[18] Theolinde Katzenmaier's black-badge block senior had a reputation for sending in negative Reports on prisoners, sometimes for trivial reasons, condemning them to punishment or having them assigned to unpleasant and even harmful jobs.[19] Sometimes it was worse: a sadistic and unscrupulous block senior could terrorize and beat her fellow prisoners, and there was no possibility of recourse.[20] In one case, a lesbian room senior used her position to pressure inmates into granting sexual favors.[21]

Another block senior, Carmen Mory, a Swiss, who herself had earlier been beaten and confined to the Bunker, was known to beat fellow prisoners, in some cases fatally. She even became a Gestapo agent "in order to combat criminal and Bolshevik influences" (her own words) inside the camp. Further, when inmates from her block (Block 10, one of the Sick Blocks, which included the notorious Idiots' Room) were selected for "extermination," she gave her full cooperation, "behaving like an SS overseer herself," according to a witness. Her appointment as block senior came only in October 1944,[22] at a time when many of the leading positions were already in the hands of German Politicals. Thus, we might speculate whether the SS made such an appointment in order to divide and rule, to offset the dominance that the Politicals had achieved in the prisoner administration.

Conversely, a benevolent block senior, particularly one with connections, could make life in her block tolerable. At a minimum, it meant restricting the stealing, fighting, and squabbling so widespread in the camp. But it often went beyond that. A caring block senior could have a prisoner put on sick call or have a convalescing prisoner assigned an easy job.[23] A good block senior would overlook minor transgressions and not send in a Report, or would unofficially permit a meeting to take place in a corner of the barracks. A certain German *Stubova* in the Polish Block was not only very nice to the Poles and allowed them considerable freedom in the barracks, but she quickly learned Polish and "renounced her own nationality."[24] But there were risks involved, and here is where connections were important. Without some connivance from the overseers, a block senior could be severely punished for bending, let alone breaking, the rules. One popular block senior at the Neubrandenburg subcamp, Maria Czapla, was arrested for allowing inmates to hold religious services in her room. When she was released from the Bunker, she was assigned to the "Shit Crew," one of the worst jobs in the camp.[25]

Needless to say, a good block senior was much appreciated by her wards. Rosa Jochmann, an Austrian Socialist, was one of the senior prisoners at Ravensbrück, and for several years was *Blockova* in Block 1, the block for "old Politicals." Not only was there no stealing or fighting in her block, but "there dominated a human atmosphere, peace and quiet, and cleanliness."[26] She reportedly never gave orders, but discussed matters and created unanimity. She avoided sending in Reports, and many "comrades" got good assignments, particularly working in administrative offices.[27] She used her camp runners to secure and pass on information of value to the network of Politicals in the camp. She protected old and sick women by exempting them from roll call and getting comfortable jobs for them. In short, "Her life was one big concern for her camp kids" (*Lagerkinder*). But in 1943, she was denounced, apparently by an informer, put in the Bunker, and later reassigned. Her career as block senior was over.[28]

Other Prisoner Officials

There were still other prisoner officials. Each work crew had an appointed prisoner foreman (*Anweisungshäftling*), but since this term was too long, everybody called them by the Polish term *Kolonkova* or the even shorter *Kolonka*. They were the crew chiefs, directly under an SS overseer. Their function was to direct and supervise the labor of prisoners, but they were not to do any work themselves. They wore red arm bands, which allowed them free movement in the camp.[29] Under them, but only in places like factories where it was necessary to watch over the inmates (mainly to prevent sabotage), were prisoner officials known as monitors (*Aufpasserinnen*). In the workplaces where they were assigned, there was about one monitor for each fifty prisoners.[30]

Until 1942, the job of policing the camp—arresting prisoners who had no authorization to be out on the camp streets, and escorting prisoners for punishment—was done by the female overseers or by overseer trainees. The growing prisoner population apparently strained this system; thus in the summer of 1942 the

position of camp police (*Lagerpolizei*) was created. They too wore
red arm bands. Inmates who had spent time at Dachau,
Auschwitz, or other concentration camps often called them
Kapos,[31] but this term was not widely used at Ravensbrück (except
in the men's camp).

Most of the camp police were recruited from the blocks of
Criminals and Asocials, and if only for this reason were both
feared and generally loathed by other inmates who thought them
"degenerate,"[32] and noted that no "decent person" would become
one.[33] Many were quite brutal in their handling of fellow female
prisoners.[34] In addition to the functions already mentioned, particularly of arresting unauthorized persons on the camp streets,
their primary purpose seems to have been as a backup force for
the overseers. Thus, when new prisoners arrived or groups of prisoners needed to be moved, the camp police were on hand to ensure
there were no incidents.[35] Also, it was the camp police who were
called upon to carry out the "controls," the shakedowns of barracks searching for stolen or unauthorized materials.[36]

The Haves and Have-Nots

Ravensbrück prisoners were of two minds concerning prisoner
officials, or at least their benefits to the inmates. The division on
this issue was fundamentally along class lines. Inmates from the
less crowded, elite blocks generally approved of the system, saying
it was "a salvation for the prisoners"[37] and in retrospect praising
their own prisoner officials.[38] Inmates from the "slums,"[39] on the
other hand, could see few benefits. To Helen Ernst, the main function of the camp police was to drive away the scavengers and beg-
gars from the "prosperous" (*wohlhabenden*) blocks.[40] Hildegard
Hansche, a Ph.D. who had experiences in the elite blocks as well
as in the slums, wrote that what she most resented about her
three years at Ravensbrück was how, most of the time, the overseers stood around with folded arms and let the prisoners do their

Nina Jirsikova, "Block Accommodations." This illustration is of the Czech block, clearly one of the elite barracks. *Sammlungen Ravensbrück.* Courtesy *Mahn- und Gedenkstätte Ravensbrück.*

Violette LeCoq, "Living Room." LeCoq's drawing is of the French
barracks, home to many "Have-Nots." From *Témoignages*. . . .
Courtesy Mme. Violette Rougier-LeCoq.

dirty work. All the real running of the camp was done by the prisoners, and what resulted was "a farce of democracy." The prisoner
officials, much better fed and cared for than other prisoners, were
surrounded by an entourage of toadies who carried out their every
wish. The prisoner officials lived in nice barracks and had their
daily warm baths. Hansche bitterly concluded: "And across from
them were the thousands of hungry, louse-ridden prisoners whom
they hated and who hated them."[41]

CHAPTER

The Camp Routine

9

Helen Ernst, "Lunch Break."
Courtesy *Stadtgeschichtsmuseum Schwerin.*

Roll Calls and Food

At 4:00 A.M., the first sirens sounded, unleashing a torrent of activity, a "dance of madness"[1] in the barracks and on the camp streets lasting several hours. The block and room seniors were the chief choreographers as they dashed about the rows of bunks yelling and shaking those still asleep. Some women went directly to the washroom and got in line; others used this time to make their beds in the militarily precise manner required. Meanwhile, the table seniors and their helpers had gone to the kitchens for that day's bread ration and a "dark liquid resembling coffee." These would be distributed, but most inmates saved their bread for later.[2]

A second siren sounded at about 5:00 A.M. This was the signal for roll call (*Appelstehen*). Now the block seniors marshaled their troops out into the roll call grounds (*Appelplatz*). Each block had its precise place, and each prisoner knew her place in the forma-

France Audoul, "Roll-call grounds, with kitchen in the background." From *Ravensbrück: 15,000 Femmes en Enfer.*

tion consisting of rows of ten. The block seniors took the roll, noting the disposition of each prisoner in her Block Book. It was usually at least an hour before all the numbers checked out and the overseers appeared. The block senior, standing on the right flank of her block, would call the block to attention when her overseer ("a cook in a general's uniform," according to one discriminating inmate)[3] approached, then would make her report. Normally, the overseer accepted this, but on occasion she walked between the rows, and if she noticed any breach of regulations, she would stop to discipline the offender, even striking her. Roll calls generally went more quickly in the morning than at night in order to get the prisoner laborers off to their workplaces. "Time was money for the SS enterprises."[4] Once all the prisoners had been accounted for, another siren sounded, indicating dismissal.[5]

Understandably, most prisoners disliked roll call, but the feeling was not universal. While Margarete Buber-Neumann was room senior of the Asocials, she looked forward to roll call because then the Asocials had to keep quiet and stop bickering.[6] Many of the Polish Catholic women used this as a time to pray.[7] And those prisoners, like Wanda Poltawska, whose sensitivity had not been dulled by life in the camp, looked forward to it for another reason: "Roll calls were our salvation, for at those times we could watch magnificent sunrises and sunsets when the sky was radiant with unimaginable colors."[8] Another prisoner wrote: "Never before have I seen such a beautiful sky. It appears to be constantly changing, always in different variations and shades of color....Sunrise, which we got to observe every morning, was really an experience."[9]

If the morning roll call had gone smoothly and not lasted too long—the length of time varied from about twenty minutes to several hours—there might be time for the women to go back into the barracks and take care of small matters like writing a letter or doing a bit of bartering. Soon, however, they would need to report to their work crews. Some of the less fortunate prisoners had no regular work assignments, but were classified as Availables (*Verfügbaren*, often called *Verfugs*). After the work crews had gone off,

France Audoul, "Knitting Detail." From
Ravensbrück: 15,000 Femmes en Enfer.

they continued waiting. Sometimes one of them would be made to take the place of an absent worker in a regular crew. But, for the most part, they were used in outside work, heavy menial labor that took no skills or training.[10]

The Availables not chosen for work in the morning could return to the barracks. They were expected to clean the washrooms and the sleeping areas, and they joined other, mostly older women, in a kind of knitting detail, who knitted socks and caps for the SS. The Availables were, however, still on call. At any moment the camp police might enter and yell: "Twenty Availables needed for unloading bags of cement!"[11]

At noon, the women who worked inside the camp returned to their blocks for lunch. The Availables brought the heavy soup kettles from the kitchens to the separate blocks, where it was divided. Old-timers could remember when, in the early days of the camp, everyone got a two-hour lunch break.[12] But the food was better then and there was more of it. By 1941, the lunch break had been reduced to thirty to forty minutes, barely enough time to eat a bowl of the thin cabbage or turnip soup, with perhaps a piece of the bread saved from that morning.[13] Then it was back to work for the remainder of the day.

Before 1941, the workday ended at 5:00 P.M., and after dinner the inmates were given a "free hour," during which they could

France Audoul, "Carrying the Soup." From *Ravensbrück: 15,000 Femmes en Enfer.*

walk around the camp and visit with friends.[14] But the workday had gradually been expanded from the original eight hours to ten hours, and by 1942, it was eleven hours for many prisoners. There was no time for a free hour when the day shift ended at 7:00 P.M. and "lights out" occurred at 9:00 P.M.[15]

As soon as the prisoners returned to their barracks, they sat

down for their evening meal. Many had been thinking about sup-
per all afternoon, and as a returning shift met the night shift
going to work, the question was always asked: "What's the soup
tonight?" [16] And the response was nearly always the same: "The
very soup we had for lunch." The actual distribution of the soup
was handled by the room senior. If she liked you, she gave you a
ladle from the bottom. "And if she didn't, she gave you from the
top, and whoever she liked she knew what to do."[17] Sometimes the
soup was "improved" by the addition of potato peelings or even a
few potatoes.[18] It was watery. It tasted terrible. But it was nourishment, and the prisoners devoured their portions. Prisoner officials received extra portions. Since there was rarely enough salt in
the soup, prisoners who had purchased salt at the canteen would
carefully sprinkle some over their bowl and perhaps share some
with a neighbor in exchange for a favor. Again, there was bread to
have with the soup, although many prisoners liked to stockpile
bread during the week so they could have a "blow-out" on the
weekend, or use it for some necessary bartering.[19]

Food was always on their minds: "Hunger was our closest com-
panion. It was with us when we woke up and it went with us to
bed, never leaving us for a second."[20] The women talked constantly of recipes and cooking; they dreamed of food.[21] If a prisoner
related a story about a past experience, somebody was sure to ask:
"And where did you have dinner afterward?" They would fantasize
about imaginary feasts and plan menus.[22] They kept secret journals of recipes and never tired of exchanging them. Halina
Nelken, a Jewish inmate at the Malchow subcamp, recalled how
in her barracks each day began with somebody asking the rhetor-
ical question: "What are you cooking today?" It turned into a
humorous little game, as from all the bunks imaginative responses were forthcoming: a Ukrainian woman was cooking pierogies,
Klara was making potato pancakes, Frau Preger was whipping
cream to make a nut torte. Then suddenly, someone interrupted
the proceedings by yelling out: "Just a minute! I have to look in
the oven to see that I don't burn the roast. On Wednesdays I

always make roast beef with dumplings."[23]

Prisoners tried every conceivable means of supplementing their meager rations. Those who were marched past the pig farm on the way to or from work hoped the pigs had just been fed, for then they would scoop up a bowl of "good pig food" as they went past.[24] When Lottie Müller's friend Elli was given some bones and rice and was ordered to cook up some dog food for the camp dogs, she discovered that what she had prepared tasted better than her own food. She, of course, sneaked some for her close friends, who also enjoyed it.[25] Micheline Maurel admitted that her preoccupation with food had changed her whole outlook: "As for me, I didn't bear love for anyone anymore. When I thought of home, it was only to see the larder in the kitchen, the basket where the bread was stored."[26]

The evening meal could be taken more leisurely than the day's other meals, but eventually the siren would sound and the women would have to assemble for the evening roll call. This was nearly always longer and more unpleasant than morning roll calls. Talking was forbidden, but during the longer sessions, prisoners whispered to each other, talking about family and food, even exchanging recipes. Sometimes during long roll calls, the conversations rose to a noticeable murmur, perhaps resulting in punishment. Roll calls sometimes lasted hours, while overseers and block seniors checked and rechecked their head counts. It was painful for all the inmates, but for the old and the sick, it could be life-threatening. It was against regulations to support anyone or help her up, so if an inmate fell over, she had to be left on the ground until roll call was over.[27]

But, at length, every roll call had to end and the women would be allowed to return to their barracks. Many of the prisoners would do little more than wash their bowls (all inmates had to maintain their own utensils) and go to bed. A few would chat, but at nine o'clock, the lights were turned out and prisoners were to be in bed. If they were lucky, they could sleep until 4:00 A.M. But their sleep was sometimes interrupted by the night watch, whose

responsibility it was to see that prisoners did not wear unauthorized clothing, such as stockings or trousers, to bed. In cold weather, most prisoners took the risk and wore all their clothes to bed
in order to stay warm, then slept lightly to detect a visit by the
overseer.[28] Even worse, there were occasional "special roll calls" in
the middle of the night, carried out purely for harassment purposes.[29]

Weekends

The women of Ravensbrück lived for the weekend. In the workplaces in and around the camp, there was a half day of work on
Saturday, followed by a roll call. But this was made tolerable by
the knowledge that it would be followed shortly by mail call, for
some prisoners the high point of the week. From then until
Monday morning, they were left relatively alone. There was a roll
call Sunday morning, but it was at a more agreeable hour, sometimes not until noon.[30] Some of this time had to be spent cleaning
and fixing things in the barracks, and there was always the possibility of a special roll call.[31]

Still, in the relative way that Ravensbrück inmates understood
better than anybody, weekends were wonderful. And the best part
of this was the "promenade," strolling on the camp streets. There
were still regulations, and the overseers were sometimes (but not
always) "picky" in enforcing them: no walking arm in arm, no
forming of large groups, no deviation in the wearing of uniforms.[32]
But what a delight! Strolling with one or two close friends,
exchanging gossip, and sometimes hearing music (including the
Berlin Rundfunk Orchestra) over the loudspeakers. The music
was not always to everyone's taste, but the advantage, soon discovered by the Politicals, was that the music made it difficult for
eavesdroppers to overhear their conversations. In fact, the
Communists took advantage of this opportunity to organize and to
exchange information.[33]

For most of the strollers, however, it was pure pleasure, uncontaminated by political or ideological considerations. The gossip was fantastic: Head SS Overseer Dorothea Binz was the Mistress of Camp Leader Edmund Bräuning, the second in command. Or this: Binz would sometimes engage in lesbian lovemaking in front of prisoners.[34] A number of groups which stressed cultural activity, including the Czechs, who by general consent had the best of several choirs in the camp, used these Sunday afternoons "when the overseers rested and the prisoners were watched over less attentively than usual" to hone their talents and to present performances.[35] While most of the strollers stayed with women of their own nationality, some took advantage of the opportunity to walk with foreigners and even to learn a new language.[36]

A Danish inmate has left a wonderful description of Sundays in the camp: All the different nationalities strolled, more or less sep-

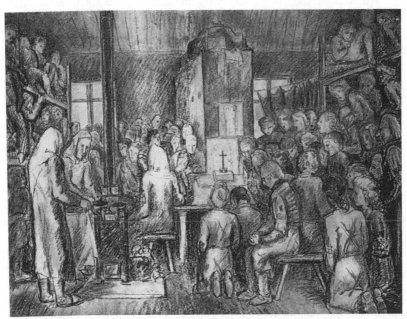

France Audoul, "Forbidden Prayers." From *Ravensbrück: 15,000 Femmes en Enfer.*

arately, on the main camp street. The French women somehow managed to look chic in their ragged prison clothes. "In spite of regulations against this, they wore their kerchiefs in a hundred different ways." At the end of the street the Czech choir was singing, surrounded by an appreciative audience. They had to post a watch in case the camp police showed up. Behind a barracks a small group of Jehovah's Witnesses sang softly.[37]

For many women, Sunday was a time for religious services. Since any form of unauthorized assembly was forbidden, and large gatherings were more likely to attract attention, it was generally safer to meet in small groups. Thus, convocations of six to ten women were typical and were to be found throughout the camp.[38] But by posting a watch, it was possible to hold larger services. The Polish blocks normally held a Mass each Sunday.[39] French prisoners performed a Mass every fourth Sunday, then met in smaller groups in between.[40]

Weekends, too, were used by prisoners to do all those little things for which there simply was no time during the workweek: writing letters, washing underwear (some women used the promenade to dry their things by holding their wet clothes between them as they strolled),[41] or maybe doing a little bartering. Many prisoners were sleep deprived and would use Sundays for a nice long nap or, in the case of the French, to practice the proverb "Qui dort dîne" ("She who sleeps forgets her hunger").[42]

Prisoners in many of the blocks took advantage of the relative freedom during the weekend to pursue a whole range of educational and cultural activities. There were poetry readings and performances of plays.[43] Lectures were given on a variety of topics, very often by real experts in their fields. Classes were offered on a vast selection of subjects. There was individual instruction, too, most often tutoring inmates in the German language, a necessary survival skill. Eugenia Kocwa, in the Polish Block, insisted that her "pupils" rise early on Sunday for their weekly English class.[44] Even the food improved on weekends. Sometimes on Sundays the soup was embellished with rutabagas or pieces of real meat,[45] and occasionally each prisoner was allotted a dab of cheap margarine and either a piece of cheese or some "war marmalade."[46]

This schedule was not immutable. In the winter months the first siren sounded at 5:00 A.M., rather than at 4:00 A.M. And in 1944, most of the factories and workplaces extended their operating hours to include all of Saturday. This left Sunday as the only real rest day, aside from Easter Monday and Christmas.[47]

Clothing and Possessions

Newly arrived prisoners had to turn in all items in their possession. After they had turned in their clothing, they were issued uniforms: "A course gray shirt, a blue-gray striped dress with no lining, a half-apron, a bandanna, a pair of wooden shoes virtually worn out, a uniform which could appear to make a relatively standard outward appearance for the prisoners."[48]

Aat Breur, drawing showing a group of prisoners in winter clothing. (The drawing has been badly damaged.) From *Een verborgen herinnering*. Courtesy Dunya Breur.

In the early years of the camp, prisoners generally were issued two complete uniforms, one for winter and another for summer. By 1943, this practice was being restricted, and by 1944, it was discontinued. There were no longer uniforms to be issued. Prisoners were allowed to keep their own clothes, but on the backs (sometimes also on the fronts) there was now painted a huge "X."[49] Diminishing supplies (and other materials, including food) was clearly a major factor in the camp administration's decision to allow most prisoners the right to receive an unrestricted number of packages, beginning in October 1942. Clothing, like food, came to be "organized" (the prisoners' term for wheeling and dealing or bartering). Those prisoners who worked in the storerooms where clothing was kept gained many advantages.[50] Warm clothing became so sought after that prisoners would trade bread for underwear. In the prisoners' letters home, one of the most common requests was for a warm jacket or socks. One young Dutch woman, who had no family, wrote to German acquaintances and pleaded with them to send her a pullover, stockings and underclothes, "even men's underpants will do."[51]

Most of the women who had had their heads shaved upon arrival were allowed to grow it back, but some were not: German women found guilty of "race defilement" were shaved upon entry, then periodically after that, usually every month or two.[52] Women assigned to the Punishment Block had their heads shaved regularly.[53] The lucky ones who had their hair were required to have it pulled back very tight or else kept under a bandanna. Women who violated camp regulations on this issue risked being given an "overseer's haircut." An overseer, backed up by the camp police, would take scissors and cut haphazardly through an offender's hair, leaving an unsightly mess of bare spots and tufts.[54]

Most prisoners had few possessions. Besides their clothing, they were issued blankets, bowls, and wooden spoons, at least up until 1943. After that, the newcomers had to supply their own, by either stealing or bartering.[55] Since theft was such a common occurrence, most inmates learned to leave their things only with trusted friends or, better yet, carry their bowls and spoons with them wherever they went. Most prisoners eventually made little bags for this purpose.[56]

It was not unusual for prisoners to have other small possessions: small crafted dolls received as gifts from other prisoners, little books of handwritten poems, a comb and other toiletry articles. Once, while taking a cold shower, Antonia Bruha had her toiletry case stolen, and it was traumatic for her: "My last possession is gone," she cried.[57] The politicals kept a copy of *War and Peace* carefully hidden, and brought it out for occasional group read-

Aat Breur, drawing of a woman making her way through the camp, carrying her possessions under her arm and her eating utensils on her belt. From *Een verborgen herinnering*. Courtesy Dunya Breur.

ings.[58] Books, diaries, journals, drawings, notebooks, were all illegal and subject to confiscation. But everyone knew these things abounded in the barracks, along with other contraband, such as knives fashioned from pieces of metal.[59]

Periodically, the prisoners could expect to be "controlled," that is, subjected to a shakedown inspection by the SS and the camp police. It was a painfully upsetting experience for the women. It worked like this: the inmates of a particular block would be taken outside their barracks and made to completely undress in the

Violette LeCoq, "Inspection." From *Témoignages* . . . . Courtesy Mme.
Violette Rougier-LeCoq.

presence of their overseer, the camp leader, and numerous SS
men. The camp police would then thoroughly go through their
clothing, item by item, checking for anything stolen from the
warehouses, or unauthorized. Meanwhile, other camp police did
the same inside the barracks, searching under beds, inside mattresses, even under floor boards. Unauthorized goods were confiscated, and the offenders were punished.[60]

The routine of daily life at Ravensbrück was anything but constant. It varied according to a multitude of factors, all of which
were beyond the control of the prisoners: the weather and the seasons, the composition of the prisoner population at a given time,
the whims of the SS, and the changing fortunes of war for
Germany. This last factor became increasingly important after
1942, when the needs of Germany's war effort caused a reorientation of the very purposes of the concentration camp system, and

when military setbacks prompted Nazi leaders to reconsider their whole program of resource allocation.

Without exception, veteran inmates who had been in the camp since its early days commented on the deterioration of conditions, particularly in the last year and a half of the war. The first years were "an idyll" compared to what came later.[61]

The changes in the camp routine and the deteriorating conditions of daily life in the women's camp were predictable factors in the whole equation of SS policies. When times became hard and there was a need for belt-tightening, the concentration camp inmates were hit first and hardest by retrenchment. While other levels of society in Germany also suffered (but not the SS leadership, who continued to enjoy luxuries such as gourmet food, maid service, and nannies for their children until the very end), the prisoner population was spared no hardship. They represented the lowest, most powerless, and certainly most expendable component of society, and by early 1945 many of them were forced into an existence that can only be described as animal-like.

Helen Ernst, untitled drawing. Courtesy *Stadtgeschichtsmuseum Schwerin.*

Friendships

Violette LeCoq, "Friendship." From *Témoignages*. . .
Courtesy Mme. Violette Rougier-LeCoq.

It was a truism of the concentration camp experience that "You simply couldn't survive alone."[1] Without friends to care for you, cover up for you, and bring you food, an illness would likely be fatal. Without trusted comrades to watch your things when you were away, most of your meager possessions would be stolen. And without confidantes to share your grief and lift your spirits, a debilitating depression was the logical outcome. Many prisoners succumbed even with this help, but without it they had little or no chance. Although we know few details about individual cases, it appears that suicide was a fairly common occurrence at Ravensbrück, most often committed by running against the electric fence.[2] Even though she herself was depressed and considering taking her own life, Hardy Kupferberg somehow mustered the strength to counsel others against suicide.[3] One unfortunate girl became so despondent that she simply lay down on the floor of the barracks and refused to get up for anybody, not even the block senior. She was taken away and was never heard from again.[4]

After their liberation, former prisoners were unanimous in suggesting that without the support networks provided by close friends, few of them would have lived to see freedom. These networks were based upon a number of ingredients, including the ties of religious beliefs and political affiliations, but language and nationality were the key determinants in prisoner groupings. Overwhelmingly, prisoners chose their immediate friends from among their fellow nationals.

Camp Families

At Ravensbrück, the most widely used mechanism for sustaining close friendships was the camp family. This could be composed of as few as two prisoners, or as many as seven or eight, but the norm seems to have been between three and five persons. Nearly all the national groups represented in the camp appear to have created such families. Red Army women called their groupings of

four to five women "communes," but in essential respects they
functioned much like the others.[5] A typical example of a camp family is that of Erika Kounio and her mother, Greek Jews who
arrived at Ravensbrück in January 1945 and were quickly dispatched to the small subcamp at Malchow. There they learned of
three other Greek girls in their barracks, and they soon became
more than casual friends: "My mother was the 'mother of the company,'" Erika noted. "Together with the three girls we were a family."[6] Through a broad-based 1978 survey of Polish survivors, we
have more detailed information on Polish camp families than
about any other group, and it is these we shall primarily discuss.[7]

Camp families came into existence in one of two ways, the most
common being an evolutionary process: Inmates who arrived
together and were assigned to the same block became friends and
somewhat informally established the ties which set them off from
other inmates.[8] The other method was a more formal process by
which prisoners consciously and intentionally asked others to join
with them in group formation. This happened to Miroslawa
Grupinska, when Kicia and a friend came to her and asked if she
wanted to join with them. She was delighted at the offer and
joined at once. Her family was called the "Cat Family" after its
leading figure, Kicia, who was called *Kätzchen* (Kitty).[9]

Ideally, families whose members worked in strategic positions,
such as in the infirmary, the kitchens, or the storehouses, were
strengthened, since this gave them connections to key goods and
services. For obvious reasons, it was crucial to have a family member who was fluent in German, and if a member happened to be
on close terms with the block senior, so much the better.[10] But the
women were not always so calculating, and many times they
joined with others to form a family purely on the basis of personal preferences or because they happened to work together.

One characteristic of a camp family was essential if the group
were to be successful, and that was the attachment of at least one
older woman, a camp mother (*Lagermutter*) to the younger
inmates. "Older" in this case is a relative term. Seventeen-year-

old Jozefa had two camp mothers, Janina and Helena, both thirty years old.[11] Camp mothers served absolutely necessary functions, not the least of which was sharing the wisdom of their experiences with younger inmates. This might mean nothing more than motherly admonitions to keep clean, but at times it meant long discussions.[12] And, of course, it included the kind of consoling for which mothers have always been known. One young woman, Urzula Broniatowska, explained how she would go over to her "Mutti" when the lights were turned out, lay her head on her lap, and find a few moments of comfort.[13]

One of these camp mothers, forty years old in 1942, described the situation from the other point of view, and in the process displayed a great deal of understanding:

> Thanks to my friendship with Urzula, I began to comprehend how much the younger women needed our motherly care. . . . How often Urzula came to me in the sewing factory where we worked, during the nightly break, and put her head on my lap for the fifteen minutes until the lights came on, in order to forget the camp. How many problems which lay heavily on the girl's mind, we were able to take care of together.[14]

The Polish prisoners had a particular advantage in that nearly all the older Polish women, having been born and raised in areas under German rule before 1918, knew German very well. Irena Matusiak would write her letters in Polish, give them to her *Müttchen* (mommy), who would translate them into German, then in turn translate the letters she received.[15] Janina Kiszka-Kalicka tutored Jozefa and her other "camp daughters" in the German language. But it was a mutual arrangement: when Janina got sick and was sent to the infirmary, Jozefa took the risk of violating regulations in order to visit her and share her own rations with her.[16]

Margarete Buber-Neumann and Milena Jesenska developed a relationship which had all the characteristics of a camp family, although they never called it that. Milena, the bisexual girlfriend of Franz Kafka,[17] shared with Margarete a disillusionment with

Communism for which they were both ostracized by the other
Politicals. They also shared a love of ideas, a commitment to
humanistic values, and an undeniable snobbishness, finding the
majority of their fellow inmates "unbearable in every way."[18]
Milena was frail when she arrived at Ravensbrück in 1940, and
her health quickly deteriorated. From the beginning, Margarete
did all she could to protect, support, and nourish her Czech friend,
but her efforts were ultimately unsuccessful. Milena died in May
1944.[19]

Another example of a family of two is that of Marcelle Pardé
and Simone Plessis. Pardé had been the directoress of a *lycée* (secondary school) in Dijon, and Simone was her secretary. Both active
members of the French Resistance, they were arrested in 1944,
brought to Ravensbrück, sent together to the subcamp at Torgau,
but after a time became separated. This separation was so disturbing to Pardé that she lost weight, became seriously ill, and
died. Her friend and confidante, Simone, was brought back to
Ravensbrück also seriously ill, and she died shortly thereafter.[20]

Four young Jewish women who arrived together from Budapest
in October 1944 took every imaginable precaution against being
separated. Under the leadership of Sara, the oldest (she was 26,
the others were 20, 19, and 16 years old) a cohesive camp family
was established. They stole vegetables from the SS and shared
with each other, they protected each other against outsiders, and
they nursed each other when they became ill. When Lily's glasses
were broken by a block senior, the others rallied to support her,
since she was nearly blind without them. They walked with her,
helped her at work, and deloused her in the evening. Like many
camp families, this one was very much turned inward. They
shared the benefits of their cameraderie with few outsiders, not
even other Jews.[21]

It was one's close-knit circle of friends that one spent time with,
went strolling with on Sunday, and for whom one did favors.
Sometimes these little cliques had birthday parties for their members, complete with little hand-crafted presents or poems. And, of

course, there were extra bread rations, carefully saved by one's friends. It was one's family, too, who mourned the deaths of their members, and in some instances held memorial services months or even years later.[22]

Those women who were fortunate enough to become part of a camp family, and not all of them were, found themselves in a rather exclusive circle. Still, we must keep in mind that families were always a subgroup within a block. In some cases, there was considerable camaraderie within a block. One had other friends and acquaintances, people one worked with, and people one stood beside for long hours at roll call. Nevertheless, one's primary social orientation was to close friends and family. They were the people you arranged jobs for, the people you shared the contents of your packages with, the ones you took risks for; they were, ultimately, the people who really mattered. And the others? It's not that they didn't matter, but one could not, after all, take risks for everyone.[23]

Intimacy and Homoerotic Relationships

Sometimes close contact and even intimacy were rather forced upon a person. But sleeping three to a bed, what could one do? At first, Catherine Roux, who was French, did not get along with her two German-Jewish bunk mates, but then she began to feel sorry for Welli, 24 years old and dying of typhus: "Welli is a little dying bird, fallen from an empty nest." At night Welli would cling to her. "She is so thin, so diminished that next to her, I feel as if I were a giant. I take her in my arms as if I could transmit some of my life to her, some of my warmth." Although they could not communicate because of the language barrier, they understood each other. "With her little head nestled against my shoulder, she spoke so sweetly to me in the German tongue, which I find so expressive, so right in its intonation."[24]

Another example of intimacy is in the personal delousing that was so common, and which "became a part of each evening's ritual, even during our literary sessions."[25] One woman, taking another's head in her lap and searching for the minute creatures was not performing just an act of hygiene; it was an act of caring: "Evelyne would ask me to tell her stories and while I did so she would delouse me."[26]

In a number of cases, of course, women of various nationalities had firmly established identities as lesbians or bisexuals before ever arriving at Ravensbrück. But the special conditions of a women's concentration camp—not only the oppressiveness, but also the absence of available men—no doubt worked to significantly raise the whole level of homoerotic behavior. Anise Postel-Vinay remembered how, on cold nights, "To warm us both up, Germaine Tillion used to slip into my bed after lights out."[27] Kvieta, a young Czech dancer, apparently developed a crush on Micheline Maurel because of a poem Micheline had written about her. Micheline's response:

> Kvieta could give me her affection if she wanted to; I would try not to let her down. I would give her as much affection as I could. This feeling was apparently as precious to her as bread. Once, as she was walking back to Block 3 with me in the evening, she suddenly caught me by the arm and kissed me. I returned the kiss. She seemed to glow with joy and then she turned and bounded away.[28]

Nearly all of the Ravensbrück survivors who wrote memoirs have commented upon the extent of lesbian activity in the camp. It was, by all accounts, extremely widespread. Buber-Neumann believed that camp life fostered strong friendships, and while those of Politicals most often remained platonic, others did not.[29] Isa Vermehren, too, noted the prevalence of homosexuality, and believed the system encouraged this. She added that one could hardly blame women for taking whatever affection they could get, including lesbian relationships.[30] Conversations among women often turned to observations of how lonely they were and how long the nights were, recalled Erika Buchmann, and she noted that women were therefore driven to other women, many of whom had no previous experience in lesbian relationships or were unsure of their own sexuality. She remembered that as they lay crammed together in their beds, they could not avoid seeing and hearing the lovemaking, "sometimes shameless and unrestrained." On occasion, if one got up at night to use the toilet, one had to wait because the "little couples" (*Pärchen*) were in the small compartments with the doors locked.[31]

At the subcamp in Neubrandenburg, Fanny Marette would often cross the yard to use the toilet at night. As she did this, she would sometimes see women making love in the shadows. Nearly always one of the lovers was a *Blockova* or *Stubova*, exchanging, she surmised, rewards for caresses. At this point, Marette was too weak to even think of physical love, and half enviously she thought: "What vitality!"[32]

In early 1942, Block 11 was so filled with homosexuals that other prisoners commonly referred to it as "the lesbian block." When Wanda Poltawska and a small group of Polish women were placed there temporarily, they were terrorized by the lesbians, who made it clear to them who was in charge. Moreover, Poltawska wrote, "propositions came thick and fast. Apparently I was in demand as a woman as well as a man."[33]

Lesbians at Ravensbrück needed to be somewhat circumspect, for according to camp rules, homosexual behavior was a punishable offense. Ironically, outside the camp, female homosexuality was never criminalized by the Nazi regime.[34] Paragraph 175, which had been enacted in 1871, had outlawed sexual acts between men, but had not addressed the issue of female homosexuality. Although under the National Socialists there was some discussion of extending Paragraph 175 to women, it was never done, and therefore sexual relations between women remained technically within the bounds of legality.[35] There is no recorded instance in which a woman was arrested and brought to Ravensbrück for being a homosexual. But inside the camp, those women who engaged in homosexual practices risked being arrested and sent to the Punishment Block, where "they found more of their kind," according to an unsympathetic witness.[36] In one notorious case, a block senior and a room senior, both Asocials, were caught in the act of lovemaking and were arrested. They were flogged, then sent off in a punishment transport. However, this particularly harsh sentence appears to have been mainly the result of camp authorities finding all kinds of contraband in their beds. Some of this was taken from other prisoners, but most of it had been stolen from SS warehouses. Many inmates were pleased at this outcome, since the offending room senior, Lena Shura, had been one of the "strong arms" who, in exchange for double bread rations, volunteered to beat fellow prisoners in the Bunker.[37]

Arrests for lesbian activity at Ravensbrück were more the exception than the rule. For the most part, and this was especially true by 1944, camp authorities turned a blind eye to the whole issue, acting as though no "problem" existed. However, by keeping antihomosexual rules on the books, they had a pretext for action and harsh punishment, which is likely what happened in the Shura case.

As one of a large transport of French women who arrived at Ravensbrück in early 1944, Denise Clark noticed quite a number of lesbian couples in the camp. She recalled that the partners in the relationship who were considered more masculine were called "Jules," and they would make a cross on the foreheads of their "steadies."[38] Denise Dufournier, another French prisoner who arrived at about the same time, described how these "Jules" were nearly always German Criminals or Asocials, very masculine in appearance and mannerisms. Further: "As night fell, couples were seen embracing behind the blocks. Any prisoner who had a recognized Jules enjoyed a certain prestige among her companions. . . . As soon as a new couple was noticed, they were the recipients of what amounted to congratulations from the rest of the camp." And while a lesbian relationship was in theory a severely punishable offense, "In practice no measures were ever taken, even in the case of prisoners caught red-handed, as the guards and *Blockovas,* whose business it was to expose them, were more often than not guilty themselves."[39] It was an open secret, at least among French prisoners, that one of their own, a young medical student from Mulhouse, had fallen passionately in love with the chief female doctor (*Chefärztin*) at the infirmary, and the two "lived together as a couple."[40]

What appears to have been happening at Ravensbrück in the last stages of the war was, first, that prison authorities were applying the same regulations concerning female homosexuality inside the camp that were applied outside; in other words, lesbianism became *de facto* legalized. Second, these authorities came to the same conclusion as have other caretakers of women's prisons in other times and places: that in the absence of men, sexual liaisons between women were probably natural, certainly unpreventable, and perhaps desirable (from the point of view of maintaining order in the camp), especially as many of these lesbian relationships were quite permanent.[41]

Social relationships at Ravensbrück ran the spectrum from platonic attachments through intimate and warm friendships to passionate lesbian love matches. In examining these, one thing seems rather clear: Overwhelmingly, these friendships which formed between women were both profound and durable. Women in the camp attached tremendous importance to their close friendships and they were intensely loyal to those friends. The literature of survivor memoirs and the "reports of experiences" verify the idea that friendships were not something the women took lightly. In fact, many of the friendships, including a few we have discussed, were ended only through transfer or death. In the transient and unpredictable world of the concentration camp, friendship was the one thing women could count on. It was more than a comfort; it was their chief survival mechanism.

CHAPTER

11

Little
Pleasures

Violette LeCoq, "Relaxation." From *Témoignages* ...
Courtesy Mme. Violette Rougier-LeCoq.

Mail

Dear Children,
   I am so happy to be able to write to you. Things are going well with me, and I hope that you're all healthy. Have you heard any news from Benoit? Write to me in the German language. Send me packages without troubling yourselves too much. I am hoping to see you again soon and I kiss you heartily. Mamany.[1]

This is in fact a complete letter, and it is absolutely typical of letters sent by prisoners at Ravensbrück. Except for the early days of the camp when inmates were allowed to write long letters with substance, prisoner correspondence was highly circumscribed and rigidly censored. Each letter was, in essence, a large-sized postcard, with spaces for the prisoner's name, number, and

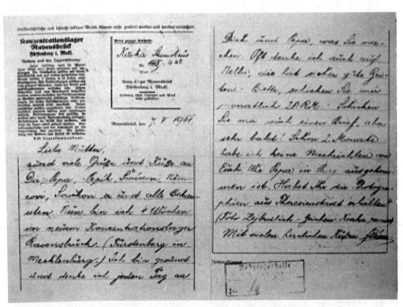

Letter to mother. The small writing in the upper left details the camp regulations concerning correspondence. *Sammlungen Ravensbrück.* Courtesy *Mahn- und Gedenkstätte Ravensbrück.*

block. Then there was a synopsis of the regulations governing correspondence. One survivor complained (in retrospect) that a letter "didn't represent much more than a sign of life, which was understandably of great importance at the time."[2]

Different categories of prisoners had different rules for mail: "Old Politicals" (those arrested before the start of the war) could write two pages twice a month. Most other prisoners were allowed to write 30 lines once each month, and they could receive a letter of 30 lines. Jehovah's Witnesses could write only five lines. Each category of letter was color coded for easy identification, and on the Jehovah's Witnesses' letter, it was printed: "I am still a Jehovah's Witness," which did not shame them at all.[3] Some prisoners were not allowed to write any letters: inmates in the Punishment Block and the NN (Night and Fog) prisoners.[4] And, naturally, some of the Special Prisoners were allowed to write longer letters.[5]

There were other restrictions. All letters, outgoing and incoming, had to be written in German. The reason for this, of course, was to make it easy for the SS censors, but it really did place a significant hardship on many prisoners and their families. All correspondence had to be written in ink, and it had to be easily legible. No money, photos, or drawings could be sent. Only one stamp could be used, and its positioning was regulated. (Indeed, consider how much information could have been conveyed by using several stamps and varying their placements. The SS had thought of everything.) And substantively, there could be absolutely no discussion of camp life, conditions, work, or the war.

The SS censors were not in the least reluctant to use what appear to have been heavy crayons to block out suspicious words or passages, or to take scissors and simply lop off whole sections of a letter. Ludwika Pretrzak felt the need to chide her mother: "Please follow the regulations exactly and write only 30 lines so that I receive the whole letter."[6] Sometimes the censors, in an apparent act of chicanery, would make big black **X**s all over a letter, making it extremely difficult to read.[7] Then, at any infraction

of these rules, they would rubber stamp it, noting "CAMP REGU-
LATIONS ARE TO BE STRICTLY ADHERED TO." Still, it was
mail, and at least one learned that one's mother or loved one was
still alive. Is it any wonder mail call on Saturdays was such an
anticipated event?

After October 1942, when the ban on receiving packages was
lifted, prisoners' letters routinely contained requests for items. As
soon as she could, Ludwika Pretrzak asked her mother to send
stockings, gloves, and "a warm night shirt."[8] Jacqueline Kerilis's
request list was even more extensive: pullover, coat, pants, towel,
handkerchiefs, jacket, soap powder, stockings (but not silk), food
— "but nothing that has to be cooked."[9]

And always there was an underlying homesickness, a pain at
being separated: "Your letters give me the strength to endure. I
am quite well, fat and always of good humor. The only thing which
tortures me is my great yearning for all of you...."[10] Naturally, this
pain was expressed in incoming letters as well: "We wait patiently for the day when you will come home. It's hard on us to have you
there, dear child. Mother and I particularly have a great longing
to see our dear daughter again. Live well, dear child."[11]

There were a few prisoners of strong personality and intellect
whose spirits had not been dulled by the concentration camp experience and whose letters rose above the mundane and the ordinary. One of these was Paula Lohagen, an old Political (Prisoner
No. 914), assigned to Block 1. Her letters to her husband, who was
imprisoned elsewhere, are remarkable for their thoughtfulness,
perceptiveness, and sensitivity. Watching two airplanes, she wrote
about the beauty she saw in their interplay and on the sun shin-
ing on them "like silver. . . . But I must then reflect on the human
spirit, which is capable of creating such things. What a path from
the first stone-throwers to modern machines. And we hardly know
what is yet to come because human history is yet so short. We
stand only at the beginning."[12] Lohagen found great joy in nature,
and even in the camp delighted in observing the birds in their separate seasons, the crows and the *Elstern* in winter, the red tails

and *Bachstelzen* in summer.[13] In late 1942, she was sent to Auschwitz. After telling her husband not to be alarmed by her new address, she wrote: "Darling, now when I look out the window, I can just see in the distance the beginning of the Carpathians. What an event it was for me to see mountains again after such a long time."[14]

Regulations were modified concerning correspondence with soldiers in the field. Their letters could be answered at once "in order to fortify their fighting will."[15] Moreover, they apparently did not need to keep within the 30-line limit required of other writers. In March 1945, a soldier, Barbl, wrote to his fiancée, Johanna Bellinger, and decorated the letter with pressed flowers and brightly painted ladybugs. This was never allowed from civilians because of the possibility of these decorations containing secret messages. The censors permitted Barbl's letter, in part because they had become less strict in the later stages of the war, but also because he appeared to be a zealous National Socialist. Twice in his letter Barbl noted that "we will be victorious." His conclusion: "And now my dear, Happy Easter and do believe in the victory of our *Führer* and our *Volk*."[16]

There was a basis for SS precautions; prisoners did send secret messages. The easiest way to do this was to make references to relatives who did not exist. The SS censors would not know they did not exist, but one's family would. Rosa Menzer had written other letters to her children in which she had referred to a nonexistent "Hilda's aunt" and they soon caught on that this meant their mother. In early 1942, Rosa seems to have learned that she would be selected and sent to the "Healing and Nursing Care Facility" at Bernburg, rumored to be a place from which nobody returned. In February 1942, she wrote her daughter: "If Hilda's aunt should have to move from her present address, I wish only that the children remain brave and not let their heads hang low .... I know her to be a woman of courage with a good attitude and a strong will."[17] In fact, not long after this, Rosa Menzer was taken to Bernburg where she was murdered in the gas chamber, another victim of Nazi "euthanasia" policies.[18]

Another method of sending secret messages was used by Polish women to transmit information about the "experimental" surgeries. Working cooperatively, some of them fashioned an invisible ink using their own urine, and they literally wrote between the lines. In order to alert the recipients about the secret message, they had the first letters of each line spell "LIST MOCZEM" (urine writing).[19]

Perhaps the most effective way of getting around the SS censors was to get someone to mail letters through the regular German postal service. Women who worked outside the camp in facilities where foreign POWs or forced workers were also "employed" had an advantage. At the sanatorium in nearby Hohenlychen, Ravensbrück prisoners worked alongside Polish forced laborers, and two of these men conspired to send and receive letters and packages for Polish inmates.[20] In some of the subcamps, sympathetic German workers mailed letters for prisoners. Although fraternization between prisoners and civilian workers was strictly forbidden, it did happen. At the HASAG factory in Leipzig, where forty to fifty Ravensbrück women worked, a young German, Hildegard Dockhorn, became acquainted with a young Russian prisoner, Ludmilla Wakulla, and deposited her letters in the postal box.[21] At Neubrandenburg, a sympathetic job foreman, *Obermeister* Jordan, mailed letters and procured medicines for his prisoner workers.[22] Similar occurrences happened even at Ravensbrück, at the Siemens factory. There a forewoman (*Vorarbeiterin*) named Frau Hintze developed a fondness for Esther Bejarano, a young Jewish woman who worked under her. On her regular trips home to Berlin, Hintze would take Esther's letters with her, to be mailed from the capital.[23]

Parcels

Except for a few Special Prisoners, inmates were not allowed to receive parcels before 1942. In October of that year, however, the policy was changed, permitting an unlimited number of packages, but only for certain groups: Germans, Czechs, and Poles, mainly.[24] In November 1942, Ludwika Pretrzak wrote home excitedly telling her mother she could now be sent anything except alcohol and cigarettes. But, she cautioned, "don't put any letters in the packages."[25]

Quite obviously, the SS had decided to allow packages, not out of concern for the prisoners, but as a means of transferring some of the cost of prisoner maintenance to their families. And the families of inmates did respond. Overnight, the packages began to roll in. Mrs. Gluck, a Special Prisoner, was made supervisor of packages for Block 1, an elite block. By 1944 her block was receiving fifty to sixty parcels each day. Some of these were sent by the Red Cross, but most were from families.[26] The effect of this policy change was two fold. First, it vastly increased the amount and availability of goods in the camp, goods that were used for the comfort and nourishment of certain prisoners, as well as for bartering. Second, it even more vastly widened the gulf between the haves and the have-nots. Most prisoners, in fact, did not receive parcels. They could only look on with envy as the rich (as they saw it) got richer. Lotti Müller's mother would bake potato fritters early in the morning, immediately mail them from the Stettin railway station, and they would arrive in Ravensbrück later that day, if not still warm, at least reasonably fresh.[27]

The infusion of packages was not only a windfall for the more prosperous prisoners, but also for the SS, and especially the overseers. Packages had to be opened in the presence of an overseer, who searched it to make sure there was no written or otherwise illegal material. In mid-1944, a minor crisis occurred when a can of sardines sent to an inmate was found to contain a map of the region.[28] All loaves of bread were cut in half, and the addressee kept only half. Anything arriving in a container was dumped out, with the addressee having to provide something to put it in, while the overseer kept the jar along with some of the contents.[29] Parcels arriving for persons who had died or been transferred to another camp were invariably confiscated. Overseers would ransack Red Cross packages, but would force the prisoners to sign that they had received them.[30] Late in the war they simply pilfered incoming packages outright for anything of value to them.[31]

Getting the News

Inmates at Ravensbrück were permitted to read newspapers, but only Nazi party papers such as the *Völkischer Beobachter* (*VB*).[32] Needless to say, these were not especially popular, but they were reading material, and they did contain some news, however slanted. Even the Communists perused the *VB*, trying to read between its propaganda-filled lines. In September 1944, the *VB* reported that Ernst Thälmann, the long time head of the KPD, had been killed during an air attack on the Buchenwald concentration camp. This news was profoundly disturbing to Communists at Ravensbrück. A few days later an Allied plane dropped leaflets on Ravensbrück. The prisoners were all ordered indoors while the SS gathered up the offensive pamphlets. But at least one "comrade" got a glimpse of a leaflet, which said, first, that the end of the war was near and that Ravensbrück would not be bombed, and second, that Thälmann had been murdered at Buchenwald.[33]

There were other German newspapers around, such as the formerly liberal *Frankfurter Allgemeine Zeitung*, now heavily censored, but still preferable to the *VB*. However, prisoners were not permitted to read these. Zenobia Dubinska remembered how she asked the civilian foreman (*Meister*) in her workplace for the newspaper after he had finished reading it. He said he was afraid of being denounced if he gave it to her. "Throw it in the waste basket," she said, and he did. She smuggled it back to her barracks, where Polish "commentators" read it and then spread the news.[34] This practice seems to have been quite common, as German civilians were often careless in disposing of newspapers.[35] Once the newspapers were in the hands of prisoners, they passed them around. Belgian Communists got the newspapers from German comrades, and they passed them on to others.[36]

The prisoner grapevine for news was well developed by 1944. French inmates at the Holleischen subcamp learned of the Normandy invasion on June 7, spread by word of mouth.[37] Communists at the main camp had learned of it a day earlier, the same day it happened. Their contacts included civilian workers and even a few SS men who gave them information orally. From there the news was spread to one's "circle of reliables,"[38] and we can assume that it took only a short time for information to travel from these circles to workplaces and barracks throughout the camp.

There were times when the prisoners got their "news" direct, right from the source. On those occasions when Hitler spoke on the radio to the *Volk*, such as after important German victories, the women would be assembled, rain or shine, and were made to listen attentively. But as German victories stopped, so did the radio. It broke down and was never repaired.[39]

Bartering

There is little evidence of any significant amount of bartering in the early years of Ravensbrück, that is, until 1941–1942. The barracks were uncrowded and the food was adequate, at least in quantity. However, with the increase in the prisoner populations by 1942, and without a significant improvement in the whole supply and food service mechanisms, the result quickly became evident: deprivation. Those inmates who were useful to the SS and its imperial system were given advantages, as we have seen. The others, those considered expendable, were provided a less than subsistence diet, prevented from receiving packages, and left to fend for themselves. "In general, each person tried in her own way to supplement her food rations."[40]

Bartering went on all the time, from the first roll call in the morning until after lights-out. Everything was traded. Everything had a price, and that price was calculated in units of bread rations, a unit being one prisoner's daily ration of bread or about 200 grams (7 ounces, not quite half a pound). One bread ration would get a person a small bag of salt, three bread rations a nightgown or a fever thermometer.[41] If a soup bowl was stolen, the going rate for a replacement was four rations, sometimes payable on an installment system.[42] When a Belgian prisoner needed a flannel cullotte, she was able to get one for only two rations.[43] Lidia Rolfi, a newly arrived Italian prisoner assigned to the Asocial Block, was approached by a woman trying to sell her a comb. Lidia became irate: "This deviate wants a whole bread ration just for one comb. I will cut my hair completely off today so I won't need a comb. Then I will eat my bread by myself!"[44]

Everything was traded for everything else: clothes for margarine, soap for salt, and so on. But the unit of measurement was still the bread ration. Reportedly, there was a lesbian prostitute in the camp who did business on weekends; her fee was margarine and sausage.[45] When Charlotte Delbo, a French prisoner, was transferred from Auschwitz to Ravensbrück in January 1944, she was amazed to see Gypsy women strolling through the camp in the evening, selling all kinds of things. Like other inmates, she assumed that all their wares were stolen. When they tried to trade roasted meat for bread, Charlotte turned them down, fearing that the meat came from the crematorium.[46]

And where did all these goods for bartering come from? Beginning in 1942, some of this came directly from the packages received by prisoners. By receiving food supplements, some fortunate prisoners were now able to trade their camp bread. Often, however, the goods being bartered were stolen, and everyone knew it. Some of it was stolen from other prisoners, but the largest part was stolen from the SS: from the kitchens, the bakeries, the administrative offices, the shoe shop, and especially from the SS warehouses. The prisoners who worked in these facilities stole things regularly. In some cases, by toadying up to their SS bosses, they had things given to them.[47] More often, SS personnel simply looked the other way as favored prisoners helped themselves. An example of this occurred in late 1944, when a group of "rich Jews" arrived from Hungary. Fifteen "trusted prisoners" went through everything, tearing apart fur coats and false bottoms of suitcases. When they had finished, there was a nice little pile of gold pieces, diamonds and other precious stones, plus jewelry. Most of this went to the SS, but there was an understanding that the "trusted prisoners" would also get their share.[48] Dagmar Hajkova, a Czech Communist and inveterate busybody, railed about how the Communists tried to work against "this dishonorable barter system," but she knew full well, and benefited from the fact, that Czechs who worked in the kitchen regularly stole food and brought it back to their block.[49]

It might have been worse. Micheline Maurel, who was transferred from the main camp to the subcamp at Neubrandenburg, noted that "living was grimmer there than at Ravensbrück." Her reasoning was that the wheeling and dealing that was so widespread at the main camp led to an amelioration of conditions. This was not the case at Neubrandenburg, where there was no stockpile of supplies to loot.[50]

Money

The prisoner-run economy was dominated by the barter system, but in fact, there was also a small money economy at Ravensbrück. Some of the prisoners came into the camp with substantial amounts of cash. Reportedly, Jews and Gypsies sometimes brought their entire savings with them, as much as 3,000

Reichsmark (RM). This money had to be turned in to the Finance Office, where it was put into an account. Then, with that office's permission, one could withdraw up to 5 RM (later on, 12) to be spent only in the prisoner canteen. In addition, it was possible to have funds transferred in (never out) from another bank account, and a few prisoners did this, allowing them to buy articles in the canteen.[51]

In 1943, the practice of rewarding prisoners for meeting or surpassing production quotas was put into place in some of the factories at Ravensbrück. The prisoner was given not cash, but a "premium," a kind of scrip that everyone called "camp money" (*Lagergeld*). It could only be spent in the canteen.[52] Prisoners could only shop there once a week,[53] and the prices were very high.[54] Moreover, Hajkova, the camp's self-appointed food critic, gave them a review that was not likely to trigger a stampede of shoppers. She claimed their offerings were not very good: "an unappetizing, greasy, green fish paté" and other equally bad products.[55] Still, the opportunity to supplement one's meager rations with red beets, margarine, cheese, and marmalade, even though of dubious quality, was irresistible for those who could afford it. If nothing else, it meant extra material for bartering purposes. Eva Busch, a former cabaret performer who had plenty of money, very much looked forward to "shopping day." She regularly bought whatever was available and as much as she was allowed. Then she would share it with her work comrades (*Kumpels*) who had no money.[56]

CHAPTER

12

The Finer Things in Life: Cultural and Educational Activities

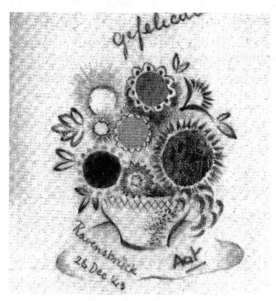

Aat Breur, "Birthday card for Marie Monee-Kremer."
From *Een verborgen herinnering*.
Courtesy Dunya Breur.

It is no small tribute to the human spirit that in the midst of all the exploitation and oppression, the suffering, even torture and death, women prisoners at Ravensbrück raised their sights above their circumstances and found the energy and vision to be creative. They sketched. They painted. They wrote poems and plays. They fashioned little dolls and purses out of scraps. They organized educational programs, with lectures and whole courses. It was an amazing and impressive outpouring of intellectual power and talent.

Poetry

Writing poetry was one of the most widespread of cultural activities at Ravensbrück. Many prisoners, both amateurs and literary professionals, engaged in this. After all, one needed only to do a little bartering for paper and pencil, easily obtained from those who worked in the SS offices. Then too, unlike painting or sculpture, the finished product was easy to hide and convenient to pass around. The verses were often learned by heart, then passed on to others orally. It is important to keep in mind that writing poetry or engaging in other forms of cultural endeavors were activities prohibited by the SS. The women were there to work, not to think, let alone create. If, during one of the "controls" so feared and despised by inmates, sheets of poetry were found, there was certain to be punishment.

On 20 June 1942, when Maria Rutkowska had just arrived at Ravensbrück, the first person to greet her and to help her was a fellow Pole, Ewa Falkowska. Rutkowska was so moved by this act of kindness that she shortly wrote a poem for Falkowska.

The Greeting

Into the measureless emptiness of the soul,
into unending misery
a wonderful gift just fell to me:
Your smile of greeting.

Its warmth melted away the ice
that had let our hearts grow hard.
The whole world was changed
by the Smiling One, by You.

And your pale countenance
appeared holy to us,
so noble was your smile,
and so like a miracle—incomprehensible.

As I read the words from your eyes
I understood what was true,
that you were stronger than the pain, because in
you was embodied Poland.

With your smile you awakened
everything that was resting inside me,
and I again found myself
in an hour of hopelessness.

Because you have done this
in the midst of the despair and the tears,
I believe that in your hour of need
God will reward you for this smile.

Tragically, their contact was very brief. On 7 July 1942, Falkowska was executed at Ravensbrück.[1]

Die Begrüssung

In masslose Leere der Seele,
in unendliches Elend

fiel eine erste herrliche Gabe:
Euer Begrüssungslächeln.

Seine Wärme schmolz das Eis,
das unsere Herzen erstarren liess.
Die ganze Welt war verwandelt
durch die Lächelnde—durch dich.

Und eure blassen Gesichter
erschienen uns heilig,
so erhaben war euer Lächeln
und so wie Wunder—unbegreiflich.

Die Worte von euren Augen ablesend,
begriff ich doch das Wahre,
dass ihr stärker als der Schmerz waret, denn in
euch verbarg sich Polen.

Du wecktest mit deinem Lächeln
all das, was in mir ruhte,
und ich fand mich selbst wieder
in hoffnungsloser Stunde.

Da du das tatest,
nahe der Verzweiflung und den Tränen,
glaube ich—Gott wird dich in der Not
für dieses Lächeln belohnen.

Another Polish prisoner, Halina Galczowa, assigned to the sub-camp at Neubrandenburg, used poetry to express her extreme dismay at working in a German factory for their war industry:

How can I come back to You

How can I come back to You?
How can I stand before You
oh my pain-filled mother
sunk in deepest sadness?

I was frightened of death,
I was afraid of agony and pain,
and now together with the enemy
I work for your undoing.

Woe is me! Days and nights
the Furies pursue me.
Damned are my hands,
damned in what they do.

My forehead bears the brand of shame,
and all in all I am damned.
How can I come back to You,
my Holy Mother—my Homeland?

Wie soll ich zu dir zurückkehren

Wie soll ich zu dir zurückkehren,
wie soll ich mich vor dich hinstellen,
oh meine schmerzerfüllte Mutter,
in tiefer Trauer versunken?

Ich erschrak vor dem Tode,
ich erschrak vor dem Leid und Schmerz,
und jetzt zusammen mit dem Feind
arbeite ich für dein Kreuz.

Weh mir—tags und nachts
stellen die Erinnyen mir nach.
Verdammt sind meine Hände,
verdammt in ihrer Tat.

Meine Stirn trägt das Brandmal der Schande,
und im ganzen bin ich verdammt.
Wie soll ich zu dir zurückkehren,
meine heilige Mutter—meine Heimat?[2]

Prisoner poets frequently dedicated their work to a dead comrade, as in this untitled poem by Antonia Bruha.

Sometimes a train travels far outside of here,
far outside, where people live free,
the birds part the sky with their flight,
treetops you see blowing in the wind.

Far outside, behind wires and walls—
wires and walls, and you are dead.
Don't you feel it? It's enormous,
and the soon-to-be sunrise is far away.

I know everything that you want to say:
"Hold on! Keep your chin up, all this will pass!
Do you want to give up so shortly before it ends?
Sometime after the night, we will be free."

You are so brave, your courage is great,
but I have blood on my hands;
today I hauled stones at the SS estate,
I'm hungry and I see no end to it.

My husband has been shot, you know that for sure.
To be free without him makes no sense to me.
Then the most beautiful sky would not be blue.
You see how disheartened I am.

In this battle, I have done my part,
but I have had it with this waiting!—
One would like to tell her many, yes many things,
but her corpse lay too soon on the electric fence.

Manchmal fährt weit draussen ein Zug,
weit draussen, wo Menschen frei leben,
die Vögel schneiden den Himmel im Flug,
Baumwipfel siehst du im Winde wehen.

Ganz weit, hinter Draht und Mauer—
Draht und Mauer, und du bist tot.
Fühlst du's nicht? Es ist ungeheuer,
und weit ist das werdende Morgenrot.

Ich weiss alles, was du willst sagen:
"Durchhalten! Kopf hoch, es geht doch vorbei!
So kurz vor Schluss willst du verzagen?
Mal über Nacht werden wir frei!"

Du bist so tapfer, gross ist dein Mut,
doch ich hab' blutende Hände;
heute schleppte ich Steine am Gut,
hab' Hunger und seh' gar kein Ende!

Mein Mann ist erschossen, das weisst du genau,
frei sein ohne ihn hat für mich keinen Sinn,
da wäre der schönste Himmel nicht blau.
Du siehst, wie mutlos ich bin.

Ich habe im Kampf mein Teil getragen,
doch dieses Warten habe ich satt!—
Man möchte ihr vieles, ja vieles noch sagen,
doch früh lag ihre Leiche am geladenen Draht.[3]

The illness of a friend, Yvonne Useldinger, and her absence
while she recovered in the infirmary, prompted Clara Rupp to
write this poem for her and to smuggle it to her.

The Desolate Day

It's a desolate day when the gray clouds
slide deeply by in the heavens,
when the trees cry and the birds fly slowly by.

The lake breathes disconsolately, and the little town
on the other side lies vaulted in gray
over pale reeds. Where have the colors gone?

I look out over the camp and its walls.
Desolately the roofs stretch out over the barracks,
and the distant voices of inmates drift away.

Where are we in the world?
Or has it already gone under?
How am I to know that this is really my life?

The camouflaged factories lie like old ruins.
The streets glimmer black and desolately,
and the windows look out mutely like empty eye sockets.
Desolately the machines hum and growl.
The pale faces of the inmates in the halls
look fixedly at the clock—when will it be over?

Everything is desolate, this world of our lives.
Only your quiet hands,
which protectively surround my heart,
are warm like red blossoms.

At the end of the poem, Rupp wrote a short note to her friend:
"This is not Rilke. [Rainer Maria Rilke was an extremely popular
poet at Ravensbrück, and Useldinger was a Rilke devotee.] Tell me
later if you like this."[4]

Der trostlose Tag

Der Tag ist trostlos, wenn die grauen Wolken
gleiten tief an dem Himmel vorbei,
wenn die Bäume weinen und die Vögel langsam fliegen.

Trostlos atmet der See, und die kleine Stadt
an seiner anderen Seite liegt grau gebogen
über blasses Schilf—wo sind die Farben geblieben?

Ich sehe auf das Lager und seine Mauern.
Trostlos recken sich die Dächer der Baracken,
und die fernen Stimmen einzelner Häftlinge verwehen.

Wo sind wir in der Welt?
Oder ist sie schon untergegangen?
Wie weiss ich, dass es mein Leben ist?

Wie alte Ruinen liegen die getarnten Betriebe.
Die Strassen schimmern schwarz und trostlos,
und wie leere Augenhöhlen stumm die Fenster schauen.
Trostlos summen und brummen die Maschinen,
die blassen Gesichter der Häftlinge in den Sälen
schauen dauernd auf die Uhr—wann hört es auf?

Alles ist trostlos, die Welt unseres Lebens.
Nur deine stillen Hände,
die sich schützend legen um mein Herz,
sind warm wie rote Blüten.

Zofia Gorska was brought to Ravensbrück in 1941 as a deeply religious nineteen-year-old schoolgirl. Her poem, "Moment of Protest," expresses some of her anguish over the issue of God's omnipotence and caring after experiencing the execution of a number of her comrades.

Moment of Protest

How is this possible, how can this ever happen?
And how can you, great God, ever witness this?
The heavens watch me through bars, like your eyes.
Can you not, after all, see how I tremble and am afraid?

Cold are your eyes, and heaven is so pale.
The clouds seem to drag by, but no lightning strikes.
How can you permit this? How can you allow it?
If you are what you are, oh God, how horribly you let me suffer.

If you are what you are, oh, God, I will turn my heart away
     from you.
I will reject your heaven. I want no more of your grace!
If you see all of this and don't reach out your hand to me,
how cruel you can be, you who are omnipotent!

Augenblick des Protestes

Wie ist das nur möglich, wie kann das nur geschehen?
Und wie kannst du nur, grosser Gott, das mit ansehen?
Durch Gitter schaut mich der Himmel an, wie deine Augen.
Kannst du denn zusehen, wie ich zittere und bange?

Kalt sind deine Augen, und der Himmel ist so bleich.
Die Wolken gleiten schleppend, aber es schlägt kein Blitz ein.
Wie kannst du es zulassen? Wie kannst du es erlauben?
Wenn du es bist, o Gott, wie schrecklich lässt du mich leiden!

Wenn du es bist, o Gott, wende ich von dir mein Herz ab.
Verzichte auf deinen Himmel, will nicht mehr deine Gnade!
Wenn du das alles siehst und mir nicht deine Hand reichst.
Wie grausam du sein kannst, du, wo du alles vermagst![5]

"Necrologue" was written by Johanna Himmler (no relation to the SS chief), a Communist and Reichstag delegate.

Necrologue

A beautiful fall day comes to a close
the workday is over in the camp.
Silent and unmoving stands the
little belt of woods that surrounds the camp.
Silent and unmoving stand
Eight thousand women at evening roll call.
Eight thousand women,
From children to old ladies!
All seems so still and peaceful
And yet there is in these faces
a gnawing question, a knowing
about something, a waiting for something...
Crack! A sudden bang!
Shots tear into the silence,
tear into the hearts and
nerves of eight thousand women.
Again deep silence, not a sound.
The faces have become paler from
the shots, heads sink, and
in many eyes tears appear.
They know that on the other side of the wall
they have female comrades who
in the bloom of youth are breathing their last,
some very young.—Yet in the morning
they went laughing and saying goodbye
into the death cells.
We can only stand and stand
and use the silence for a kind of
inner farewell ceremony, a
roll call for their great and courageous deaths.

Eight thousand women!
Who would ever have this honor?
The evening is already fading,
the darkness hides everything
in its peaceful haze, even
covering up the crimes which have been
born out of blind hatred.
From the hearts of eight thousand women
comes the unuttered scream:
How much longer? How much longer?

Nekrolog

Ein Schöner Herbsttag geht zu Ende
Im KZ ist Feierabend.
Schweigend und unbeweglich
steht der schmale Waldgürtel,
der das Lager umschliesst.
Still und unbeweglich stehen
8000 Frauen zum abendlichen Appell.
8000 Frauen,
Vom Kind bis zur Greisin!
Alles scheint so still und friedlich
und doch steht in der Gesichtern
eine bange Frage, ein Wissen
um etwas, ein Warten auf etwas...
Krach!—Ein kurzer Knall!
Schüsse zerreissen die Stille,
reissen an den Herzen
und Nerven von 8000 Frauen.
Wieder tiefe Stille, kein Laut!
Die Gesichter sind noch um einen Ton
bleicher geworden, Köpfe senken sich
in manchen Augen stehen Träner.-
Sie wissen:
Jenseits der Mauer hauchen
Kameradinnen ihr blühendes Leben aus
einige Blutjunge! — Am Morgen noch
gingen sie lachend und abschiednehmend
in die Todeszelle.
Wir können nur stehen und stehen

und die Stille zu einer inneren
Abschiedsfeier benützen, zu einem
Appell eurem grossen, mutigen Sterben.
8000 Frauen!
Wem wurde jemals diese Ehre?
Der Abend sinkt bereits,
Die Dämmerung hüllt alles
in ihren friedlichen Schleier, der auch
das Verbrechen zudeckt, das aus blinden
Hass geboren wurde!
Aus den Herzen von 8000 Frauen
kommt der verhaltene Schrei
Wie lange noch? Wie lange noch?[6]

Paintings and Drawings

There was an understandable rationale behind the SS's suspicion of prisoners who made drawings of the camp and of camp life. Prisoners would hide their drawings, but when the SS searched a barracks and found them, they were always destroyed. Of the roughly four hundred drawings produced by Maria Hiszpanska, hardly any made it to the end. It is probable that most of the drawings and paintings done by prisoners before the liberation of the camp were destroyed. If their creators did not survive, they are gone forever. Fortunately, a few drawings from before April 1945 survived the SS *Kulturkampf*. Fortunately too, some of the artists lived, and immediately after the war were able to recreate many of their original drawings. Over and above their artistic and aesthetic appeal, these drawings are enormously valuable in giving us firsthand mental images of camp life. Without them, our understanding of life and conditions at Ravensbrück would be much diminished.

Helen Ernst was one of two of our group of prisoner artists who had had professional training in art and the only one known to have made a living as an artist before the war. In Weimar Berlin, she had worked as a fashion artist and drawing teacher. Then, in the politically charged atmosphere of the times, and influenced by Käthe Kollwitz, she turned toward the KPD. She fled Germany for Holland in 1934, but was arrested in 1940 and brought to Ravensbrück in April 1941. She held many jobs during her years as a prisoner, including being chief of the painting crew, a position which could have offered her little artistic satisfaction, as the crew mainly painted barracks. Nor was the position likely an easy or comfortable one to fill, for most of the painting crew was composed of German Asocials, "veritable monsters," according to a French crew member, Denise Dufournier, who noted that many of these women were lesbians and very abusive to the French. But Helen Ernst was decent to them. Dufournier's evaluation of her was rather mixed; she spoke perfect French, had traveled widely, and "was a person of considerable culture." Further, "she was an adventuress, attractive in some ways, possessing an unquestionable physical charm, but somewhat spoiled by typical German coarseness."[7]

Helen Ernst later became "court painter" (*Hofmalerin*) for the SS, in which role she mainly did fashion drawings for some of the overseers. In her new, more privileged position, she attracted the suspicions of fellow prisoners who believed she had become an SS agent. In her defense, she later wrote: "I lived so much in my own world, which I hoped to later build for myself, that I not once concerned myself about what other people thought of me."[8] After the war, her reputation was restored and her works, some of which show a definite influence by Kollwitz, are now prominently displayed in the Historical Museum of Schwerin.

Having been a cabaret dancer and professional choreographer in Prague, Nina Jirsikova discovered a hidden talent for drawing in the confines of Ravensbrück. Her works are wonderfully realistic and unsentimental glimpses into the nooks and crannies of daily life in the camp. Additionally, she was the creator of the "Ravensbrück Fashion Magazine," a tongue-in-cheek look at the things inmates could do to their uniforms to be really high-fashion.[9] They were not, of course, actually allowed to do this, but fellow inmates appreciated Jirsikova's humorous approach to camp life.

Yvonne Uselinger was a Communist from Luxembourg who was arrested for resistance activities and brought to Ravensbrück in 1943. Unlike the drawings of most of the other artists, who were attempting to document the life and suffering in the camp, hers were generally of a personal nature. She drew plants and flowers, and when her friend, Mila Janu, the Czech doctor who had nursed her back to health, died, she drew a posthumous portrait.[10] In February 1945, the first and only child was born at the Siemens camp. Eight days

Yvonne Useldinger, "Portrait of Mila Janu." *Sammlungen Ravensbrück.* Courtesy *Mahn- und Gedenkstätte Ravensbrück.*

later, Useldinger made a drawing of the infant and gave this as a gift to the mother, Anni Hendriks, who was from Holland. Something of Useldinger's personality is perhaps expressed in a journal entry she made in March 1945: "Today I saw something really special. A swan on the little pond offered a wonderful scene to draw. Nature here is always full of surprises. Although one always sees new wonders in the same view, the electrified barbed wire brings us quickly back to reality."[11]

Aat Breur was the other prisoner artist of our group who had professional training, in her case at an academy in The Hague.

Aat Breur, "Double Portrait." The artist did this because of a lack of paper. The woman in the upper part of the drawing is a Dutch woman, Wil van den Heuvel-Bertholée, arrested in 1942 for sabotage. The woman in the lower part of the drawing is unknown. From *Een verborgen herinnering*. Courtesy Dunya Breur.

Following the German invasion of their native Holland, she and her husband joined the Resistance, but were denounced, then arrested in November 1942. Breur and her infant daughter, Dunya, were put in a prison at Utrecht, while Breur's husband was sent to a concentration camp. A few months later, in February 1943, he was killed. That summer, Breur was transported to Germany, leaving Dunya in the care of her grandparents. In September 1943, she arrived at Ravensbrück.

Breur's reputation as a talented artist spread quickly in the camp. Soon fellow prisoners were bringing her paper, pencils, crayons, then asking her to make drawings for them, sometimes portraits. She did most of her drawing from her top-story bunk, where it was safest, cleanest, and easiest to hide her drawings; she could reach up and stow them between loose ceiling boards. In October 1944, some comrades who knew of her talent managed to get her a work assignment at the book bindery, where she was provided with materials and given more time to draw. Some of the SS personnel learned of her abilities, and asked her to make drawings of their children, which she did.

Breur's drawings en- compass a wide range of activities, from a small child holding the hand of her *Lagermutter* to corpses lying in a wash- room. The life of the camp in its last year and a half of existence was carefully and objectively docu- ment ed in these draw- ings. Unfortunately, ma- ny were given away and have become scattered; others were destroyed or became badly damaged. One whole genre of her drawings — posthumous portraits of recently de- ceased prisoners, done at the request of comrades

Aat Breur, "Portrait of Violette LeCoq." From *Een verborgen herinnering.* Courtesy Dunya Breur.

and then given to them — have virtually disappeared. Only two are known to have survived. Nevertheless, Breur's extant draw- ings offer the most comprehensive body of visual images we have of Ravensbrück, reflecting both the personal side of camp life as well as its misery and horrors. Her portfolio of original drawings was largely saved from destruction in the closing stages of the war when confidantes smuggled them out on Red Cross transports. Aat Breur herself remained behind to help in the infirmary.[12]

Another artist who came to Ravensbrück at about the same time as Aat Breur was Violette LeCoq. She was brought to Ravensbrück in October 1943 as part of a transport of French Resistance workers, the Night and Fog prisoners. Because she spoke German, she was assigned to the tuberculosis block. In a series of more than thirty ink drawings which she called

France Audoul, "Portraits of Comrades." From *Ravensbrück: 15,000 Femmes en Enfer*.

Témoignages (Evidence), she captured much of the horror of Ravensbrück in its last year and a half of existence. Her drawings were so highly regarded that they were in fact used as evidence in the Hamburg Trial of SS personnel in 1946–1947.[13]

France Audoul entered Ravensbrück in February 1944. Although little is known about her, she later made her purpose clear: "I was deported to the fascist concentration camp, and I wanted . . . to report about what women had suffered, about the unimaginable mistreatment which was imposed on them, and about the last minutes in the lives of so many women who never returned home."[14] Her drawings are indeed a report on what women had suffered, but she went beyond this. In a series of portraits of her fellow female prisoners, she truly captured their variety, their inner beauty, and their strength of personality.

And all of this on paper stolen from the SS.

Handicrafts, Singing, and Storytelling

Prisoners were not allowed to take anything from their work-sites, not even scraps of paper or small pieces of wood. Yet we know that there was an active trade in all sorts of materials illic-itly obtained from workplaces, along with articles that entered the camp legally through the mail. After these items had served their original functions, handy inmates refashioned them to meet new purposes. Worn-out toothbrushes were elaborately carved and made into crucifixes. Snippets of cloth were carefully embroidered and transformed into doilies, handkerchiefs, decorative scarves, or dolls.[15] Gypsy women were noted for creating little wooden spoons ("God only knows how," according to one inmate), then trading them for one or two bread rations.[16] Although some of these products were made for the purpose of barter, the great majority were intended as gifts and presented to close friends on special occasions.

Handcrafted items by anonymous prisoner-artists. Photographs by the author. Courtesy *Mahn- und Gedenkstätte Ravensbrück.*

Handcrafted items by anonymous prisoner-artists. Photographs by the author. Courtesy *Mahn- und Gedenkstätte Ravensbrück.*

The museum at the Ravensbrück Memorial has a number of these handcrafted articles on display. For the most part, little is known about the creators of these objects or for whom they were intended. What is unmistakable, however, is the force with which these many unpretentious little items speak of altruism, of affection, of a level and quality of human contact which helped to make even the concentration camp experience somewhat bearable.

Singing was another activity that made the lives of women inmates more tolerable. The SS encouraged this, to a point; the women were often ordered to sing as they were marched to and from worksites outside the camp, as this created a rather benign impression for bystanders. Even this form of group singing was tightly controlled; only German songs could be sung, and they had to be sung in German. Moreover, no popular songs (*Schlagerlieder*) were allowed—only traditional songs.[17]

Inside the camp, singing of any kind was further circumscribed. Inmates were allowed to sing only during their "free hour" between evening roll call and lights-out, and this was only to take place inside the block.[18] But, as with all else related to camp regulations, women took calculated risks and bent the rules. Unauthorized or not, they sang their own songs, most often folk songs, and they sang them whenever and wherever they could, sometimes at work,[19] sometimes in the barracks at night after the watch had made its rounds.[20] Their soft voices filled the barracks with musical resonances, reminding everyone of homeland and happier times.

Inmate musical activities went beyond this. As part of the Forestry Crew, Eugenia Kocwa and her work partner, Alina, sang operatic duets in the relative solitude of their isolated worksite.[21] At evening gatherings, artists with musical talents were asked to perform, and they were glad to do so.[22] Many national groups formed their own choirs within the camp, practicing after lights-out and performing on weekends.[23] The benefits for all these musical activities far outweighed the risks.

Storytelling was another form of cultural activity which was widely practiced and became highly developed in the women's concentration camp. Since prisoners were not permitted to keep books, even handwritten ones, they would sometimes gather and describe to each other in some detail the contents of books they had read before their imprisonment. Some prisoners, such as those who peeled potatoes at night in the kitchen, were able to tell stories while they worked, but storytelling mainly took place in the evenings, as inmates gathered around the bunks in the barracks. Of course, some cultivated the art of storytelling naturally and they would quickly gather an appreciative audience once they began. Some women were able to recite whole plays from memory. In the Polish Block, one of the most talented and popular storytellers was Helena Tyrankiewicz, whose repertoire included Polish works by Mickiewicz as well as foreign literature, such as the *Song of Roland* and the *Nibelungenlied*, along with a number of Greek dramas.[24] After a recitation, there were often discussions. Not infrequently these sessions eventually drifted into talk of recipes and feasts of the past.[25] Real or imaginary, it didn't matter;

France Audoul, "Conference." From *Ravensbrück: 15,000 Femmes en Enfer.*

stories took the minds of all who listened far away from the reality of turnip soup and coarse bread.

Educational Programs

The eagerness with which women prisoners pursued culture
and learning seems to have been almost as intense as their zeal to
discuss food. Examples abound: Belgian prisoners had their own
chorus, readings of literature, and even organized language courses.[26] Almost all the other national groups acted similarly, frequently having readings or discussions of important works in
their own language.[27] As a group, the Communists do not seem to

have been as culturally active as some others, but they had different priorities. They had discussions of Marxist theory, and for a time they held readings of *War and Peace* in their barracks.[28]

The learning of languages was pursued relentlessly. In nearly every barracks there was instruction in the German language, although this no doubt had as much to do with the survival instinct as with a love of learning. There was quite a lot of English instruction as well. In the elite blocks, where conditions were more conducive to learning, Gemma Gluck taught both a basic English course and an advanced conversation class.[29] Rita Sprengel, who already knew English, French, and German and worked as an interpreter in the camp, took advantage of the opportunity and learned a fourth language, Russian.[30] Textbooks and little dictionaries, all of them handwritten and small enough to be easily hidden during work, were passed around and copied hundreds of times. Eugenia Kocwa, who gave English lessons, wrote her own textbook on 80 sheets of toilet paper.[31]

In none of the blocks was education and learning pursued with more vigor than in the Polish blocks. Isa Vermehren, mercilessly objective when it came to discussing nationalities, including her fellow Germans (whom she mostly despised), judged that the Poles had an intellectual level unmatched by any other group in the camp.[32] The fact that the earliest transports from Poland were composed of many teachers undoubtedly contributed to this. They set a tone and a standard which were never relinquished or surpassed.[33]

What distinguished the Polish educational effort from that of the other national groups was not only its scope and breadth, but also the fact that it was a system, not just a random offering of talks. Systems need organization and leadership, and this was provided early on by Helena Salska, an experienced educator, a Master (*Magister*) in history. Salska taught, but more important, she gave the program a sense of direction.[34]

Lists are generally boring, but take a quick look at the list of subject areas taught (and the wide range of instructors) in the

Polish underground educational system:

Polish Language and Literature: Winska, Bromowicz, Panakowna, Swiebodzianka, Szartowska
Chemistry: Chorazna, Dydynska
Physics: Tyrankiewicz, Sierakowska
Geography: Peretjatkowicz, Mazurek
Mathematics and Astronomy: Prof. Milweska, Modzelewska, Babinska-Dobrowlska
Anatomy: Dr. Maczka
European History: Salska
Cultural History, Education: Lanckoronska
Ancient History: Panenkowa
German Language: Karier-Westfalowa
French Language: Jordan, Krasicka
English Language: Kocwa
Latin: Madlerowa, Zawadzka[35]

The people who taught in these areas were well qualified, in many cases experienced teachers. In the winter of 1942, every morning between roll call and work call, a group of women met for half an hour in a corner of Block 15. There Urszula Winska, a trained specialist in Polish studies, offered a course in Polish literature. At first, there were six participants, later twenty.[36] Irena Panenkowa's lecture on Socrates was so well received that she was asked to repeat it, and ended up giving it on five different occasions.[37]

Polish teachers conducted lessons from memory, sometimes using sticks and dirt in place of chalk and blackboards.[38] They held discussions and study sessions. They granted no diplomas or degrees, but after the war Stanislawa Czajkowska was given credit for her second, third, and fourth classes in the *Gymnasium* (college preparatory high school) for the academic work she did at Ravensbrück.[39] More significantly, these programs helped to give the Polish women a feeling of camaraderie, a sense of purpose, and an awareness of their self-worth that was vital to their survival.

CHAPTER

13

Keeping Clean (and Other Personal Matters)

France Audoul, "At the Showers." From *Ravensbrück: 15,000 Femmes en Enfer*.

Lice and Delousings

The first noticeable infestations of lice occurred in 1942. There were delousings and even quarantines, but the problem never abated. By 1943, there was a full-fledged scourge of lice and fleas in the camp, which lasted until liberation.[1] Except for some of the lucky few in the elite barracks or in the Siemens camp, everybody had lice to one degree or another. If prisoners were sensible, each evening they would spend some time examining their clothes, themselves, and each other for "nits."[2] The French women turned the chore into an evening game: "What a refined and delightful occupation, the hunt for one's lice. . . . The problem is multiple: track them down into the minutest folds, in the most surprising recesses, and kill them all. Count them in a whisper and then call out your score."[3] Sometimes the game continued at work: "We would catch the little beasts while stroking our necks; then, holding them between our fingers, we would crush them on the workbench in front of us. We would keep a tally and see who could line up the most hunting trophies before noon."[4]

As sensible as personal delousing practices were, they hardly touched the root of the problem. "The dear little beasts were everywhere: in the blankets, in the straw mattresses, in the cracks" of the barracks.[5] Women who worked with the clothing turned in by soldiers could not avoid getting lice and fleas, and bringing these back to their own barracks.[6] There were prodigious numbers of cockroaches too, but while many women were nauseated by their presence[7] they did not truly represent the health threat posed by their smaller kin.

About 1943, the Office of Sanitation Service (Sanitätsdienst) was created, under the direction of the infirmary staff. The Sanitation Service now assigned a block nurse to each barracks. They were to look after the cleanliness and general health of their fellow prisoners, taking care of bandaging and minor health and first-aid problems. They were clearly meant to relieve some of the pressure on the infirmary staff. Although they were authorized to

Maria Hiszpanska, "Searching for Lice." *Sammlungen Ravensbrück.*
Courtesy *Mahn- und Gedenkstätte Ravensbrück.*

send inmates to the infirmary, their main job was delousing. It was an impossible task. In the first place, block seniors did not like acknowledging that there were lice in their barracks, and they were often uncooperative.[8] Even when a general delousing of a barracks was called for and carried out, it was only minimally effective. The barracks' inhabitants would be ordered outdoors. They would undress, have a shower, and put on clean clothes. Meanwhile, their quarters would be disinfected, but not thoroughly—it was simply impossible to fully disinfect the barracks, particularly the overcrowded ones. The three-storied bunks were so tightly packed that one could not get under them, and that was where most of the filth was.[9]

Prisoners assigned to the SS administrative offices or certain of the workplaces where cleanliness was required were expected to be free of lice, but they were given preferential treatment in terms of living accommodations and sanitary facilities. Many of them got

Violette LeCoq, "Hygiene." From *Témoignages*. . . . Courtesy Mme.
Violette Rougier-LeCoq.

to shower every day, and have a fresh change of clothes.[10] When
one of the young women who worked in the sewing factory in
town, where cleanliness was demanded, was found by her overseer to have abundant lice, there was a nasty scene. The young
woman, Maria Schneider, was made to walk through both halls of
the factory totally naked, showing off her many louse and flea
bites.[11] How this form of punishment was supposed to change anything is not clear. In many of the blocks there simply was not any
soap (prisoners could buy this at the canteen), and if there was
water, it was almost sure to be ice cold. Nevertheless, most
Russians and Poles washed completely in it. They chided the
French for only washing their hands, and believed this explained
the higher than normal mortality rate among the French women.[12]
Whether French women in general avoided the cold showers is not
known, but one French woman was so determined to get a shower that she arose before the normal wake-up call: "It's better to
take a cold shower and shiver than to let the vermin eat at you."[13]

A Russian prisoner noted long afterward that whenever they were changing clothes or in the showers, SS men were always trying to look at them. They became accustomed to the cold showers, but not to the leers.[14]

Menstruation

Most of the women were already amenorrheic upon arrival at Ravensbrück. The trauma of arrest and separation from family, the weeks and, in some cases, months spent in detention centers or other concentration camps, and the general state of physical and often emotional exhaustion had already taken its toll. Of the group of French women accompanying Fanny Marette to Germany, none menstruated.[15] The same was true of Jewish women, mostly from Auschwitz, who were delivered to Ravensbrück in the winter of 1944–1945. A few thought the SS were giving them drugs to sterilize them and prevent menstruation,[16] but there is no real evidence of this. Miriam Litwin, a Jewish medical doctor brought to Ravens-brück in 1944, relat-ed how after only a few weeks of mis-treatment and poor nourishment, almost none of the roughly thirty women in her group still menstru-ated.[17] This may have been a blessing, since camp authorities made no provision for feminine hygiene, not even providing rags for the relative-

Violette LeCoq, "Vermin." From *Témoignages* . . . . Courtesy Mme. Violette Rougier-LeCoq.

ly few women who continued to menstruate.[18] In this situation, those women who were able to barter for some rags did so; those who had nothing to use had to let the blood run down their legs, often incurring the wrath of overseers or *Blockovas* for this unsightliness.[19]

Dysentery

A much more serious and widespread problem involved diarrhea. This was not an occasional bout of loose bowels caused by food poisoning, but a chronic, long-lasting version that sapped the strength of its victims. The diarrhea epidemic in the camp no doubt had many causes, one of which was almost certainly food poisoning, as prisoners often could not clean their bowls or utensils carefully.[20] Another was the prisoners' diet, insufficient in itself, but especially poor in fiber. Micheline Maurel was probably correct in blaming her condition on the soup.[21] Other inmates believed that contaminated water was causing their diarrhea, and some tried to avoid drinking the water at the camp.[22] But what choice was there? In any

Nina Jirsikova, "In Line for the Toilet." *Sammlungen Ravensbrück.* Courtesy *Mahn- und Gedenkstätte Ravensbrück.*

event, while all of these explanations have merit, the primary cause of the diarrhea epidemic was neither the food nor the water, but typhus, carried by the lice.

The problem of dysentery was exacerbated by the lack of toilet facilities and the policies concerning their use. There were simply never enough toilets; there were only eight in the original barracks and in the elite blocks, twelve in the "slums." When the overcrowding set in, this became woefully inadequate.[23] Moreover, the plumbing frequently broke down, not only creating a stinking mess, but also forcing many women to go outside to relieve themselves. In the winter of 1944–1945, the plumbing system failed, and almost none of the toilets in the barracks worked. Pits were then dug outside with a kind of seating apparatus (called the "chicken roost") built over them:[24] Outdoor privies without any privacy.

Even worse from the inmates' point of view were the camp's policies concerning the use of toilets. Inmates were never allowed to excuse themselves from roll calls, no matter how long they lasted. Women with diarrhea had no choice but to let it run down their legs. After a roll call, one could almost always see little piles of watery excrement,[25] "the unmistakable signs of our sickness."[26] One inmate tried to prevent this by tying strings around the legs of her underwear.[27] In the workplaces, prisoners were generally allowed only a midmorning and a midafternoon break to use the toilets.[28] There were quite a number of exceptions to this, however, which allowed more frequent usage. At night, in the barracks, the problem continued. Prisoners could use the toilets, but the crowded conditions and the physical weakness of many of them did not make it easy. Plus, some women had simply become incontinent: "Everything was full of shit. Many didn't even have time to get out of bed. Each bed had three stories, so the shit ran down on the floor or on the other prisoners."[29] Naturally, this led to a certain amount of grumbling and irritability among the residents, along with an effort to claim the upper bunks.[30]

Ostensibly, to prevent the further spread of dysentery, and

because so many prisoners suffered from diarrhea, one of the SS doctors, Dr. Treite, proposed isolating these cases in a special barracks. Needless to say, it immediately gained the name, "the Shit Block" by the other inmates. One of the nurses who visited there said, "Words can hardly describe this shit barracks." The women who were shoved in there were nothing but skeletons wallowing in their own filth.[31]

It is clear that many of the unfortunate women who were assigned to the "Shit Block" in the winter of 1944–1945 were what prisoners and SS alike had for some time called the *Schmuck-stücke*. Literally, this means "piece of jewelry," but the phrase was always used sarcastically, as in: "Isn't she a real piece of jewelry?" French prisoners, as was their custom, gave the word a Gallic twist and called them *schmoustique* ("low life").[32] Germaine Tillion has written a detailed description:

> A *Schmuckstück* was a seemingly human creature, the likes of whom I had never seen anywhere but at Ravensbrück, far past what is usually called emaciation and almost at a fatal stage of malnutrition (autopsies found all organs greatly reduced in size—a liver the size of a rabbit's); incapable of personal or social discipline, unwashed, resigned to the lice, clothed in unbelievable rags, and covered with every kind of running, infected sore. They were beaten, with or without reason, by all the more sturdy Germans (female guards in the SS or other prisoners—their impulses were the same); they would throw themselves flat in the mud to lick up the remains of an overturned soup bowl; without friends, hope or dignity, and apparently without thoughts; transformed by fear and hunger, and finally destined to be gassed like rodents after one of those manhunts known as "selections." Each day of existence for these poor grubworms defied everything one might have believed about nature and hygiene. It was no surprise that they died; they were already removed from life.[33]

It is impossible, in retrospect, not to feel the greatest pity for these wretched specimens of humanity. Many were women who had arrived in the camp already sick and who had never become part of a camp family or circle of friends. In camp families, the old-

er members would often exhort the younger ones to keep themselves clean, reminding them of the revulsion everyone felt for the
Schmuckstücke.[34] Reportedly, many of them were Asocials, for
whom there already was considerable aversion. It is difficult to
believe that it was anything other than a deliberate policy on the
part of the SS to send these inmates to their deaths by placing
them in conditions which made recovery unlikely, if not impossible.

Rape

After the liberation of the camp and returning to France,
Micheline Maurel gave talks and took part in meetings discussing
her experiences. She remembers how everyone expected her to
talk about being raped and tortured, but all she talked about was
hunger. Hunger was a reality; rape was not.[35] Her experience is
echoed by the testimony of hundreds of Ravensbrück survivors.
Not one of the women who wrote memoirs or "reports of experience" after the war claims to have been raped by a German male.
None of the women who were taken by the Red Cross to Sweden
at war's end mentioned having been raped at Ravensbrück,
although a few said rapes sometimes occurred as prisoners were
being transferred from one camp to another.[36] Wanda P., a Gypsy,
told how at Auschwitz she and other young Gypsy women lived in
constant fear of being raped by SS men, but she said nothing
about this problem after being transferred to Ravensbrück.[37]

"Of course we weren't raped," a survivor once told me emphati-
cally. "What man would want to rape women who looked like we
did?"[38] Other survivors reiterated this theme about being ugly and
louse-ridden:[39] "We stunk and we had no hair." That's why there
were no rapes at Ravensbrück, according to another survivor.[40]
Now, it is quite true that the majority of women prisoners at
Ravensbrück were kept in a relatively unpresentable, unattractive condition, but not all were. Prisoners who worked for the SS

administration were expected to be clean and neat in appearance. Moreover, anyone who has seen photographs of recently-freed Ravensbrück inmates taken in April 1945[41] has to have noticed the dichotomy between emaciated creatures on the one hand and hearty, wholesome women on the other. Aside from the fact that rape is an act of violence, without regard to the victim's appearance, the argument that there were no rapes at Ravensbrück because all the women were so unattractive does not hold up.

Reportedly, there were instances of consensual sexual relations between SS men and Ravensbrück inmates. A French prisoner learned by chance that her block senior was the mistress of an SS official,[42] and the affair between Gerda Ganzer, a German prisoner-nurse, and SS Dr. Rosenthal became, for a time, the talk of the infirmary.[43] Other prisoners have confirmed the suspicions that there were occasional sexual trysts between male personnel and female prisoners.[44] Given the inequality inherent in these relationships, however, it hardly seems fitting to think of these sexual liaisons as truly "consensual." An even more grievous example of this inequality and the powerlessness with which women confronted their captors occurred when women prisoners "volunteered" for brothel duty. SS men were known to occasionally "try out" a volunteer before rendering a decision on her qualifications.[45] Nevertheless, it should be emphasized that all the evidence suggests that these sexual encounters between SS men and women prisoners mentioned above were exceedingly rare occurrences. The issue deserves further investigation, but for now we are left with the tentative conclusion that camp regulations against fraternization between the SS and prisoners were overwhelmingly obeyed, and that the SS's code of conduct forbidding intimate relations with "inferior types" was strictly adhered to. In any event, perhaps the one bright spot in SS-prisoner relations is that women prisoners at Ravensbrück with all of their other concerns and worries, including the constant voyeurism, did not live in fear of being forcibly raped by their SS captors.

CHAPTER

Two
Factories

14

Women working at the straw shoe braiding workshop. (SS Photo.)
Sammlungen Mahn- und Gedenkstätte Ravensbrück.
Courtesy U.S. Holocaust Memorial Museum Photo Archives.

For all of its eventual scope and complexity, Ravensbrück was but a small part of a massive economic empire operated by the SS. Ultimately, the tentacles of this empire reached into every corner of Germany and all of the countries occupied by Germany. The running of this huge system required the labor of millions of men and women and brought in billions of Marks. It was an incredible money-making endeavor, and its considerable profits went in several directions. The Reich got a share; the SS as an institution became fabulously wealthy; and private interests—German companies, as well as individual civilian and SS entrepreneurs—had the opportunity of getting rich, and many of them did.[1]

The foundation of this economic empire, and one reason for its immense profitability, was its widespread use of slave labor. Ravensbrück was, in fact, a pioneer in the SS experiment to effectively exploit concentration camp labor. By the time Ravensbrück began functioning, the early concentration camp purposes of preventive detention and political re-education had been largely replaced by the newer goals of removing undesirables from society and exploiting their labor. In 1942, these goals were brought together in the "extermination through work" (*Vernichtung durch Arbeit*) program which characterized SS labor policies from that point until the end of the war.

Ravensbrück inmates were employed in four different types of economic undertakings. First, they worked in the SS-owned textile factories inside the camp. Second, they were rented out to private firms nearby and in the subcamps. The largest of these enterprises was the Siemens firm which built a major productive facility next to the main camp. Third, they formed the crews (*Kolonne*) that basically did the work of running the camp itself, doing everything from collecting the garbage to repairing the furniture. Finally, they worked in the administrative offices of the SS, handling much of the secretarial work.

The SS Textile Factory

In 1940 an agency called the Association for Textile and Leather Utilization, Ltd. (*Gesellschaft für Textil und Lederverwertung, GmbH*), opened at Ravensbrück. It was a company created and owned by the SS.[2] Some called the enterprise the Dachau Industry because of the location of company headquarters, but most simply called it the SS textile factory.

The initial stages of the SS textile firm were modest in scope: a few workshops mainly producing prisoner uniforms or modifying the black SS uniforms for newly created units. But the SS seemingly had grander plans all along, and the coming apart of *Blitzkrieg* strategy by late 1941 led to a reorientation of the war economy.[3] Expansion in facilities and in the workforce continued steadily, particularly during 1942. By September of that year, over 5,000 women were put to work there, with the factories turning out a variety of products, including uniforms and other items of clothing for the Waffen SS.[4]

The SS textile factory had four main subdivisions: a sewing plant (*Schneiderei*), a fabric plant (*Stoffweberei*), a furriers' shop (*Kurschnerei*), and a straw-weaving plant (*Strohflechterei*). By 1943, the entire operation employed about 3,000 women, working in two shifts of eleven hours each.

With the possible exception of the fabric plant, prisoners abhorred working in any part of the textile factory. The work was physically difficult, the conditions were appalling, and the SS personnel there were the most feared in the entire camp.[5] The night shift was particularly disliked because prisoners who were assigned to it had difficulty sleeping during the day, and were therefore nearly always sleep-deprived.[6] The heart of the operation was the sewing plant, where hundreds of women worked in each shift behind cutting machines, steam presses, buttonhole machines, and, of course, sewing machines. One of these women has left a description:

The first time a person entered the hall, they must have thought they had just been transferred either to hell or to a lunatic asylum. Aside from the noise and the stuffy air [there was no ventilation system, but windows were sometimes opened twice a shift to bring in fresh, but cold, air which took away everyone's breath], one heard from every corner the bellowing of the SS personnel. . . . One saw only pale, fearful-looking fidgety women working at the machines. The closer the SS man came, punching as he went, the more giddy and restless became the tormented creatures. "Your quotas! Your quotas!" was their slogan.[7]

Quotas had been introduced in 1943, as a means of stepping up production. Starting in 1944, workers who exceeded their quotas got a premium (scrip), generally worth either 50 Pfennings or 1 Mark, which could be spent at the canteen.[8] (During most of the war, the official exchange rate was RM 2.5 = $1 U.S. or RM 1 = 40 cents.) Only a few workers got these.[9] Most workers detested the system, as it placed so much additional pressure on them, and punished those who didn't meet the quotas. And the quotas kept increasing; originally it was 120 jackets per month, later it was 220.[10] For a worker who did not reach her quota, in addition to

Female prisoners stand at attention during an inspection of the strawmat-weaving workshop. These mats were used to reinforce roads in swampy areas, mainly on the Eastern front. (SS Photo.) *Bildarchiv Preussischer Kulturbesitz.* Courtesy USHMM Photo Archives.

Women working in the straw-weaving workshop. (SS Photo.)
Sammlungen Ravensbrück. Courtesy USHMM Photo Archives.

rations being withheld, she risked getting her ears boxed, and
Binder, the SS man in charge of operations, was not reluctant to
do this.[11]

The straw-weaving plant was originally set up to produce straw
overshoe liners for the SS. It continued doing this, but expanded
production to include straw handbags and sandals, most of which
were sold on the civilian market (handbags RM 5, sandals RM
3.75). Reportedly, SS big shots from Berlin and Oranienburg were
first in line to get these products. One branch of the straw weaving plant, the reed-mat weaving plant (*Rohrmattenweberei*), produced straw mats and packing material.[12] Women disliked weaving the straw because the straw tore up their hands, causing infections. In addition, the air was filled with straw dust. Mainly
Gypsies were assigned to work here, some as young as fourteen
years old. The SS knew full well how distasteful this work was, for
in 1942, after Heydrich's assassination, they assigned nearly all
the Lidice women to this plant as a form of special punishment.[13]

Among the many peculiarities of Ravensbrück was that it had
an Angora rabbit hutch. These rabbits were raised not as pets, but
for their fur. This fur was sent to the furriers' shop to be used in
cap linings which were then sent "to the east." The furrier's shop
also bought pelts for this purpose, but most of their furs came

from fur coats either turned in by patriotic Germans to aid in the war effort, or, more likely, taken from Jews. Some of these furs confiscated from Jews were sent from camps and ghettoes in Poland, on direct orders from Himmler.[14] After the SS and overseers had helped themselves to the choicest coats,[15] the others were then taken apart—the workers were watched quite closely because sometimes they found money or other valuables sewn inside—and then reassembled as new coats or liners. It was hard work, and the furs, having been stored for some time in the SS warehouses, were often filthy and vermin-infested. A teenage seamstress working here once asked a workmate to poke her with her needle so she could wake up from this nightmare she was having.[16]

The fabric plant produced fabrics and materials which were used in the sewing plant to make uniforms and other garments. There were two halls of the plant, one containing twenty hand looms, the other about fifty mechanical looms. It was very hard work, especially manipulating the hand looms, and the same quota system was in place here as in the sewing plant. But the prisoners didn't mind working here as much, for the SS men in charge—reportedly, older, less fanatic, more reasonable men—were decent to the women, and tried to help them. Not once was a Report on a prisoner ever sent from the fabric plant.

Inside the sewing workshop at the SS textile factory. (SS Photo.) *Sammlungen Ravensbrück.* Courtesy USHMM Photo Archives.

Prisoners at work in the spinning workshop. (SS Photo.) *Sammlungen Ravensbrück.* Courtesy USHMM Photo Archives.

Initially, the SS had assigned mainly Criminals and Asocials here, but this had not been a happy experience—reportedly, they wasted too much of their own and their crew leader's time on petty accusations. After that, mainly Politicals were employed. Soviet army women were especially preferred, as they were strong enough to operate the heavy hand looms.[17]

Organizationally, the SS textile factory came under the direction of the WVHA (*Wirtschafts- und Verwaltungshauptamt*), the Main Economic and Administrative Office of the SS. Its chief, *SS-Obergruppenführer* Oswald Pohl, moved his family to a comfortable estate near Ravensbrück, perhaps signaling the importance of the women's camp in SS economic planning. Although the textile factories were inside the camp, they were technically autonomous (in late 1944, they officially became a separate subcamp) and hired their workers from the concentration camp authorities, paying 50 Pf. (1/2 RM) per day per unskilled worker, and RM 1 for technicians.[18] This was quite a bargain, considering that outside employers were paying three to five RM per worker. Technically, the factories sold their products to the various branches of the SS—although much of this was a paper transfer—

and to others, including the *Wehrmacht* and private firms. Sales
soared, going from RM 575,000 in 1940–1941 to RM 1,214,000 in
1942, and then to RM 15,500,000 in 1944.[19]

The Siemens Factory

Whether the success and profitability of the SS textile factory
at Ravensbrück served as a model for other companies is not
known. What is known is that leaders of Germany's second largest
manufacturer of electrical components, the Siemens Corporation,
had taken steps to maintain good relations with Himmler,[20] and in
mid-1942, it opened a factory just outside the camp walls. Eighty
women prisoners were employed at first, but expansion was under
way, and by late 1944, the Siemens camp had become a complex
and imposing system alongside the main camp. By then its fifteen
work halls employed some 2,500 prisoners and around 80 civilians, not counting SS and overseers.[21]

Inmates who worked at Siemens in 1942 and 1943 remember
being marched the short distance (less than one km, or 2/3 mile)
to and from the main camp every morning and evening.[22] Then in
late 1944, Siemens opened barracks for its own prisoner workers,
located next to their factories. The Siemens barracks differed from
those in the main camp in that they were much smaller and there
were no toilets. There was one central toilet/washroom, an incon-
venience at night, and there were not enough facilities for the
inmates.[23] But these disadvantages were more than offset by the
feeling that the barracks were nicer, with more light, and not as
crowded as those in the main camp.[24]

The Siemens factory at Ravensbrück produced electrical components and specialized electrical equipment for the military, such
as radios for submarines, electrical relays and coils, switchboards,
and parts for V-2 rockets.[25] The work was technically demanding,
and their workers needed to be both bright and alert. Apparently,
as part of the arrangement with the SS, Siemens was given the

pick of prisoners, requiring both an intelligence examination and a physical test for dexterity.[26] It is little wonder that they were considered the "aristocratie du camp" by many of the prisoners.[27] For all the controversy surrounding Siemens' use of concentration camp slave labor and its subsequent refusal to pay compensation to any but a few of their former concentration camp workers,[28] it needs to be said that the Siemens directors at Ravensbrück apparently understood that the workers' productivity could be increased if they were given adequate nourishment along with a good night's sleep. Almost to a person, those women who were assigned to the Siemens camp have testified that, compared with the main camp, it was a much nicer place to work, and also to live. Irma Trksak, a Slovak from Vienna, once told me she attributed her survival at Ravensbrück to "luck"—she spoke German, and she got a job in the Siemens camp.[29]

Workers at the Siemens camp were given an hour's break at midday and were provided a substantial lunch.[30] Inmates were permitted to move around the camp freely, visiting friends whenever they were not working.[31] Almost never did the kind of interminable roll calls occur that so distressed prisoners in the main camp. The barracks were cleaner and less crowded. There were only two stories of bunks, rather than three.[32] A Belgian prisoner later reflected: "In the relative peace of the Siemens camp, it was possible to exercise our intellectual faculties."[33] And in her diary entry of 11 March 1945, Yvonne Useldinger could write, almost as though she were back home in Luxembourg: "My usual walk with F.M.E.J."[34]

The workplace and conditions of work were relatively pleasant. The factories had large, high windows that let in plenty of light, but were too high to see out of. Unlike the SS factories, the Siemens plant was totally directed by civilians, and they were more interested in getting things done than in harassing people. Workers were allowed to use the toilets once each hour, and nobody bothered a worker who got up and stretched. There was an incentive system in effect whereby workers could get extra food (bread, wursts) for good work and, as in the SS factories, premiums for special productivity, which could be spent in the canteen.[35]

There is no question that prisoners at Siemens were forced to work very hard. Their individual productivity was carefully recorded, and if quotas were not met, there were unpleasant consequences. This could include beatings and even Reports. A prisoner who got a Report would likely be sent back to the main camp. Another negative feature was the number of work-related injuries which could easily have been prevented by sensible safety practices.[36] This was a common problem in concentration camp enterprises. The SS placed almost no demands on employers concerning the safety or welfare of the workers, and the result was that the companies did whatever they pleased.

Complicating the issue of work and safety even further, there were, in fact, five- and six-year-old children "working" in the factories at Siemens. The company has consistently maintained that this was not their policy, that it was the mothers who wanted to keep their children close to them and the company acquiesced.[37] From what is known about the lives and conditions of children at Ravensbrück, it seems reasonable that a caring mother would have been much less worried about a child who was with her— even in a factory—than left alone or with other people all day long in some other location.

Overseers in the Siemens plant were called monitors (*Aufpasserinnen*), and they were mainly there to keep a watchful eye against sabotage, of which there was a fair amount. When they found evidence of it, or even suspected it, there was no holding them back. They beat the prisoner on the spot, then sent her back to the main camp for "real punishment."[38]

However, for the most part, life and work in the Siemens camp proceeded without too much abuse or arbitrary misbehavior by the SS or camp leaders. This was likely the outcome of company policy; terror was kept under control and captive workers lived and labored in tolerable circumstances which could maximize their productivity.

15

Work Crews

Women working outside the camp. (SS Photo.) *Sammlungen Mahn- und Gedenkstätte Ravensbrück.* Courtesy U.S. Holocaust Memorial Museum Photo Archives.

With the exception of the Siemens Plant, where nearly all the prisoners worked in relatively tolerable conditions, elsewhere one's circumstances depended on "the luck of the draw." If one were lucky and had a decent overseer and a good crew chief, eleven hours of work in the right place could be a relatively benign assignment. Otherwise, not—and it was mostly not.

Ravensbrück, by 1941, had become a complex operation with a surprising amount of self-sufficiency. Not only did prisoners produce their own gray-striped uniforms in the SS textile factory, but they also grew cabbages and potatoes in SS-owned fields close to the camp. At the height of the growing season, about 200 prisoners worked in these fields. Later, after the harvest, many worked in the potato cellar. About three dozen were assigned to the SS estate, located close to Fürstenberg, where there were horse barns, straw sheds, and pig pens. Additionally, six to eight inmates were regularly assigned to a nearby chicken farm.[1] Some of the produce from these facilities, such as the chickens, were destined for the tables of the SS rather than the prisoners.

Prisoners at work in the shoe repair workshop. (SS Photo.) *Sammlungen Ravensbrück.* Courtesy USHMM Photo Archives.

Moreover, inside the camp, all those activities that were designed to feed, clothe, house, and care for the inmates (to the extent they were cared for) were run by the inmates themselves. There were more than sixty work crews (*Kommandos* or *Kolonnen*) having to do with the internal operations of the camp. Some of these were very small crews, like tool maintenance and plumbing repair, which generally had only a few crew members. Others, like the laundry and kitchen crews, were sizable, containing dozens of workers.[2]

Administrative and Kitchen Work

A number of prisoners were utilized as support staff for the SS, chief among them being the administrative workers. The dozens of secretaries, steno-typists, and accountants were not there just to "keep the books" on fellow inmates, but to maintain the SS's own records, at least those related to the female overseers.[3] Prisoners cleaned all the office buildings as well as the private residences of SS officials. There was even a prisoner hairdresser for the female overseers.[4]

The job assignments that carrried the most prestige as well as benefits were those in the administrative offices, particularly in the commandant's headquarters. Because the constant drain of SS personnel to the front created a situation of chronically under-staffed administrative offices, this in turn led to an increased reliance on prisoners in those offices.[5] These workers were assigned to one of the elite blocks where conditions were comfort-able, and they got daily baths, as well as extra uniforms.[6] SS high-er-ups, after all, did not want to work in close proximity to foul-smelling, lice-infected women. Some of the prisoners who worked in these offices were SS toadies,[7] but others tried to maintain a balancing act between meeting the demands of the SS and help-ing fellow prisoners. A few of the women who worked in the Day Room, or Writing Room (*Schreibstube*) as all the prisoners called

Kveta Hnilickova, "Work Crews."
Sammlungen Ravensbrück. Courtesy *Mahn-
und Gedenkstätte Ravensbrück.*

it, functioned as a kind of listening post for the camp's grapevine. They often learned in advance if there were to be transports or selections, and could get the word out through camp runners.[8]

Kitchen workers were another elite group, if only because they had access to all that food. There were actually three kitchens at Ravensbrück, but all were connected. The kitchen for the SS leadership prepared gourmet meals, served in their own dining room. Another kitchen was for the SS and overseers. The largest of the three was for the prisoners. There the cabbage and potato soups were prepared in 600-liter pots. Because of the night shifts, it was a 24-hour-a-day operation, and a sizable one at that. In 1944, about 250 women worked in the kitchens, seventy of them on the night shift. Most were Polish, some were Czechs, and all lived in Block 1. It was more or less expected that kitchen workers would help themselves to table scraps and take some back to the barracks, but they went beyond this and stole real food. While Maika, "the Bread Queen," worked in the bakery, the Czechs always had plenty of bread.[9] No kitchen worker ever went hungry, nor did most of her friends.

Female prisoners in front of the camp kitchens. (SS Photo.)
Dokumentationsarchiv des Österreichischen Widerstandes. Courtesy
USHMM Photo Archives.

Gardens and Farm Work

Women who were assigned to the gardens and farms could
expect to keep their bellies full, too, at least during harvest. One
of the most pleasant work assignments was the Garden Crew,
where the head gardner, an SS man named Loebel, was a nice fellow "who had retained his Catholic faith." For those prisoner officials with connections, it was a good place to send an inmate who
needed convalescing. Loebel was satisfied if half of his crew of
twenty women were working at any one time. Anise Postel-Vinay,
who was there recovering from TB, remembered: "We took turns
resting or sun-bathing behind the huts. . . . "[10] Loebel also understood that prisoners would eat their fill of vegetables and even
smuggle a few back into the camp—getting their bounty past the
guards was a problem, but it was worth the risk. Buber-Neumann
used her connections to be assigned there, and she spent much of
her time creating terrariums and aquariums. In the gardens and

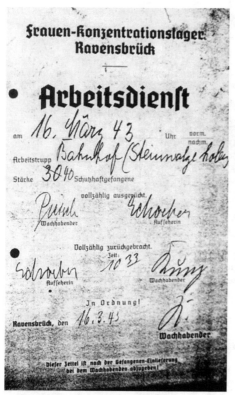

Frauen-Konzentrationslager Ravensbrück

Arbeitsdienst

am *16. März 43*   Uhr vorm.
                                          nachm.
Arbeitstrupp *Bahnhof (Steinwalze holen)*
Stärke *30/40* Schutzhaftgefangene

                    vollzählig ausgerückt.
Wachhabender   Aufseherin

                    Vollzählig zurückgebracht.
                              Zeit: *10 33*
Aufseherin   Wachhabender

                    In Ordnung!
Ravensbrück, den *16.3.43*
                                    Wachhabender

Dieser Zettel ist nach der Gefangenen-Einlieferung bei dem Wachhabenden abzugeben!

Report of a prisoner work detail. The report indicates that on 16 March 1943, thirty prisoners were requisitioned (forty were actually sent) for a work detail which involved going to the railroad station and hauling back a number of stone rollers. The detail was finished by 10:33 A.M., and one can assume that other work awaited the prisoners upon completion of this task. *Sammlungen Ravensbrück.* Courtesy *Mahn- und Gedenkstätte Ravensbrück.*

greenhouses, "We led a relaxed and happy life," she recalled.[11]

Other prisoners were rented out to farmers in the area for three marks per day. This was the more preferable assignment, for not only could the women feast on fruits and vegetables in season and take some home, but also on these civilian farms there was the possibility of meeting people (mostly Polish workers and French POWs) "who thought of us as friends rather than enemies," wrote one prisoner.[12] Although contact was forbidden, in the relatively relaxed atmosphere of fields and orchards, there were exchanges.[13]

The fields and farms where the prisoners worked were scattered around Fürstenberg in every direction. Two elderly sisters who lived their whole lives in Fürstenberg described how "endless columns" of prisoners were marched through the town, morning and night, as they went to and from work. The sisters recalled how when they came back in the evening, they always sang very prettily as they marched through the streets of town, giving the impression that things were "in order" and that they were all healthy and robust.[14] We know now that *Schmuckstücke* and their likes were kept well out of sight of the townspeople.[15]

Internal Work Crews

One of the largest work crews was the Street-Building Crew (*Strassenbau-Kolonne*), whose strength varied from 40 to 160 workers, depending upon needs. It was hard and unpleasant work: digging, moving earth, hauling sand and gravel, leveling, and—the worst—pushing and pulling the gigantic street rollers used to pack down the road bed. It took about a dozen women to move one, and if there was any sign of a slowdown or loafing, the overseer was not loathe to beat the women. A crew member left this description:

Original stone roller, in front of the Bunker. Photograph by the author, 1997.

We scattered gravel on the paths, then smoothed it down with a huge, heavy roller. Ten to fifteen people pulled the roller. Sometimes we were lucky and were able to come behind the rollers with our wheelbarrows of gravel. It was much more difficult work otherwise. If you loaded too little gravel in your wheelbarrow, the overseer sent you back to do it again and besides that, gave you a good boxing on the ears.[16]

But even a crew like the Street-Building Crew on occasion had its lighter moments. There was a brief period in 1941 when, because of a temporary lack of road-building materials, the crew was sent off to its workplace with only a crew chief as supervisor. This particular crew chief was a jovial type, a green badge imprisoned for having had an abortion. In the absence of an overseer and with no real work to do, she allowed her crew to sit around and talk about whatever they liked. They told each other about their former lives and really became acquainted. They called themselves "the Prominents," and they renamed their crew, "The Crew

Female inmates engaged in construction. (SS Photo.) *Sammlungen Ravensbrück.* Courtesy USHMM Photo Archives.

of general merrymaking Prominents" (Kolonne der Prominenten allgemeine Heiterkeit). They joked about "the imminent fall of Hitler," and each Prominent got her chance to hold court. Some gave little lectures or talked about Marxism. Anni, from Prague, regaled her audience with the story of how, when she learned of Rudolf Hess's flight to England, she got so excited that she immediately packed up all of her things, believing that it would be "only a matter of a few hours until Hitler was overthrown." The "Most Prominent of the Prominents," Käthe Leichter, a Jewish sociologist and socialist publicist from Vienna, wrote an original play as her contribution to the group.[17] In this play, titled "Schum Schum," (roughly "Befuddled"), two Jewish prisoners, a man and a woman, escape to an island inhabited by savages. Through peculiar and humorous circumstances, the pair is accepted by the savages as their king and queen, and everybody lives happily ever after. Beneath the funny songs and slapstick humor, however, there was penetrating social criticism and subtle sarcasm directed at the SS.[18] The play was performed, complete with costumes, in the Jewish barracks before an appreciative audience. One non-Jewish admirer wrote: "Something like this could only have come out of the Jewish barracks." Unfortunately, before the performance was finished, the SS found out. Everyone who was involved was punished, and the entire Jewish Block was denied food for three days.[19] Polish women, however, moderated the effects of this by sharing one day's bread rations with the Jewish Block.[20] Not long after this, the little band of "Prominents" was again back at work, pushing the heavy rollers and, no doubt, reminiscing on occasion about their good times.

There was never a time in the six-year history of the Ravensbrück concentration camp that there was not construction going on. Even before the original camp was finished, work had begun on the housing development for SS officers and their families immediately to the north of the main camp. There was a major expansion of the main camp which opened in 1942, about the time that the construction began for the Siemens factories. There was

Female work crews engaged in construction at the SS housing development. (SS Photo.) *Sammlungen Ravensbrück*. Courtesy USHMM Photo Archives.

Female inmates digging sand and loading a hopper car. (SS Photo.) *Sammlungen Ravensbrück*. Courtesy USHMM Photo Archives.

always something being built: garages, kennels, storage sheds (some of them underground and huge in size), office buildings, and so on. Some of the heavier construction work was done by male prisoners from the main camp, or brought in from Sachsen-hausen,[21] but much of the physical labor was supplied by the women prisoners. They dug, loaded dirt onto carts and moved it to other parts of the camp, then piled it up. And they dug sand. The region is built on sand, which was thus readily available for all sorts of construction projects. It only had to be moved. "A mind-numbing endless digging of sand began. . . . We had to dig for nine hours in the glowing heat of the sun."[22]

The prisoners worked four to a cart, and chastised each other if one did not do her share. Antonia Bruha was too weak to lift a full shovel of sand, and her Russian crewmates got after her, thinking she was German. When she told them she was Austrian, they were more accepting of her.[23]

Slackers were not generally tolerated, either by other prisoners or by the SS. Women who could not work or, in some cases, would not work, were put in the "Idiot's Room". Moreover, some prisoners who genuinely could not work were mistreated. In April 1940, Susi Benesch, an Austrian, fainted doing construction work. A doctor examined her and pronounced her capable of work, but the next day she fainted again. The commandant, Koegel, called this sabotage and had her put in the Bunker. Three days later she was dead.[24]

Susi Benesch's death came two years before Himmler and his inner circle formulated their policy of extermination through work (*Vernichtung durch Arbeit*). The "principle" was to make use of the labor of the expendables, particularly Asocials and Jews, and work them until they were no longer work-capable (*arbeitsfähig*), then let them drop.[25] Susi Benesch was neither an Asocial nor a Jew, but she was clearly an expendable, and her death in 1940 indicates that the policy was being practiced long before it was officially formulated.

Some of the work crews operated with a surprising amount of

independence. Charlotte Müller had been an apprentice plumber under her father while growing up, and although she never got a license, she knew much about plumbing. In early 1943, she volunteered to repair plumbing fixtures in the camp, and she was so successful at this that she soon got to choose helpers, creating the Plumbing Crew. A Communist herself, she chose only fellow Communists. They had the run of the camp, and were able to use this mobility to gather information and help their comrades throughout the camp.[26]

Another example of a relatively pleasant work assignment, purely by the accident of its having tolerant and congenial personalities, was the Forestry Crew (the Poles called it the Wood-Cutting Crew). The crew was composed mostly of Poles and was headed by a Polish crew chief named Myszka Liberakowa, whom everyone called Mother Liberak. The overseer was a 19-year-old German, Shenja, a good-natured girl, but a bit lazy. And there was a kindly forester, a German civilian named Kretschmar. He liked to tell stories, and the larger his audience, the better. Sometimes when the crew was working in the woods, he would indicate that it was time for a break. The women would then lay down their implements and sit around him, listening enraptured as Kretschmar spun tales. The crew normally worked hard, felling trees and stacking wood, but they were allowed frequent breaks, and they went about their business without any harassment or fear of punishment. Shenja liked to take naps in a little hut, and she did so on Mother Liberak's promise not to let anybody run away. In addition, the group liked to sing songs, especially Polish patriotic songs, while they worked. Shenja not only allowed this, but she and Kretschmar enjoyed this so much they often sang "tra la la" along with them. But those overseers like Shenja who believed they were safe underestimated the risk. One day a crew member named Eugenia Kocwa sneaked away. There were terrible repercussions, and overnight this Forestry Crew ceased to exist.[27]

The "Availables"

By general agreement, the worst work assignment at Ravensbrück was to be an Available. It was not uncommon for most prisoners to spend a short time in this category before being placed in a more permanent position. Most prisoners, especially those with skills, either political or vocational, were drafted into a more secure assignment within a few weeks. But some inmates spent months as Availables, and it was extremely distressing for them. They were always being called upon to form a special loading or unloading detail, or helping out in the Street-Building Crew when it needed more workers. It was also the Availables who formed the Corpse Crew (*Leichenkolonne*), those unfortunates who had to take carts around to the different blocks and carry bodies away. This was not a crew requiring many workers until the winter of 1944–1945, when the number of deaths increased dramatically.[28]

Perhaps the most negative aspect of being an Available was not the actual work, but that the impermanence of these crews meant they lacked the camaraderie and helpfulness of regular crews. Prisoners would do nearly anything to get out of this category and into a regular job. "Better the rack," one said, "than continuing as an Available."[29] In mid-1944, ten women from Ravensbrück volunteered to be sent to the Barth subcamp in order to escape continuing as Availables, not knowing that at Barth their lives would be even more hellish.[30]

Prisoner Prostitutes

One of the most bizarre and perverse examples of SS entrepreneurial activity began in 1941 when Himmler and his economics chief, Oswald Pohl, conceived the idea that production in the concentration camps could be increased through an incentive program. Prisoner workers would be paid premiums for meeting or surpassing production quotas. They would then be able to spend these premiums for tobacco, food, clothing, or in the case of male prisoners, for sex. Whorehouses would be created in the concentration camps, and male inmates would be permitted to visit there once or twice a week upon payment of a small fee.[31]

In 1942, the first SS-sanctioned whorehouse for prisoners opened at the concentration camp at Mauthausen. Pohl visited the facility, liked what he saw, and almost immediately went to Ravensbrück to interview women prisoners for work in a similar facility at Buchenwald.[32] In 1943, brothels were opened in Buchenwald, Sachsenhausen, and Auschwitz, and the following year in four other camps. Ravensbrück prostitutes were sent to all the camps except Auschwitz.[33]

Contrary to rumor, no Ravensbrück women were forced to become prostitutes.[34] But to claim they were all "volunteers" is to stretch the point. Considering the conditions of their existence and the promises made to them if they volunteered, it is not surprising that many Ravensbrück women took the offer. They were all promised better food, private rooms, pretty clothes, more comfortable conditions, and best of all, most of them were told they would be released after six months.

Himmler preferred to recruit women who already had "reputations" so as not to corrupt German women who could still be made part of the Folkish Community (*Volksgemeinschaft*).[35] Thus, the majority of women who were accepted (not necessarily the majority of those who volunteered) for brothel duty had been prostitutes before entering Ravensbrück.[36] Most of the women who volunteered were, indeed, German, but there was an effort to recruit others. When the block seniors approached the women in their blocks about volunteering, there were some interesting responses. Not surprisingly, inmates in the Punishment Block volunteered in great numbers in an effort to escape their oppression.[37] In the French barracks, some of the women whose German was less than perfect raised their hands to volunteer because they thought they were being asked to go to Bordeaux rather than to a *Bordell*. Their mates quickly corrected them.[38] In another barracks composed mostly of non-Germans, the offer produced quite a commotion, but after that, several names were volunteered. The block senior began to write them down until she realized that the names she was being given were the oldest women in the block, all seventy years old or older.[39] The Polish women were so outraged at even being asked that they sent a delegation to the commandant to protest, and were all punished: no mail for two weeks.[40]

Those women who volunteered for brothel duty were taken to the infirmary where they were checked out, naked, by SS officers and a doctor. In an episode involving four volunteers, two were accepted and the other two (rejected for health reasons) were returned to their barracks that evening, where they faced the scorn of the other women.[41] Some of the more attractive women were recruited for the whorehouses of the SS and the *Wehrmacht*,[42] where presumably the pay was somewhat better, but most were intended for concentration camp brothels. Those who were chosen were immediately relieved of duty and the obligation to stand roll calls, and were allowed to loaf for a few days. Meanwhile, warehouse workers scoured their bins to find suitable lingerie, including black panties, to replace the unerotic prison underwear.[43] Then they were shipped out to their new duty posts.

Frau W. was one of the women who volunteered to be a prostitute in order to leave the Punishment Block. She was one of the few prisoner prostitutes who allowed herself to be interviewed, and her recollections provide us something of a rare insider's view. She had been in the camp since December 1939, and in the summer of 1943, when she got the chance to improve her conditions, she took it. She and fifteen other women were paraded nude in front of the SS officials, and those chosen were sent by train to Buchenwald. There they were put in a nicely furnished barracks, where they could sleep until 8 A.M., lounge around all day, and work two hours each evening. Each "girl" was expected to service eight men in that time. The customer paid two Marks, of which the prostitute kept one. There was a peephole in each room, partly for the benefit of SS voyeurs, but also to make sure that "things" were being done right. Only the missionary position was allowed, but the women would cover the peephole when their own *Lieblings* (sweethearts) paid a visit.

One of the women in Frau W.'s "crew" justified her decision to become a whore at Buchenwald: "Better this than to get beaten every day, have to work hard, and get nothing to eat."[44]

The SS had kept its word except on one important point: None of the women were released after six months, as originally promised. Many worked longer than six months (a few of the original Ravensbrück "girls" were still working at Buchenwald in March 1945); however, most were returned to Ravensbrück after a few months suffering from venereal disease, but with money in their accounts. One fellow prisoner noted, with a combination of envy and disgust, that these "whores" (*Dirnen*) had come back with about 3,000 Marks each.[45] Those who returned were exchanged for other volunteers.[46] There was no shortage of desperate women at Ravensbrück.

CHAPTER 16

The Subcamps

France Audoul, "Groundbreaking." From *Ravensbrück: 15,000 Femmes en Enfer.*

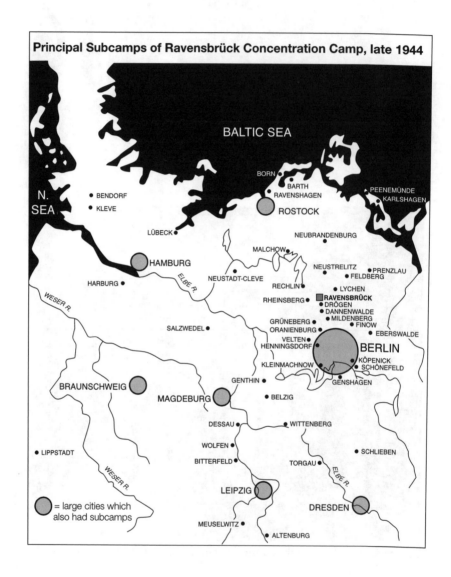

Principal Subcamps of Ravensbrück Concentration Camp, late 1944

BALTIC SEA

N. SEA

BORN
BARTH
RAVENSHAGEN
PEENEMÜNDE
KARLSHAGEN

BENDORF
KLEVE

ROSTOCK

LÜBECK
NEUBRANDENBURG

MALCHOW

HAMBURG

NEUSTRELITZ
FELDBERG
PRENZLAU

HARBURG
ELBE R.
NEUSTADT-CLEVE
RECHLIN
LYCHEN

WESER R.
RHEINSBERG
RAVENSBRÜCK
DRÖGEN
DANNENWALDE
MILDENBERG
FINOW

GRÜNEBERG
ORANIENBURG
EBERSWALDE

SALZWEDEL

VELTEN
HENNINGSDORF
BERLIN

KLEINMACHNOW
KÖPENICK
SCHÖNEFELD

BRAUNSCHWEIG
GENTHIN
GENSHAGEN

MAGDEBURG
BELZIG

DESSAU
WITTENBERG

WOLFEN
LIPPSTADT
SCHLIEBEN

WESER R.
BITTERFELD
TORGAU
ELBE R.

= large cities which
also had subcamps

LEIPZIG
DRESDEN

MEUSELWITZ
ALTENBURG

Overview of a Mini-Empire

The first subcamps (called *Aussenlager* or sometimes, *Neben-lager*) of Ravensbrück were created in 1941–1942. The subcamp at Grüneberg, meant to provide labor for the munitions factory, *Grüneberg-Metallwerk*, was constructed during this period with help from female prisoners from Ravensbrück. When construction was completed, many of the women stayed on to work in the factory, producing bombs and shell cartridges.[1]

From this point, thus coinciding with the new economic emphasis of the entire concentration camp system, the expansion of the subcamp system was more like an explosion. By 1944, Ravensbrück was the center of a mini-empire of its own. The system of subcamps that it directed stretched from Königsberg to Hamburg and from the Baltic to Bavaria. Over seventy subcamps were encompassed in this system, more than half of which had inmate populations numbering in the hundreds. One of these camps, Neubrandenburg, held five to six thousand women and might eventually have become an independent camp in the way Dora-Mittelbau had broken off from Buchenwald, or Neuengamme became independent of Sachsenhausen. This did not happen, but some of the subcamps originally created and run by Ravensbrück were transferred to these larger camps. Here is a listing of the more important subcamps controlled by Ravensbrück.

Ravensbrück Sub-Camps	Maximum Pop. 1944	Primary Type of Work
1. Barth	2,000	Aircraft, V-1 & V-2 components
2. Beendorf	250	Aircraft parts
3. Berlin	1,200	AEG: Electronics
4. Berlin- Genshagen	500	Daimler-Benz: Aircraft Motors
5. Berlin- Henningsdorf	800	Weapons
6. Berlin-Klein Machnow	800	Weapons

7. Berlin-Köpenick	1,000	Rubber, cables
8. Berlin-Schönefeld	850	Aircraft
9. Bitterfeld	300	I.G. Farben
10. Braunschweig	500	Steel
11. Breslau	450	Munitions
12. Dessau	700	Aircraft
13. Dresden	700	Universelle: Aircraft Motors
14. Dresden	750	Zeiss Ikon: Explosives
15. Eberswalde	800	Munitions
16. Finow	300	Munitions
17. Fürstenberg	200	Heinkel: Aircraft parts
18. Fürstenberg	80	Grahl Textile Factory
19. Genthin	850	Munitions
20. Grüneberg	1,800	Munitions
21. Hamburg-Wandsbeck	300	Rubber products
22. Karlshagen	1,200	Artillery, V-weapons
23. Leipzig	3,000	HASAG: Munitions
24. Lippstadt	530	Iron and steel
25. Lübeck	250	Ikaria: Weapons
26. Magdeburg	1,100	Polte Fabrik: Munitions
27. Malchow	500	Chemicals, Explosives
28. Meuselwitz	150	Munitions
29. Neu Bohlen	250	
30. Neubrandenburg	6,000	MWN: Munitions
31. Neurohlau	450	Porcelain
32. Neustadt-Glewe	4,000	Arado Flugzeug Werk: Aircraft
33. Oranienburg	1,200	Auerwerke: Aircraft parts
34. Peenemünde	300	V-Weapons
35. Penig	750	Junker Plant: Aircraft parts
36. Ravensbrück	2,500	Siemens & Halske: Electronics. Officially became a subcamp in the summer of 1944.

37. Ravensbrück	2,500	SS-Textile Factories. Officially became a subcamp in October 1944.
38. Ravensburg	250	
39. Rechlin	1,800	Airfield construction
40. Rostock	1,500	Aircraft
41. Salzwedel	1,170	Cables, Metal products
42. Stargard	500	Technical equipment
43. Torgau	600	Munitions
44. Velten	500	Munitions
45. Wattensted	1,300	Hermann Goering Werk: Steel
46. Wittenberg	500	Arado Flugzeug Werk: Aircraft
47. Zwodau	1,500	Siemens: Electronics

There were smaller subcamps spread from Königsberg in the eastern Baltic (where women prisoners worked on airstrips), to Ansbach in Bavaria (where they worked in a *Lebensborn* home). Not surprisingly, there was a cluster of small subcamps in towns not far from Ravensbrück, in Dammenwalde, Hohenlychen, Neustrelitz, Feldberg, and in nearby Drögen, where there was also a Gestapo school.[2] It was a massive system, and exceedingly complex. Keeping track of the labor and personnel needs of this far-flung empire was a major undertaking and required the efforts of numerous office workers, but labor was plentiful and cheap. Surviving SS records contain many reports detailing the movement of prisoners between the main camp and subcamps. Prisoners were being shuttled almost every day, sometimes for a permanent assignment, but often for temporary labor needs for a specific work project. Once Germany began to experience the impact of Allied bombing raids, prisoners were frequently dispatched to a site for purposes of clearing rubble.[3] Many inmates went back and forth between the main camp and one or more subcamps a number of times.

Life and Work in the Subcamps

Conditions for both living and working varied enormously among the subcamps, perhaps even more than between the various sections and work assignments of the main camp. As always, much depended on the personalities and dispositions of individual leaders in these camps. It's also necessary to keep in mind that some of these subcamps were really quite small, containing perhaps a dozen or so inmates. There might only have been one overseer, and if that overseer had a touch of humanity, conditions there might have been relatively tolerable. A Danish prisoner who was assigned to the subcamp at Torgau for five weeks noted that their overseers were, in general, "not the worst sort." They were local women, and they lacked the "special training" of the overseers in the larger camps. They would sometimes even chat with the prisoners when they knew they were not being observed.[4]

An illuminating example of the precariousness of inmate existence is afforded by the little subcamp of Holleischen, in the Sudeten area. Working in what was essentially a type of cottage-industry production, the prisoners made casings and shells for the military. The commandant, a man named Edmond, was a kind of enigma. He did beat the women for infractions of the rules, but in other ways he was solicitous of them and of their needs as women. Since so many of them had arrived with their heads shaved, he issued bandannas to them immediately. He allowed them to wear their dresses with some consideration for feminine notions of taste. He had a mirror placed in their washroom. Little things, but they made life just a bit more pleasant for the women prisoners. Then Edmond was transferred, and "From that moment on, the little camp at Holleischen entered into a period of irreversible horror. Diabolical delousings, beatings, slow degradation, systematically brutalized by the horsewhip, by hunger, cold, fatigue, and lack of sleep. We were spared nothing. The precarious equilibrium of the camp disappeared with our first commandant."[5]

In the subcamp at Barth, on the Baltic Sea, a situation had arisen that was very much an anomaly and which would never have been found at the main camp. By 1944, the camp was largely populated by non-Germans, which was not so unusual. But these non-Germans, Czechs in particular, were the dominant element and were openly hostile to German prisoners. In June of that year, a group of German women had voluntarily transferred to Barth to escape a continued existence as Availables in the main camp. At Barth, they were assigned to the Gypsy camp. There, they encountered another anomaly: a Gypsy block senior. Put simply, the Gypsy women terrorized the Germans. They took the best for themselves at mealtimes, stole from them relentlessly, bribed the overseers for favors, and lost no opportunity to oppress their underlings.[6] Perhaps this was retaliation for all the mistreatment the Gypsies had endured at the hands of Germans.

Neubrandenburg

Some time during 1943, Rintelen, the director of the Neubrandenburg Engineering Workshops (*Mechanischen Werkstätten Neubrandenburg Gmbh* or *MWN*) made the short (a little over an hour) trip to Ravensbrück. His company was already deeply involved in the production of munitions and aircraft components, especially making bomb sights, and more workers were needed. By this time, there was a severe labor shortage in Germany, and one of the few places to "recruit" good workers was at the concentration camps. Rintelen was leaving nothing to chance. By going to Ravensbrück he could personally interview and examine potential employees. Female prisoners were examined for good teeth and healthy hands. Gray-haired women were automatically rejected, as were any who showed signs of being sick or weak.[7] Not unnaturally, women who were examined in this way found the process upsetting and humiliating. To Ilse Reibmayr, an Austrian, they were being "bought . . . just like slaves."[8]

From the point of view of the MWN, the partnership with Ravensbrück was a happy and profitable arrangement. Everywhere there was expansion: in production, the factory, and the camp. The positive experience led the MWN to increase facilities, add shifts, and staff them exclusively with female prisoner laborers. By late 1943, about 2,000 women worked at the MWN factory, and another two to three hundred were kept behind to maintain the camp. A year later these figures had just about tripled.[9]

For the women, the experience at Neubrandenburg does not appear to have been quite so salutary. Most women who made a comparison thought that Neubrandenburg was a much worse camp than Ravensbrück.[10] But our sample might be warped because the only two memoirs written by Neubrandenburg survivors, of which I am aware, were written by French women. At Neubrandenburg, the French did not have their own barracks. They were a minority surrounded by a Slavic majority; the two groups hated each other and fought constantly.[11]

Because the factory was located between the town and the camp, at some distance apart, each day the prisoners were marched to and from work. As they walked along the roads, local civilians would sometimes turn their backs to them or even spit at them.[12] A French inmate recalled: "On our way to work, the local Germans watched us pass. They never showed the least sign of pity. The children threw stones at us, which pleased the guards."[13]

Nearly all of the subcamps hired civilian workers, at least as foremen. Prisoners generally called them "masters." Many of the camps had lots of civilian workers, but Neubrandenburg did not. Moreover, while at some camps there was a kind of equality between masters and overseers, this was not the case at Neubrandenburg, where the overseers definitely had the upper hand.[14] In the workplaces there seems to have been an unusually large number of physical beatings; the foremen were frankly afraid of the overseers and reluctant to interfere. "They [the overseers] hit us for looking at them the wrong way, for being a minute late coming from roll call, they hit those who had put paper under their clothes to keep from freezing. They beat us for the slightest cause and even without any cause."[15]

Dresden and Leipzig

Not all of the subcamps were as oppressive as the ones we have discussed. At Dresden, for example, the Universelle Factory, which before the war was a cigarette factory, had been producing pumps and pressure regulators for the military for some time. In 1944, it expanded production by bringing in 500, and later, another 200, female prisoners from Ravensbrück to supplement their civilian workforce. For the concentration camp inmates, it was a self-contained system. The factory was in the lower stories, the next story was the kitchen and dining area, and the upper stories were the sleeping rooms. There, each prisoner had her own bed, and the mattresses were made of wool rather than straw. According to survivors' testimony, the rooms were all heated and the food was adequate. Still, it was hardly a utopia. Prisoners had to work 12-hour shifts (which had become almost routine in the camps by early 1945) with only a half-hour break. The punishments were severe, although not as arbitrary as at Neubrandenburg. (Some of the prisoners were being punished in a cell somewhere in the city on the night of 13 February 1945 when the city was leveled by American bombers. Their bodies were found much later.)[16]

We know something else about the Universelle Factory from an internal investigation done by company personnel, which resulted in a confidential report. Apparently, relations between civilian workers and women prisoners had become rather chummy in the factory. The report cited a number of cases in which workers were not only friendly to prisoners, but had also given them food, clothing, and cigarettes, even mailing their letters for them. The report concluded by noting that this was not to be taken lightly, for if the Gestapo learned of this, they could be expected to take action and "remove" the people involved. Surprisingly, and this may be the most illuminating aspect of the report, the implication is clear that company officials had no intention themselves of volunteering this information to the Gestapo.[17]

This appears not to have been an isolated situation. A fairly similar development occurred at a subcamp in Leipzig at the Hasag Factory, where the predominantly Polish and Russian female inmates worked alongside German civilians, mostly women. In one work crew, a congenial atmosphere was established by the master, Holstein, who was "only as strict as necessary" and talked with the prisoners privately, even though this was forbidden. The German women shared their bread and other provisions with the inmates.[18] In other parts of the factory, these contacts were carried even further. Germans volunteered to mail letters for prisoners. In one case, a real friendship developed between a young German woman, a civilian worker named Hildegard Dockhorn, and a Russian prisoner, a medical student named Ludmilla Wakulla.[19]

Ravensbrück inmates who were assigned to the Grahl Sewing Plant in nearby Fürstenberg later noted that the SS overseers there were quite nasty to them. Regulations against fraternization were very strictly enforced, so they did not become acquainted with other workers—in fact, they did not even know that about fifty of the workers were Polish "volunteers." But, in general, the civilian workers treated them well. The factory director, a man named Bruggemann, once interceded to save the whole crew from a Report.[20] Overwhelmingly, those prisoners who worked outside the main camp, either in subcamps or in work crews near Ravensbrück, remembered later that the civilian supervisors—the Masters, most of whom were somewhat older men—were nice to them.[21] The women who worked on the assembly lines making Messerschmidt aircraft for the Heinkel Factory in Berlin-

Schönefeld report being treated brutally by their masters, but not as badly as by the female overseers.[22] This was, however, the exception. Most of these men treated the women prisoners who worked under them with some consideration, but probably none were as considerate to their workers as Denise Dufournier's master was to her. When he noticed that she was looking sick and weak, he took her to his workshop and fed her a large plate of potatoes, "cooked to perfection."[23]

Neustadt-Glewe and Malchow

In 1943, English bombers destroyed the aircraft factory of the Dornier firm (a subsidiary of Arado Aircraft), located at Wismar, on the Baltic Sea. The plant and its managers were soon relocated about 75 km (45 miles) inland, to the town of Neustadt-Glewe, where the firm hoped to resume operations shortly. A few workers transferred there, and advertisements placed in local papers brought in others, but this did not suffice. The decision was then made for the firm to become a subcamp of Ravensbrück in order to tap into the supply of female workers. Facilities were quickly constructed, existing structures were renovated, and by late summer of 1944 the Dornier factory was again producing aircraft.[24]

The subcamp at Neustadt-Glewe was designed to hold between 800 and 1,000 female prisoners. By December 1944, it had about reached capacity: 900 women, mostly Polish, working two shifts of twelve hours each. Each prisoner had her own bed, and the food was nearly adequate, at least in quantity.[25] The guards were not SS, but *Wehrmacht* personnel, mostly older men who were not considered suitable for combat. Survivors of the camp overwhelmingly commented on how decently these men acted toward the women inmates, even sharing their food with them on occasion.[26]

Neustadt-Glewe was hardly a workers' paradise, and yet all the indicators suggest that in its early stages, conditions at the camp were tolerable. What changed this was not increasing workloads or growing SS oppressiveness, but simply overcrowding. Beginning in January 1945, with camps in the east sending prisoners west, Ravensbrück itself became terribly overcrowded and the SS administration there attempted to minimize its own problems by dumping their excess populations onto certain subcamps. From January to April 1945, the prisoner population at Neustadt-Glewe went from 900 to about 5,000.[27]

Most of these newcomers, probably about 60%, were Jews. Most had come from Auschwitz, and all had come through Ravensbrück. Many had spent only a few days at the main camp before being forwarded, generally by train, to Neustadt-Glewe. In their reports and memoirs, survivors recalled how totally unprepared their new camp was for their arrival. Many had to wait days before they were fed by the SS; if it had not been for other prisoners' willingness to share provisions, they would have starved.[28] There was virtually no work for them. The aircraft factory was running at capacity and needed no additional workers. A few women were organized into work crews for special purposes, such as digging defensive trenches on the edge of town, but most just sat around all day talking and exchanging recipes, their favorite pastime.[29]

In spite of the increased numbers of inmates, no new barracks were constructed, and the old barracks were reserved for the original inhabitants who still worked in the aircraft factory.[30] Presumably, the Dornier management wanted to make sure their workers got sufficient sleep, for these workers were the only prisoners in the camp who had beds. Some additional space for the newcomers was created by converting other buildings, apparently some hangars, into barracks. However, these makeshift barracks had no facilities, neither beds nor toilets. Prisoners slept on the floor, in close proximity to buckets that served as chamber pots.[31]

By March 1945, the combination of overcrowded barracks, unhygienic conditions, and inadequate nutrition had begun to produce the same results at Neustadt-Glewe as in the main camp; the death rate began to rise significantly. A Dutch civilian, a conscripted male worker, remembered seeing a work crew of eight to ten women making the rounds every day, picking up corpses, then hauling them into the nearby woods for burial.[32] After the war, some of these mass graves were located, but most were not. This fact, coupled with the destruction of SS records, has made it extremely difficult to determine the death toll in the subcamp. Karl Heinz Schütt, whose study of Neustadt-Glewe is the most substantive we have for any of Ravensbrück's subcamps, estimates the number of dead at 500 to 560,[33] about 10% of the total number of women prisoners.

A quite different picture emerges in examining the neighboring subcamp at Malchow. Many of the initial conditions were the same as at Neustadt-Glewe: it was a small camp which serviced local industries, in this case a chemical plant and a factory that made paper cartons. As at Neustadt-Glewe, the guards were older army men, rather than SS, and they did not generally mistreat the women prisoners. In addition, food and housing were adequate.[34] Beginning in January 1945, the authorities at Ravensbrück began sending some of their surplus population, again mainly Jewish women, to Malchow. But while Neustadt-Glewe became unbearably overcrowded, Malchow did not. Conditions worsened, particularly as food became scarce, but Malchow never reached the point at which the survival of significant numbers of prisoners was threatened. Indeed, many survivors commented upon how relatively comfortable the surroundings were, right up to the end.[35]

Why Malchow should have remained relatively comfortable, while Neustadt-Glewe did not, is one of the many unanswered questions related to the subcamps. Indeed, Ravensbrück's sub-camps are only now being given attention, and very little at that. Not much is known about the relationship between the main camp administration and that of the subcamps or why some sub-camps remained relatively free from life-threatening conditions, while others did not. Was it principally a matter of personalities at the local level, or did it represent part of a larger plan, perhaps engineered at the main camp? More basic research must be done on this issue if real sense is to be made of it. This will not be easy, especially without the SS's own correspondence and other official records. But studies, like that of Karl Heinz Schütt on Neustadt-Glewe, point in a promising direction.

German Civilians and Ravensbrück Prisoners

The issue of the relations between the German civilian population and the concentration camp inmates is an important and sensitive topic deserving of more substantive treatment than it has so far been given. The issue automatically raises a number of questions, one of which is: how much did civilians know about the women prisoners of Ravensbrück, whether at the main camp or in subcamps? After all, everyone was aware of the prisoners; they saw them marching through towns or being escorted from camp to camp, often by train. We have seen examples which suggest that at this level, the level of casual contact, the behavior of most Germans toward the female prisoners was simply deplorable, and many survivors remember these experiences with an understandable degree of bitterness.[36] There were, fortunately, some exceptions to this treatment, however rare. A French prisoner, Charlotte Delbo, remembered being part of a group of prisoners escorted from Auschwitz to Ravensbrück in January 1944. At a train station in Berlin, while most onlookers looked at them with suspicion, a German mother told her child: "These are unfortunate women. Give them a smile." And she herself smiled kindly.[37] This small act of considerateness immeasurably brightened Delbo's trip, and remained indelibly in her mind long after.

Delbo's experience was the rare exception, but the probability is very strong that at this level of contact, the civilians knew very little about the prisoners, let alone about their treatment. The common attitude was that they were criminals and as such were being rightly punished for their misbehavior. Keep in mind that even in the workplaces, let alone in a train station or on the street, it was a strictly forbidden and punishable offense for prisoners to converse with civilians or vice versa. And for those few civilians who were sympathetic and might be inclined to show kindness to prisoners, there was the undeniable factor of fear. Those sisters in Fürstenberg who daily observed columns of prisoners on their street had heard stories about how a man from their town had given some bread to prisoners. Then the man, a carpenter, had just "disappeared." According to rumors, his act of benevolence earned him a year or two in jail.[38]

Ravensbrück Concentration Camp was located just across a small lake from the town of Fürstenberg, at most a kilometer (2/3 mile) in distance. No civilians ever worked in the camp, but local business people, such as the butcher, Reimann, sometimes went inside the gates to make deliveries.[39] Some of the SS men and overseers lived in the town, and although it was forbidden for them to discuss the goings-on across the lake, we can assume that occasionally little pieces of information were leaked. A better source of information would have been local farmers who hired groups of prisoners, or the masters of some of the work crews. They were not permitted to converse, and the prisoners were watched by overseers. But, one knows how easy it is for a few words to just slip out. And then there were those bodies being delivered to the town crematorium. At first there were only a few—in 1941–1942, not even averaging one each day. In 1943, the deaths began to mount, and in 1944, the numbers soared.[40] But how many knew about this, and if they did, what were they to make of it?

Daniel Goldhagen's assertion that "the regime made no serious effort to spare the German people from exposure to these institutions of violence, subjugation, and death"[41] appears to have little validity when applied to the camp at Ravensbrück. Obviously the townspeople knew about the concentration camp across the lake, and obviously many of them had heard bits and pieces about unsavory practices behind the camp walls. There were reports that

Original sign, which reads: "Attention! Approaching the
fence as well as hanging around on the road alongside the
camp and making photographs is forbidden!" This message
is signed by the Waffen-SS of the concentration camp and
the camp commandant. *Sammlungen Ravensbrück.*
Courtesy *Mahn- und Gedenkstätte Ravensbrück.*

on occasion gunshots were heard coming from the direction of the
camp.[42] But unless *all* the information that floated around the
town would have been systematically gathered up—and that
would have required asking a lot of questions, a very risky venture—not much would have been known about the camp. Even
then, it would have been difficult putting the information together and making any sense of it.

A somewhat different picture emerges when we examine those
situations in the subcamps where Ravensbrück prisoners worked
in close proximity to German civilians. They were not supposed to
converse, but there is evidence they did. In the relative security of
a workplace with a sympathetic master and a not-too-attentive
overseer, German workers probably began by asking questions of
their uniformed work companions, followed by other questions,
brief answers, offers of bread. One thing led to another, but it

seems reasonable to assume that at the point at which German civilians were offering to take the risk of mailing letters for prisoners, they had become fairly well acquainted. One suspects, too, that these civilian workers had gained information and insights into the lives of the prisoners which went well beyond what most other German civilians, including the townspeople at Fürstenberg, ever acquired. What they did with this information we can only surmise, but one thing appears quite certain: unlike those Germans who only saw the prisoners from a distance, the Germans who worked alongside or in close contact with Ravensbrück prisoners often treated them with kindness and sympathy. Everyone knew there were great risks involved. In the Walter John Firm, a small subcamp of Ravensbrück that made drainage and sewer pipes, a situation developed in which civilian workers were supportive of their prisoner-workers, giving them rest breaks and treating them kindly. Probably as the result of a denunciation, in 1944 all of the civilians were arrested and put in camps themselves.[43]

In the late stages of the war, German civilian workers were themselves living anything but lives of plenty. Everything was rationed, and many essentials were unavailable. The weekly bread ration was "adjusted" from 2 1/2 to 2 kg. (5 1/2 to 4 1/2 lbs.) per person in 1942.[44] This was still almost a third more than what an inmate received: 280 grams per day versus 200. While the caloric intake of most Germans hovered above minimal levels (1,800 calories per day being considered minimum) for the greater part of the war, in 1944 it dropped below this level.[45] Moreover, there was a continuing extension of working hours: from 49 per week in 1939, to 52 in 1943; then to 60 (women were held to 56). Some workers in key industries were required to work 72 hours a week.[46] By contrast, Ravensbrück prisoners generally worked 65 hours per week.

There is no question that in the last year of the war that mythical creature, "the average German," the one the Germans themselves parody as the hapless "Michel," always wearing his nightcap, began to live a life of hardship. The Nazi state, having long before this imposed want and misery on its neighbors, now had to watch its own people be engulfed in similar conditions. In this context, the extension of acts of kindness, the giving of bread and clothing by German civilians to their concentration camp workmates of various nationalities, is all the more remarkable. For all of their privation, they had come to know and appreciate that these poor women were even worse off than they were. In the otherwise bleak landscape of human relations during the period of Nazism in Germany, surely this is one of the bright spots.

17

Crime and Punishment

Aat Breur, "In the Bunker." From *Een verborgen herinnering*. Courtesy Dunya Breur.

By the time the women's concentration camp at Ravensbrück opened in 1939, the system used to punish inmates was well established. It was called the Dachau Model because it had been devised for Germany's first concentration camp by Theodor Eicke (the second commandant of Dachau, and also head of the concentration camps from 1934 to 1939), then was later extended to all the other camps. The theoretical basis for the system was Eicke's "Disciplinary and Punishment Regulations for the Prison Camp" (*Disziplinär-und Strafordnung für das Gefangenenlager*). This was meant to suggest that if prisoners followed the rules they would have no problems.[1] Eicke's regulations created a graded system of punishments to be standardized throughout the entire concentration camp system. However, these written procedures were more than slightly offset by Eicke's oral pronouncements to SS guards wherein he urged them to be ruthless and show no pity to these "dangerous enemies of the state," the inmates.[2]

"Minor" Punishments

In theory, women were informed about camp regulations during their period of quarantine, shortly after arriving. Although this was done, there seems to have been considerable variance in the scope and quality of these orientations. For many prisoners, this was a very confusing time, for the sessions were given mainly in German. The result was that many inmates had a faulty understanding of the rules, at least initially. Moreover, there were so many regulations, it was difficult to keep them all straight. Many of these were simply picayune. For example, one could be punished for having a button unbuttoned, for not tucking in one's blanket at the bed corners exactly to specifications, for not responding properly to an overseer's command (not understanding German well was no excuse), or for any violation of the dress code.[3] For any of the official punishments, it was necessary for an overseer to send in a Report and have it approved by the commandant's office. But judging from the number of punishments, such approval was not difficult to obtain.

The simplest and most common form of punishment was *Strafstehen*, literally, "punishment standing." The offender was made to stand, more or less at attention, for a specified period, anywhere from one hour to several days. Sometimes whole blocks were given this punishment, which was normally administered on weekends, or in the evenings after roll call for short sentences. During *Strafstehen*, there was to be no talking, eating, or moving around.[4] An inmate left this description of her block being punished because of illicit communications between the men's and women's camps:

> You come back to the camp about seven o'clock, dead tired from hard work. Your feet burn intolerably. You have torturous hunger. But don't think that you can go somewhere and sit in peace and eat your supper; you've got to stand for a couple of hours as punishment. In long rows, one against the other, all equally hungry, equally tired, equally dirty, equally confused. You stand, because somewhere another letter was found, stupid as the words taken from a ten-Pfenning novel, from some Asocial to some almost unknown male prisoner. You stand, still and disciplined, bitterness in your heart, full of bewilderment. A few rows behind you, those whose inconsiderateness was responsible for the block's punishment loudly and nonchalantly amuse themselves.[5]

To increase the severity of this punishment, overseers would sometimes capriciously order offenders to stand barefoot, even in cold weather or snow.[6]

Deprivation of food, withholding of mail, and confinement to barracks were other mild punishments for minor offenses. Often whole blocks were punished for the misdeeds of one individual, thus forcing the members to police their own ranks. On one occasion, because two Jewish women spoke to each other during roll call, their entire block was made to stand from noon until evening in driving snow.[7] This tactic also caused disharmony within groups. When camp authorities tried to recruit young Polish women for brothel duty, they were so outraged they sent a delegation to the commandant to protest. For this audacious act, their entire block was punished: no mail for two weeks, and their packages were given away. The older Polish women were angry, at least for a time, at those younger women who had seemingly brought this on.[8]

Depending upon the mood and disposition of the overseer, normal punishments were frequently accompanied by punches and kicks or even worse. Wanda P., a young Gypsy, was observed by an overseer as she tried to make contact with her husband, whom she presumed was in the men's camp. It was not the first time she had attempted this. Consequently, in addition to ten hours of *Strafstehen*, she was beaten badly about the face and had several fingernails pulled back for good measure.[9]

The "Idiots' Room"

An example of both the underlying inhumanity of the system and the chicanery of the SS was to commit troublesome prisoners to the so-called Idiots' Room. This was a relatively small room in one of the sick blocks where women were placed who were considered mentally unbalanced. Some of them were indeed mentally ill, and a few were even dangerous. It was an absolutely horrendous scene, according to the few observers who reported on it. The room was packed with forty to sixty women in a space about 4 x 5 meters (12 x 16 feet). There were no beds. Maybe half the inmates had blankets. Some of the women were totally naked; a few were partially dressed. Some of the women sang intermittently, others danced, and one played an imaginary piano. One woman pretended to be a dog and was known to bite her companions.

A bucket placed in front of the door was filled to the rim with excrement. Excrement stuck to the emaciated bodies.

Aat Breur, untitled drawing of women from the "Idiots' Room." From *Een verborgen herinnering*. Courtesy Dunya Breur.

They smeared it on the walls and lay in it. The smell in this little room was frightful, the noise gruesome. Animal-like screams of deranged women mixed with childlike sobbing of those who were despondent. One woman laughed hysterically and another sang at the top of her lungs. All were skin and bone, naked under a bloodstained blanket they shared with a half dozen others. Among them were normal people like you and me, wild bewilderment in their eyes, incorporated into this inferno as punishment. In a few days, they would either be dead or mad like the others.[10]

The SS had obviously decided that these prisoners would not have long to live, and thus they were given only half-rations. Inmates of the Idiots' Room were periodically transported, not to be heard from again.[11] Being sent to the Idiots' Room was technically not punishment, rather a reassignment. But, of course, it was considered punishment by any who were sent there, even for a few days. Incredible stories (not much worse than the reality) circulated about conditions there, and thus prisoners understandably harbored great fears about this place.[12]

The Punishment Block

Of all the blocks at Ravensbrück (the Bunker was not a block), the most feared was the Punishment Block (*Strafblock*), in part because the overseers and block seniors there were rumored to be the most brutal in the camp. Prisoners there were segregated from the rest of the camp by a barbed-wire fence. They had no postal privileges. They worked only in the hardest outside jobs, with no days off. Prisoners were sentenced to the *Strafblock* for major violations of camp regulations, such as stealing, or talking back to a superior. Many were there for repeated violations of smaller offenses.[13]

Women who were released from Ravensbrück were forbidden to speak with anyone about what they had seen, heard, or experienced. Those who were found to have talked were rearrested and sentenced to two years in the Punishment Block.[14] Moreover, it was customary for prisoners to be assigned to the Punishment Block upon release from the Bunker. In addition, the Gestapo sometimes sent prisoners there for reasons of their own.[15]

Punishment Block inmates performed not only the hardest work, but also the dirtiest. Generally, it was inmates from this block who formed the "shit crews" (*Scheisskolonne*) whose job it was to clean out the toilet pits. The only way to do this was to get down in the pits, standing up to one's knees in human waste, and shovel the excrement into buckets, which were then pulled out and dumped into carts and hauled away out into the countryside, where it was spread onto fields. If the crews were lucky, some of this filthy work would have already been done by hapless Availables.[16]

From the point of view of many prisoners, the most negative

feature of the Punishment Block was neither the work nor the conditions, but the company one had to tolerate. The majority of Punishment Block inmates were Criminals and Asocials, many of whom had been brutalized by long years in detention, and whose only remaining instinct, seemingly, was self-preservation. A Polish inmate noted: "They looked out from behind the barbed wire entanglements like wild beasts, always squabbling with each other. It was a hard life for any woman who was physically weaker or more intelligent finding herself among them—they persecuted and harassed her."[17]

Theolinde Katzenmaier, who later became a nun, observed that the fourteen days she once spent in the Punishment Block gave her a very negative view of human nature.[18] Another prisoner observed that the Punishment Block increasingly took on the character of "a lesbian whorehouse."[19] Women in other parts of the camp risked being arrested and sent to the Punishment Block for making homosexual advances or for engaging in homosexual activity. But once they were there, no further punishment appears to have been forthcoming for continuing these activities. Indeed, a French inmate believed it would have been impossible for a woman to survive the Punishment Block without at least tacitly going along with the prevailing lesbian relationships and hooking up with a "Jules."[20]

Among the treasures in the Ravensbrück Archives is a little gem of a report which tells us something about life in the camp, as well as crime and punishment there. In 1943, a work crew from the Punishment Block was doing some work at the water treatment plant. The overseer was an 18-year old. A crew member later recorded: "There were some real high times going on in this crew. The overseer flirted with the prisoners and the prisoners flirted with the overseer. Then there were some parties and the like put on in a nearby wooden shack. Nobody wanted to leave this crew because it offered us many advantages." Another of the crew members was a woman named Zippzack who was apparently somewhat disgruntled. Secretly she was keeping a diary about the goings-on in this crew, probably taking note of the illegal fraternizing with its homosexual intimations. When Zippzack's note-taking was brought to the attention of the young overseer, she tried to get her removed from her crew, but Zippzack objected and threatened to go to the commandant. The overseer then conspired with three prisoners to kill Zippzack. She had them pick a fight with her and throw her into one of the pools of the water treatment plant. When Zippzack tried to climb out, the overseer repeatedly hit her hands with a shovel until she lost strength and sank into the pool. They waited quite some time before sounding an alarm and retrieving the body.

A criminal investigator of the camp established premeditated murder, and all four perpetrators were placed in the Bunker that same evening. *SS Obersturmführer* Bräuning personally went to the Punishment Block to gather information and concluded that the overseer, who up until then had "carried out her duties loyally and well," had been led into this murder by three prisoners "who no longer deserve to live among humanity." The three prisoners were hanged shortly thereafter, and the overseer was sentenced to eight years' imprisonment.[21]

It would be invaluable to have the SS's own report on this incident, but it is missing and will likely remain so. Therefore, conclusions must be drawn without it. Two issues about this case appear to stand out: First, in the investigation, the word of the overseer was likely given far more credibility than that of any of the other eyewitnesses. It is probable that she was given an eight-year sentence more for her fraternization and for allowing developments in her work crew to get out of hand than for her participation in a murder. Second, the fact that this was a crew from the Punishment Block made it all the easier for the authorities to punish them severely.

The Bunker

The Bunker (the word is the same in both English and German) or Cell-Building (*Zellenbau*), was an innocuous-looking structure located just inside the camp walls in the main area of the camp. It contained 78 primitively furnished cells, 39 in each of two stories. To be sentenced to the Bunker was to experience the most severe form of official punishment that Ravensbrück had to offer.

Prisoners who were sent to the Bunker had been charged with quite serious offenses. One cannot say they were guilty of these offenses since there were no legal proceedings to determine guilt or innocence. The mechanism was this: an overseer made a Report, perhaps on the recommendation of a prisoner official, which was sent to the camp leader. He could hold an investigation and/or order incarceration in the Bunker for up to three days. Longer incarceration required the approval of the commandant. There was no hearing. The evidence was whatever the overseer said it was.[22]

Inmates assigned to the Bunker did no work. Except for a few cases in which groups were placed in cells temporarily, the rule was solitary confinement. One prisoner recalled being delivered to her cell:

> My shoes were taken from me. Then Binz [the head over-seer] led me down a corridor over behind an iron staircase into a cell on the lower floor. . . . The door closed and it was completely dark. In groping around, I bumped into a stool which was fastened to the floor . . . opposite the little folding table in the left corner a plank bed; by the door the toilet, against that the water pipes and to the right of the door a cold radiator. High on the wall above the door was a small window which through a shade could be made light-tight. The cell was 4-1/2 paces long and 2-1/2 paces wide.[23]

Detention in the Bunker, particularly under Head Overseers Mandel (April–October 1942) and Binz (August 1943–April 1945) was simply torture. Prisoners were kept in almost total darkness, and often went days without being fed. In the winter, the cells on the lower floor were generally unheated, and inmates were not always provided blankets. High pressure hoses were sometimes turned on prisoners, pummeling them until they were black and blue.[24] The corpse crew, which was assigned the unenviable task of picking up the bodies of deceased prisoners from everywhere in the camp, was sometimes ordered to the Bunker. Emmi Handke, a veteran member of this crew, later noted that almost all the bodies of dead women which they hauled out of the bunker showed signs of having been beaten. One of her worst experiences was having to remove the body of a twenty-year-old pregnant woman who was from her own block. Not only had she been beaten; her body was frozen to the floor of the cell.[25]

Corporal punishment had been in use at Ravensbrück since Himmler's visit in 1940. Prisoners were beaten by the head overseer in the presence of the commandant and a doctor. Two years later, Himmler ordered "sharpened" corporal punishments. Prisoners were now to be whipped or caned on their bare buttocks, still in the presence of camp authorities, but now the flogging was to be done by inmates rather than overseers. Foreign prisoners were to be given small bonuses of food or cigarettes to flog fellow prisoners. Himmler stipulated, however, that foreigners were never to flog Germans. A special room, the Caning Room (*Prügelraum*) in the lower floor of the Bunker was outfitted to accommodate this procedure.

A detailed description of one of these canings was left by the victim, Martha Wölkert, a peasant woman. She was arrested for race defilement (*Rassenschande*) for supposedly having sex with Polish forced workers while her husband was away serving in the military. She claimed she only gave them some of her husband's old clothes because she felt sorry for them. But somebody informed the Gestapo about her indiscretion, and her fate was sealed. After having her head shaved publicly in the main square of her town, she was sent to Ravensbrück. Once there, she and twenty-two other women were escorted to the Bunker to take their punishment, one by one. Her account:

> [Head Overseer] Binz read me the warrant for my arrest and my punishment: twice 25 lashes [*Schläge*, "hits"]. Then [*Commandant*] Suhren ordered me to step up to the rack. My feet were fastened in a wooden clamp, and the Green Badge strapped me down. My dress was pulled up over my head so that my entire backside was exposed. (We had had to take off our underpants before we left the barracks.) Then my head was wrapped in a blanket, presumably to muffle the screams.
>
> While I was being strapped in, I had taken a deep breath so I wouldn't be strapped in so tightly. When Suhren noticed this, he knelt down and pulled the strap so tight it caused me considerable pain.
>
> I was ordered to count each of the strikes out loud, but I only got to eleven. I only heard, rather groggily, how the Green Badge kept counting. I also cried out, which seemed to lessen the pain. Then I noticed somebody taking my pulse. My bottom felt like it was made of leather. When I got outside, I felt horribly dizzy.

Less than a week later, Martha Wölkert returned for her second 25 lashes. This time she only could count to seven before virtually passing out. Afterward, her sympathetic block senior took her to the sick barracks.[26]

Sabotage and Escapes

The two most serious offenses a prisoner could engage in were sabotage and attempting to escape. In spite of all the precautions and the surveillance by overseers, there was a fair amount of sabotage in the workplaces of Ravensbrück. Even the *Strickerinnen*, women who sat in the barracks knitting socks for the SS, got into the act in a small way. Many were proud of the fact that of their quota of sixty socks per week, no two were a matching pair.[27] Much of the sabotage, like work slowdowns to decrease production, was relatively passive. At the Siemens factory, the head prisoner crew chief, Anny Vavakova, used her position to slow production by moving people around. She placed "reliable people" in key positions and replaced women who were overly industrious.[28] It was risky business, however. After Simone Lévy was suspected for the second time of causing a work stoppage at the Holleischen subcamp, she was hanged as an example to other would-be saboteurs.[29]

Some of the sabotage was very active. French prisoners at Neubrandenberg would routinely grab a handful of small parts as they left work, then throw them into the woods as they were marched back to camp.[30] Prisoners at the Siemens plant learned if they rubbed garlic on precious metal contact points in electronic relays, it ruined them. Once the Siemens personnel caught on, anybody who had garlic in her possession was sent directly to the Bunker.[31] On another occasion at Siemens, twelve women were found to have removed tiny rubber o-rings from a device and put these in their pants. The women were first beaten, then sent to the main camp, where reportedly they were all shot.[32]

Soviet army women who worked in the SS textile factory sometimes threw screws and tiny parts into the highly sensitive sizing machines, rendering them inoperable. They would then need to be taken apart, components sent to Berlin, then reassembled—a work stoppage of at least three days.[33] But the authorities became increasingly quick-tempered when sabotage was suspected. In one instance, a young Polish woman whose machine broke down was accused of sabotage, arrested, sent to the Bunker, and shot—all in short order.[34]

In the Ravensbrück Archives, there is preserved the tragic story of a Russian woman, Anna Pankratowa, who worked in the SS textile factory sewing buttons on trousers for German soldiers. When she thought of all the Russian soldiers who were freezing, and how she was really helping the German army to keep warm, she decided to act. She sewed the buttons without firmly fastening the threads. This way, after the second or third buttoning, the buttons would pop off, leaving the German soldiers with a cold draft in a place where no man likes being cold. She did this for two weeks, dreaming of the wonderful effects of her patriotic handiwork. But she was found out by the overseer, who called in Binder, the notoriously brutal director of the SS textile factory. Binder beat her into unconsciousness on the spot. From there she was taken away, not to be heard from again.[35]

One February night in 1941, a Gypsy woman named Weiss (or Waitz), an inhabitant of the Punishment Block, crawled out over the SS canteen and used a blanket to insulate herself from the high voltage wires, then leaped to the ground and headed for the woods. In the morning, when she was reported missing, the entire camp was ordered to do *Strafstehen* until she was found. After a day, apparently, the camp authorities relented, allowing all but the Punishment Block to resume normal activities. Those from the Punishment Block were made to continue standing, and were also deprived of food.

It was the first escape from Ravensbrück, and the SS did not take it lightly. A massive manhunt was launched, combing the woods and farmlands for some distance. On the third day she was captured and brought back to the camp. An eyewitness remembered: "We stood there as she was pushed past us. It was a pitiful sight. The poor miserable little figure whose clothes had been torn to shreds by the dogs now struggled under the kicks and blows of the huge commandant. As she moved past us, she left a trail of blood."[36]

Weiss was taken back to the Punishment Block, where the other inmates still had not eaten, and had been kept standing since her escape. Zimmer, the overseer, turned her over to them and told them to finish her off. What followed was a scene out of a nightmare, as the other women kicked, beat, and even bit the little Gypsy woman. She was to have been sent to the Bunker, but she was already dead.[37]

There were other escapes, almost all of them unsuccessful, until May 1944, when Eugenia Kocwa walked away from the relatively

pleasant confines of the Forestry Crew. In spite of a widespread
manhunt, she was never found. Hers was a meticulously planned
escape, prepared for a year and postponed several times until circumstances were just right. The hardest parts were putting
together a respectable-looking civilian outfit and obtaining German money, but these were accomplished through the barter system. Kocwa's escape was facilitated by several factors, not the
least of which was that she was exceptionally intelligent and well-
educated. She spoke perfect German, and she had the good sense
to not tell another soul of her plans. After leaving her work crew,
she put on the civilian clothes that she had hidden in the woods,
walked right through the center of Fürstenberg, and continued
walking toward Berlin. She trekked all night, and twenty-four
hours later was in Birkenwerder, on the outskirts of the capital.
Once in Berlin, she went to the brother of a fellow inmate, who
helped her. Five months later, she was home in Cracow.[38] Meanwhile, back at Ravensbrück, things were not going well. Ramdohr,
the local Gestapo chief, interrogated everybody involved, but
learned nothing. The entire crew was sent to the Punishment
Block. Both the crew leader, Liberakowa, and the overseer,
Shenja, were kept in the Bunker for months.[39]

In another instance, two young Russian women who were
attempting an escape were electrocuted. Late that night, a special
roll call was held, and all the inmates were forced to witness the
scene. The SS turned searchlights on the lifeless forms still dan-
gling from the electric fence. Just in case any prisoners failed to
get the point, the SS kept repeating: "This is what happens if you
try to escape."[40]

Executions

According to the militarily based disciplinary system that operated in the camp, some "crimes" carried with them the death
penalty: sabotage, attempted escape, conspiracy. An SS order of 22

January 1943 required that executions of women inmates be carried out in ways that would attract the least possible attention.[41]
This was in marked contrast to executions in the men's camp,
which were done openly. Whether this secrecy was done out of concern for female sensitivities is not known, but the SS stayed strictly within this policy. On only one occasion did a female inmate witness an execution, and that was by chance.[42] As a result of this policy, however, very little is known about executions at the women's
camp.

Most executions at Ravensbrück were carried out by shooting.
Sometimes these took place outside the parameters of the camp,
in wooded areas to the south, but on occasion, the executions were
performed in the main part of the camp, in what was known as the
"shooting corridor" (*Erschiessungsgang*). The only women who
ever saw this were those who were condemned, for it was located
outside the camp walls and was approachable only through the
crematorium. The positioning was not happenstance; once a victim had been shot, her corpse could be thrown through an open
window into the crematorium.[43] A male prisoner, Horst Schmidt,
who worked in the crematorium at one time, witnessed the execution of two women by two SS men who administered shots to the
neck at close range (*Genickschuss*). Sometimes the women prisoners would hear gunshot fire close by (the shooting corridor was
located just a few feet from the main enclosure, separated only by
a high wall), but they did not know where this sound came from.
In the case of the execution witnessed by Horst Schmidt, however,
there was almost no sound, as the weapons were apparently outfitted with a silencing device.[44]

We know that there were hundreds of women executed at
Ravensbrück, a few by hanging, but mostly by shooting. We know
the names of some of the victims, but for the most part the details
of these grisly murders are missing. The combination of obliterat-
ed SS records along with the regrettable, yet understandable,
reluctance of the perpetrators to step forward and provide information means, in all likelihood, that our knowledge of this issue

will remain forever incomplete. Perhaps the most fitting testimony to the victims is the poem "Necrologue," by their fellow inmate, Johanna Himmler (see pp. 155–157).

The Nazi system gave virtually free rein to those who agreed with its principles and who were in positions of power, such as SS overseers. For all the pretense at there being regulations governing their actions, female overseers at Ravensbrück, as far as can be determined, were rarely disciplined for abusing prisoners. The SS's records concerning the punishment of overseers at Ravensbrück are gone, but Irmtraud Heike has examined the records for the women's camp at Lublin. There, while one female overseer was sentenced to three months for stealing Reich property, another was given five days' incarceration for fatally wounding an inmate.[45] One has the right to wonder what would have been, in the long run, the future of a system that so thoroughly deprived itself of those features, such as respect for human life and adherence to legal frameworks, without which civilized living seems tenuous at best. Quite possibly, the nihilistic tendencies long observable in National Socialism would have eventually engulfed the entire system.

CHAPTER 18

Sickness and Health

Violette LeCoq, "Fit for Work." From *Témoignages* ...
Courtesy Mme. Violette Rougier-LeCoq.

Sick Call and the Infirmary

In the mornings before roll call, a prisoner who was feeling ill would try to contact her block senior (or after 1943, the block nurse) to gain permission to report for sick call. These block authorities would make a preliminary check of the prisoner's condition, and if they granted approval, the prisoner would be escorted to the infirmary (*Revier*).

At the infirmary, there would be a line, and as the prisoners waited, most of them were thinking, "If only I have a fever, then I can go to bed."[1] They knew body temperature was the primary determinant for being placed on the sick list. A temperature of 39° C (102° F) got one admitted.[2] Anyone with a temperature lower than that was sent off to work. The examinations were gener-

France Audoul, "Sick Call Lineup." From *Ravensbrück: 15,000 Femmes en Enfer*.

ally rather cursory at best, but sometimes the examining doctor didn't want to get near a patient, and would curtly tell her: "You have lice. Take care of that!"[3] and send her back to her block, destined for work. Then, too, there were the usual nationality issues which complicated everything, even sickness. Infirmary workers were notorious for showing favoritism to certain national groups and prejudice against others. Dr. Benno Orendi, a Romanian who volunteered for the *Waffen SS*, had a reputation for disliking and mistreating French prisoners.[4] Dr. Rolf Rosenthal's prejudices against Jews and Russians were so well known that other infirmary workers would try to dissuade those women from even trying to be admitted while he was on duty.[5] A Danish block nurse, Sunneva Sandoe, had such a problem with some of the German infirmary workers repeatedly sending genuinely sick patients back to work that she personally accompanied her wards through their examinations. The infirmary staff did not take kindly to her presence, but the tactic generally worked.[6]

Those women who were rejected at the infirmary, along with those like the Jehovah's Witnesses who intentionally avoided going there, could hope to get some care and treatment from fellow prisoners, particularly if they lived in one of the "better" blocks. In fact, there was a small but active illegal trade in medicines at Ravensbrück. Some of these were stolen from the infirmary or from the SS pharmacy at nearby Drögen, where about fifty female prisoners and a smaller number of male prisoners worked. A prisoner pharmacist named Max Hamawald regularly smuggled medicines into the camp by hiding these among dirty towels and linens being sent back to the camp laundry.[7] But some of the medicines came from the Fürstenberg pharmacy whose owner, Paula Schulz, was an anti-Nazi. Through a circuitous route, she was able to deliver medicines to prisoners, often without the expectation of any payment.[8] In addition, prisoners made some of their own medicines, such as coal tablets, considered useful as a cure for diarrhea. More importantly, prisoners who worked on farms and orchards would frequently bring back "vita-

mins": wild plants like goose thistle (*Gänsedistel*) and goose foot
(*Gänsefuss*), peppermint and chamomile for making teas, and
sometimes fruits and vegetables.[9] These were invaluable supplements to the diets of sick prisoners.

Many hazards awaited the "lucky ones" who were accepted into
the infirmary. Most witnesses agree that conditions there were not
observably better than in a regular block. In 1943, Ramdohr, the
local Gestapo officer, investigated the infirmary and found conditions there "deplorable." There was filth everywhere, and bed
linens were almost never changed.[10] Dr. Orendi claimed to have
repeatedly criticized conditions and brought this to the attention
of superiors, but the only result of his endeavors was retribution:
he never got promoted.[11] Others, particularly prisoner doctors,
believed he was not promoted because he was incompetent.[12]

Infirmary workers were automatically classified as prisoner
officials, and in the jargon of other inmates, were "Armbands."
They wore yellow armbands, giving them unrestricted movement
anywhere inside the camp. Most lived in Block 3, one of the elite,
less crowded blocks, and because of the nature of their work, they
never had to stand roll call. They were considered by most inmates as a rather privileged class, but at the same time, they were
generally admired. The feeling was widespread among inmates
that only the prisoner doctors and nurses treated patients with
any measure of human consideration,[13] and even that was sometimes conditioned by national prejudices.

Until 1942, when the prisoner population of Ravensbrück had
not yet exceeded 7,000, the infirmary was a relatively small operation. Its three interconnected barracks, its three medical doctors
(none of them prisoners), and a staff of 35 were sufficient to handle the roughly thirty to seventy prisoners who would report for
sick call two or three days a week.[14] Until mid-1942, the number
of patients convalescing in the infirmary averaged only about sixty at any one time,[15] an entirely manageable number.

Extermination through Work

The year 1942 was pivotal in the history of Ravensbrück, bringing with it many changes. Most basically, the camp population more than doubled during that year, increasing from about 7,000 to 15,000. Even with the physical expansion of the camp in that year, the facilities were simply inadequate for this number of people. Thus began the overcrowding of the camp which only worsened in the following years, until the war's end. It was also in 1942 that other developments, certainly interconnected, occurred. First, the Nazi program for the extermination of Europe's Jews, enunciated at the Wannsee Conference in January, was set in motion. Second, military setbacks, particularly in Russia, now forced Germany to more fully mobilize its economy for war. Labor, especially that of foreigners, was to be systematically exploited. Labor Minister Fritz Sauckel's program called for these foreign conscripts to be "fed, housed, and treated in such a way as to exploit them to the greatest possible extent at the absolute minimum of expenditure."[16] This was already in practice in the concentration camps, but now a new element was added. Goebbels and Himmler were in agreement that for Jews, Asocial elements, Poles, Czechs, and even Germans serving long prison terms, "the idea of exterminating them by labor is best" (Goebbels). In September 1942, Himmler set in motion the Extermination through Work (*Vernichtung durch Arbeit*) program in which the concentration camps would play a central role.[17] Finally, in 1942, Ravensbrück was assigned a new commandant, Fritz Suhren, a somewhat enigmatic figure, but one who was unlikely to go against policy. Under Suhren's leadership, extermination through work became the operating principle: Feed the women as little as possible, work them as much as possible, and when they can no longer work, push them aside and let them die.

The infirmary and its staff were a key factor in the SS's effort to extract as much labor as possible from the women inmates. The staff's primary function in this regard was to make decisions concerning which prisoners were work-capable and which were not. Those who were still potentially useful would be cared for, at least minimally. Those who were judged by the staff doctors (prisoner doctors were never involved in these decisions) to be incapable of working could be dealt with in several ways. First, they could be sent to work anyway. Prisoner doctors have testified that Dr. Orendi sometimes refused to treat genuinely ill prisoners, forcing them to go to work details that were likely to be fatal.[18] Second, prisoners could be sent to one of the special blocks known as Bed Card Blocks. The theory was a sensible one: issue sick prisoners a "Bed Card" which would entitle them to avoid roll calls and work assignments, while they stayed in bed and convalesced. In reality, however, conditions in these blocks were dreadful. Created in 1943, the following year they evolved into the typhus and tuberculosis blocks.[19] Finally, beginning in 1942, camp doctors played their part in selections, literally choosing certain prisoners to be

Aat Breur, untitled drawing of a sick prisoner being carried to the infirmary on an old coat. From *Een verborgen herinnering*. Courtesy Dunya Breur.

sent to their deaths. In January 1942, the SS inaugurated its euthanasia program cryptically labeled "14f13," aimed at killing mentally ill prisoners.[20] A few months later, a *Transport* of women from Ravensbrück was sent to the Healing and Nursing Care Facility (the Nazis loved euphemisms) at Bernburg, where they were murdered by carbon monoxide poisoning.[21] Some 68 of them had been inhabitants of the doomed Idiots' Block, but others, like Rosa Menzer, were merely old or Jewish. She was both.[22] The killing had started and it would get much worse before it was ended in April 1945.

By late 1942–early 1943, there were large numbers of very sick women at Ravensbrück, and these numbers were growing daily. Contributing to this problem was the fact that most of the subcamps did not have their own infirmary, so they sent sick prisoners back to the main camp to be exchanged for healthy women. By 1943, the number of women reporting for sick call had more than tripled from the previous year, to between one hundred and three hundred per day. A year later the number had tripled again.[23]

Medical Experiments

As if Ravensbrück did not have enough sick women, beginning in 1942 and continuing into 1943, SS medical doctors conducted a series of experimental operations on female prisoners. In this synthesis of SS racial and wartime political policies, the SS could get rid of, or at least incapacitate, non-German women who had proven troublesome to them. In fact, with only one exception, the seventy-five women chosen for these experiments were Polish. Most of them had arrived at Ravensbrück on 23 September 1941, part of a 400-person special transport from Lublin. Almost all had been arrested for their connections to the Polish resistance group, the ZWZ, and they had already been given death sentences.[24] Some of these women were executed in April 1942, before the medical experiments began. In addition, certain SS doctors, backed by

Himmler, were eager to test new medicines, notably some involving the treatment of wound infections. Germany's changing fortunes of war, particularly the increasing numbers of casualties on the eastern front, gave an apparent urgency to these tests.

SS doctors had been discussing the usefulness of conducting medical experiments on humans, but there was a deadlock between factions, and no decision was reached. The deadlock was broken by the 27 May 1942 assassination of Reinhard Heydrich, second in the SS only to Himmler, by Czech partisans. The bombing attack had punctured Heydrich's body with all sorts of foreign matter and bacteria. Dr. Karl Gebhardt, Himmler's physician and chief surgeon of the Waffen SS, was called in, but in spite of all efforts, Heydrich died, essentially of infected wounds. Hitler's own physician, Dr. Theo Morell, let it be known that Gebhardt had relied too heavily on surgery and not enough on antibacterial drugs. Within weeks, a branch of the Hohenlychen clinic headed by Gebhardt was established at Ravensbrück, and preparations were going forward to experiment on humans.[25]

On 27 July 1942, seventy-five women were yanked from their work and taken to the commandant's headquarters, where they had their legs examined and their papers verified. Although most of these women were shortly sent back to their workplaces, it was from this group, chosen by Dr. Herta Oberheuser, that all of the experimentees were eventually taken.

The first experimental operations took place a few days later, and over the next several months, usually in groups of six to ten, the women were operated on, then allowed to convalesce while the effects were studied. The experimental operations were basically of two types: In the first type, the doctors made an artificial wound in the patient's leg, then inserted strains of bacteria (staphylococcus and streptococcus) into the wound. Then SS doctors, directed by Gebhardt, attempted to check the effectiveness of certain new drugs (Cibazol and Albucid) in treating the infections.[26]

Among the first two groups of experimentees, involving fifteen women, none died. SS Dr. Grawitz then questioned the validity of the experiments on the grounds they "did not replicate battlefield conditions." As a result, in the experiments that followed, women were given authentic gunshot wounds, after which dirt and other foreign materials were stuffed into the open wounds. In one experiment, in October 1942, four women were infected with gangrene. Only one survived. Gebhardt could have saved some of these women through amputations, his preferred method, but he refused. Grawitz and Himmler wanted "sacrifice of blood" (Blutopfer) and he would deliver this.[27]

The second type of experimental operation carried out by SS doctors, notably Dr. Stumpfegger, involved severing muscles and breaking bones, sometimes using hammers, ostensibly to learn more about regeneration. About twenty Polish women were subjected to these methods, and although this was not in itself life-threatening, it left the women permanently crippled. Another ten women from Ravensbrück were taken to nearby Hohenlychen, where experimental operations involving amputations and bone transplants were performed on them. These procedures had direct military applications, for the hope was to use concentration camp inmates as a source of "spare parts" for wounded German soldiers. The victims, all of whom were mentally ill (and very likely chosen for that reason) were killed by injection. Because of faulty medical procedures, such as the use of unsterilized instruments, the results were compromised and little of perceived scientific value was learned through any of these medical procedures.[28]

There were other experiments, some of them bordering on the perverse. Sigismund Rascher, a physician protégé of Himmler's, easily gained his chief's approval to use Ravensbrück inmates in experiments he and Himmler devised to resuscitate military personnel suffering from acute hypothermia. The half-frozen men (male prisoners from Dachau) were placed between two women, all of them naked. The goal was to revive the men through sexual stimulation and ultimately coitus. The results were inconclusive.[29]

All the medical experiments were carried out in considerable secrecy. The experimentees were never informed of the nature and purpose of the operations, but were told only that their compliance would save them from being executed. (This was not true. In March 1943, eight of the special transport women from Lublin, including two victims of medical experiments, were executed.) No prisoner doctors or nurses were directly involved with these operations or even allowed in the convalescent wards.[30] The affected women were often sent back to their own blocks, so it is now possible to piece together some of the details.

Rumors of the medical experiments spread rapidly through the camp, and the victims elicited great sympathy. The "rabbits" (*Kaninchen*) as they were called because of their hobbling walk, were sent food, blankets, and underwear from many different blocks.[31] Women who had had the operations and survived were no longer assigned work, or if they were it was light work, such as knitting socks.[32] One of them gloated: "We were old hands, high in the hierarchy of camp prisoners."[33] But some of the other Polish women chastized them both for going off to the operations "like sheep" and for later leading lives of leisure.[34] Still, in August 1943, when the SS ordered more "patients," the Polish block, backed by their block senior, went on strike. In spite of punishments, they refused to turn over any more women.[35] Later, in early 1945, when it was rumored that the "rab-

Aat Breur, portrait of Stanislawa Bafia-Czajkowska, one of the Polish women subjected to medical experiments. From *Een verborgen herinnering*. Courtesy Dunya Breur.

bits" were to be killed, fellow inmates hid them. By this time, there were only about two dozen of them still alive, but the women of Ravensbrück showed real solidarity in protecting them. Not one was informed upon, and in the closing stages of the war, the camp underground gave them new identities. Eighteen "rabbits" were successfully evacuated from Ravensbrück on Red Cross transports.[36]

Typhus and Tuberculosis

At Ravensbrück, the first symptoms of typhus seem to have appeared in 1942: fever, skin rash and itching, aches and pains, lethargy. Most of the so-called *Schmuckstücke* had these symptoms. The disease is carried by a micro-organism which is a parasite of the human body louse. "The louse has an unfortunate proclivity for defecating while it sucks blood from its human host. The feces contains the germ, which is then rubbed into the skin through the feeding punctures by the understandable scratching on the part of the human host."[37] By the midpoint of the war, Ravensbrück was the perfect incubator for typhus: thousands of undernourished women living in overcrowded conditions, surrounded by filth and unable to practice even minimal hygiene. It is easy to understand why the disease was more widespread in the "slums" than in the elite blocks.

The camp authorities were not blind to the problem. They understood that the main culprit was the body louse, and they forced inmates to undergo periodic delousings. In 1943 they created a special new health officer, the block nurse whose primary goal was to rid her block of lice. It was a hopeless task, even for a conscientious nurse, for the authorities altered none of the other conditions. It did no good to disinfect a barracks if the prisoners had to change into other vermin-infested clothes and had no soap when they showered.

The same conditions that nurtured typhus in the camp—inade-

quate nutrition, low standards of hygiene, and the constant strain
of overwork—also predisposed many inmates to contracting tuberculosis. Indeed, since some of the symptoms are the same—loss of
weight, fever, fatigue and lethargy, loss of appetite—it is probable
that many inmates were misdiagnosed, especially considering the
often perfunctory nature of camp medical examinations. Ravensbrück SS doctors were not interested in treating and curing disease; they isolated the chronically ill from the rest of the prison
population and let nature take its inevitable course. There was
both a Typhus Block and a TB Block by late 1944, but according
to eyewitness descriptions, they were handled identically. Sick
inmates were jammed into these barracks, sleeping three or more
to a bed. There was no pretense at adequate medical care—the SS
doctors would not visit these barracks—and food rations for these

Violette LeCoq, "The Morgue? No, The Hospital." From *Témoignages*. . . .
Courtesy Mme. Violette Rougier-LeCoq.

prisoners were further reduced.[38] Inmates suffering from either typhus or tuberculosis were not expected to recover. A seventeen-year-old girl, afflicted with tuberculosis, accepted the finality of her condition and uttered the following prayer: "I'm going to die today. I'm sure about this. But I have one great and last request: I have not had my own bed for so long, please God, let me die in my own bed."[39]

Other prisoners understood this too, and sometimes called the TB Block the Cemetery.[40] When Charlotte Müller and her maintenance crew discovered two Political "comrades" in the Typhus Block, Müller conspired to get them transferred to another block where their chances of survival were improved.[41] It was the only sensible thing to do for a person one cared about. By the end of 1944, these blocks had become nothing more than dumping grounds for prisoners who were not expected to survive, and for whom the camp authorities were not inclined to make further investments of food, medicines, or any other resources. Moreover, with new transports of prisoners arriving almost daily, it was necessary to make space available for those who were work-capable. Ravensbrück was, after all, a slave labor camp.

CHAPTER

The Men's Camp

View of the camp showing ongoing construction, ca. 1941–42. The photograph was taken from approximately where the Men's Camp was located. (SS Photo.) *Sammlungen Mahn- und Gedenkstätte Ravensbrück.* Courtesy U.S. Holocaust Memorial Museum Photo Archives.

Male prisoners from the nearby Sachsenhausen Concentration camp were brought to Ravensbrück to perform the initial construction work in building the women's camp. Then, before the new camp officially opened in mid-May 1939, the men were sent back to their home base. Of these, a large number were released on 20 April 1939, the occasion of Hitler's fiftieth birthday.[1] Periodically, men from Sachsenhausen would be returned to Ravensbrück to engage in heavy labor projects, mostly in construction, which were apparently considered too physically demanding for women. While on these temporary assignments, they were housed in one of two barracks that had been built as part of the original construction.[2]

Because of the ongoing construction projects at Ravensbrück, particularly the additions to the SS textile factories and the expansion of the barracks area, it was apparently decided that a permanent men's camp at Ravensbrück would be a more sensible and efficient arrangement. Thus, in the spring of 1941, three new barracks for men were constructed, along with a service building. A few months later, the men's camp got its own infirmary and kitchen, having been dependent for these services on the women's camp until then. This small complex was then surrounded by a high wall, forming an enclave on the southern periphery of the women's camp.[3]

The new men's camp at Ravensbrück opened in April 1941, manned by 350 prisoners who were permanently transferred from Sachsenhausen. As in the women's camp, the prisoner population soon began to rise sharply. By August 1943, there were 3,100 inmates, and by the end of that year, there were 8,000 to 10,000. Just over 20,000 male prisoners were registered between 1941 and 1945, and about 7,500 of them were sent out to one of eight subcamps. Wanda Kiedrzynska, in addition to her analysis of the women's camp, has also made a brief examination of the men's camp. Her findings show close parallels to the women's camp: over 80 percent of the inmates were Politicals, about 16 percent were Jews, and the nationality breakdown follows the same order:

1. Poles (6,400)
2. Germans (4,000)
3. Russians (3,850)
4. French (2,250)[4]

In one particular feature, the men's camp differed markedly from the women's camp. In spite of the numerical superiority of the Politicals, the Criminals dominated the prisoner hierarchy. They held the key positions and they ruled with a ruthlessness that was, on the whole, absent in the women's camp.[5] In this sense, the men's camp was more typical of other concentration camps than was the women's camp.

Unlike the women's camp, the men's camp had a camp senior with real power. From the early stages of the men's camp, until 1942, Camp Senior Leonard and his entourage, all of them Criminals and all called *Kapos*, ruled through a system of favoritism that was probably more harassing and humiliating than it was brutal. There were rumors that Leonard and his *Oberkapo*, Schmel, "lived like in paradise," giving favors to young men in order to seduce them. According to a collective report by male Czech prisoners, Leonard and his cronies liked to call a daily "lice inspection," done not just to control the vermin and degrade the prisoners, but to give the leaders the pleasure of seeing all those naked men.[6]

In the winter of 1941–1942, a huge transport of some fifteen hundred prisoners from Buchenwald arrived, instantly causing significant overcrowding. The group was of mixed nationality, but many were "greens" and "blacks" (Criminals and Asocials). Almost immediately the "Buchenwalders" took over. The old leaders kept their positions for a time, but *de facto* the newcomers called the shots. When a report for theft sent in by Camp Senior Leonard on a Buchenwalder was intercepted, there was a showdown. A group of Buchenwalders ganged up on Leonard and murdered him. When other groups of new prisoners arrived from Flossenburg and Neuengamme shortly after this and joined forces with the

Buchenwalders, the transfer of power was complete.[7]

For most of the prisoners in the men's camp, the victory of the Buchenwalders did not signal any fundamental change in the structure or operating procedures in the camp. It had been a dispute between factions, not one over methods of governing. The "grüne Aristokratie"[8] continued their dominance, and if the new faction's rule was increasingly marked by physical abuse of fellow prisoners, the difference was a matter of degrees rather than of kind.

The SS too played a role in the continuing brutality at the men's camp, not only by looking the other way as the criminal elements exercised their power plays,[9] but by their own disciplinary methods. Whereas in the women's camp, executions were carried out behind the scenes, normally with much concern for secrecy, in the men's camp the SS conducted them openly. When a prisoner was to be hanged, the other prisoners were made to form a closely ranked square around the gallows. The victim carried in his own coffin and placed it under the gallows. Then, in the presence of the commandant and other SS personnel and observed by his fellow inmates, the trap door was sprung. As many as five men were sometimes hanged in one session.[10]

Like the women, the men prisoners had work assignments both inside and outside the camp. And, as with the women, much of one's circumstances and chances for survival depended on getting a good assignment. The men did not get any of the jobs working in orchards, gardens, or farms, which offered fresh air and the opportunity to supplement one's food rations. These were given exclusively to women prisoners. But men could hope for assignments that were at least relatively free from harassment. Two Polish prisoners, Albert Pollak and Stanislaw Ostasz, had the good fortune to be assigned to the firm of *Kuhn Bau und Möbeltischlerei* upon their arrival in April 1941, and they worked there until the war's end. The Kuhn firm, located only a ten to fifteen minute walk from the camp, on the near side of Fürstenberg, was a small woodworking plant, specializing in the production of furniture and cabinets. Not only were the prisoner-workers there never mis-treated, but the owner, Erich Kuhn, treated them like family, inviting them for dinner and for vespers, and to take part in spe-cial family gatherings, such as birthdays. In addition, with as lit-tle fuss as possible, the owner frequently left bread and fruit for the prisoners at their workplaces.[11]

Many of the male prisoners had to go into the women's camp on a daily basis, some for regular work assignments, others for con-struction projects. In fact, more than half the work crews formed at the men's camp were in construction. For example, men did almost all of the roof repairs and electrical work for the entire camp, simply because men were more likely than women to have had prior training or experience in these fields.[12] For the same rea-son, men had a monopoly on automobile and truck repairs; the camp garages were a purely male domain. But when women could be found who had the skills, as Charlotte Müller did in plumbing, or Johanna Sturm did in woodworking, the camp authorities pre-ferred that they do the work inside the women's camp.

For the most part, male and female prisoners were kept rigidly segregated in the camp, but, as always, there were exceptions. Some men worked in the clothing storehouses, if not alongside, at least in close proximity to women. It was absolutely forbidden for those of either sex to converse with their counterpart, or to reach out to them in any way. Even waving or nodding at them from a distance was a punishable offense.[13]

Still, some men and women took the risk and did reach out to each other. They had conversations during which they got acquainted and found out about each other's lives.[14] Joseph Rehwald was a Jehovah's Witness who worked in the automobile repair shop, which bordered the women's camp. When female Jehovah's Witnesses noticed his lavender triangle, they found ways to speak with him, eventually sending him bread and under-wear. Further, when they learned that he was the son of *Oma* (Grandma) Rehwald, who was in the women's camp, they arranged a meeting between them. Joseph recalled: "How over-

joyed we were to see each other again! A few months later, shortly before our liberation, my mother died. She had remained faith-
ful to Jehovah until her death."[15]

A clandestine mail service moved letters and packages between
the men's and women's camps, particularly appreciated by husbands and wives who were both at Ravensbrück. But almost any
kind of goods could be exchanged, and were. For example, once the
women learned of the almost complete lack of leather shoes in the
men's camp, they sent quantities of them through their underground parcel service.[16]

In at least one case, the contact between men and women
inmates at Ravensbrück went beyond the merely casual. Willi
Kostusiak, a green badge whose wife, ironically, was an overseer
in the women's camp, preserved the following story about his best
friend, Viktor Dietrich. He was a carpenter whose job frequently
required him to work inside the women's camp. Viktor was a
young man, and in the course of his activities (in opposition to the
regulations, not to mention common sense), he met a young
woman, a prisoner like himself, and in that disabling condition
known as being in love, decided to act. He put on an SS cap he had
found, commandeered a bicycle from somewhere, and rode over to
the women's camp to rendezvous with his beloved.

Which of us would not care to know what transpired during
Viktor's escapade in the women's camp? Unfortunately, that information is not available. What we do know is this: somehow he was
missed and reported. When he returned to the men's camp,
Commandant Suhren was waiting for him. He was shot later that
day.[17]

In another episode, occurring shortly after male prisoners
began to work inside the women's camp, a Polish woman bribed a
camp police official to loan her a red armband. With this, she could
go wherever she pleased in the camp, and she went directly to
where a group of men were working. She spent some time with a
Polish man inside a building, but was observed when she came
out, and then was arrested. She was given six months in the

Bunker for her misbehavior. The Polish man got twenty five lashes and a reassignment to a worse job.[18]

Most women prisoners at Ravensbrück lived and worked in settings which allowed virtually no contact with men prisoners. Naturally, they knew about the men's camp, but their knowledge about it was generally second- and thirdhand. It may have been accurate, but it was not very direct. In any case, what emerges from the memoirs and recollections of women survivors, if they commented on it at all, was the notion that the male prisoners in the camp had to endure an even worse set of conditions than the women did. Comparisons and generalizations on this issue are very risky, not to mention controversial. Indeed, Lawrence Langer has questioned whether gender-based studies deserve the kind of emphasis in Holocaust research that they have recently been receiving.[19] The debate ultimately addresses the issue of whether women were more adept than men at surviving the horrors of the concentration camps. Langer argues that the evidence does not allow a conclusion to be drawn, while others, notably Sybil Milton, contend that women certainly had survival skills that were superior to men's, and that this largely explains the higher survival rate of women in the camps.[20]

A comparison of the death rates between the women's and men's camps would be extremely valuable, but unfortunately the data are not available in any complete form. On a micro level, one survivor of the men's camp, Wlodzimierz Kulinski, has analyzed the death rates for his fellow Polish prisoners. In examining the first 2,000 registered male inmates, he found that 581 were Polish men, and of these only 73 survived, a survival rate of only 12.5 percent.[21] A more broadly based survey is presently being undertaken by Bärbel Schindler-Saefkow, who is meticulously studying all the documents listing Ravensbrück prisoners, male and female. Her goal is to create a computerized listing of all Ravensbrück inmates, with an indication of what happened to each.[22] The overall conclusion of her study is perhaps a few years away, but she has found that up to December 1941, the 206 death notices sent out by the camp administration were divided equally between male and female inmates.[23] Considering that in late 1941, the women's camp held over six thousand prisoners and the men's camp certainly less than one-third this number, it does indeed suggest a markedly higher death rate for men than for women.

Many factors influenced the survival of prisoners, both as individuals and as groups, in the concentration camp. In Ravensbrück, as we have seen, certain categories of women were given priviliges and conditions that significantly enhanced their chances of survival. The same holds true for male prisoners. Jewish men, for example, were often subjected to humiliations and punishments not imposed on "Aryan" men.[24] It may be that the SS was, in general, simply more brutal in its handling of male prisoners than females, and this then explains the higher death rate for men. Our examination of the men's and women's camps at Ravensbrück is inconclusive on this point.

What is not inconclusive, however, judging purely from what is known of the men's and women's camps at Ravensbrück, is the notion that in the men's camp a more violent and inhumane system prevailed than in the women's camp. It was not just the institutionalized terror of the SS, in the form of beatings and public hangings, that created this. It was also caused by the brutish behavior of the male prisoners toward each other. There were, as we have noted, rare cases of women prisoners murdering other women prisoners. But this was not condoned by the SS, nor did this ever include the murder of prisoner officials, as happened in the men's camp. At times, this prisoner-generated terror extended beyond the men's camp itself. When two *Kapos*, Schweizer and Huterer, who were thought to have been cruel in their treatment of fellow prisoners, were transferred to Dachau, word got around quickly. At Dachau, where they now had no rank, they were both murdered by other inmates.[25]

Male prisoners not only handled their disputes more violently than did the women; their writings and reports almost totally omit any discussion of the kind of self-help mechanisms, such as camp families and educational-cultural programs, that were so important in ameliorating conditions in the women's camp. At best, what seems to have developed among the men was a kind of buddy system. It is difficult not to draw the conclusion that a more dog-eat-dog world existed in the men's camp than in the women's camp.

In the last year of the war, with the army and SS becoming desperate for manpower, male prisoners were recruited for military service. Some Russians were enlisted into the anti-Communist "Vlasov Army,"[26] and others were encouraged to join a special *Waffen-SS* unit known as the *Dirlewanger Brigade*, destined for the Eastern front.[27] Joining the penal brigade did not bring great prestige, but it got these prisoners out of the concentration camp. Those prisoners who remained were all sent back to Sachsenhausen when the men's camp at Ravensbrück was closed on 13 March 1945.[28]

20

Children

Aat Breur, "Child holding her mother's hand." From
Een verborgen herinnering. Courtesy Dunya Breur.

Children in the Camp

There were few children at Ravensbrück in the early stages of its existence. We know that some Gypsy children accompanied their mothers to the camp in June 1939, as did some Czech children from Lidice in July 1942. In addition, a few children were born at the camp in its early years.[1] The fate of these children is simply unknown. Survivors' memoirs from this period hardly mention them at all, and SS records are missing.

A few children were brought to Ravensbrück in 1943, and during 1944 children were brought there in considerable numbers. Most came from Eastern Europe, from those regions occupied by German forces. Other children, mostly Gypsies or Jews, were transferred from camps or ghettos in the east. But some came from almost all the countries occupied by Germany, and eventually they represented about as many nationalities as the adult women.

Although children were arriving in large numbers throughout 1944, and from all parts of Europe, there were three main groups of children. The first was composed of Gypsy children transferred to Ravensbrück from Auschwitz between April and September 1944, when the Gypsy camp at Auschwitz-Birkenau was closed. Ceija Stojka, whom we discussed earlier, arrived in one of these shipments along with her mother and a sister. The second group of children was brought in, mostly with their mothers, from Poland following the suppression of the Warsaw Uprising after September 1944, and from Hungary as a result of the closing of the Budapest Ghetto in October 1944. Finally, the third group were those children, infants, who were born in the camp. For the most part, their mothers were Polish women who themselves or their husbands had been implicated in the Uprising. By late 1944, there were around five hundred children at Ravensbrück, almost half of them Gypsies, and this number does not include infants.[2]

The introduction of several hundred youngsters into the life of the concentration camp inevitably affected the social dynamics. At first, all of the women inmates paid them great attention: "Angela was the first. She was a Gypsy girl about nine years old, a little Indian beauty. As she went down the camp street, surrounded by her numerous relatives, all the women gazed at her with aching, motherly eyes. They hugged Angela. They sent her their bread. And they all thought of their own children."[3]

Aat Breur, drawing of a child on a potty chair. From *Een verborgen herinnering*. Courtesy Dunya Breur.

For some of the women, the children eventually became a nuisance, as they went from barracks to barracks, hounding and begging.[4] But overwhelmingly, the arrival of the children, many of them orphans, awakened in the women deep and powerful maternal feelings which were a joy as well as a relief to be able to express. Odette Fabius, herself a mother, was one of a group of French women who adopted a Gypsy girl of about eight: "through her, we felt ourselves to be mothers once again."[5] Moreover, this no doubt distracted some of the women from their own miseries. Virtually every child who came in without her (or his) mother was "adopted" by a woman, who became the child's "Camp Mother." It was a position which carried great responsibility; the camp mother not only saw to the child's provisions, but also had to coordinate caretakers during working hours; and she took it upon herself to shield the child as much as possible from the vicissitudes of camp life, particularly the capriciousness of the SS. It was a task the inmates delighted in. Antonia Bruha adopted a girl from Holland who called her *Tante* Toni. And when Aunt Toni returned from

work, the child would ask her: "Do you have anything for me?"[6]
The Communists made arrangements to bring seven Russian girls
into their block, and since this was one of the privileged blocks,
they could and did "spoil" the children.[7]

It was naturally easier to care for children in one of the better
blocks, but they were just about everywhere (except in the
Punishment Block). Even the Tuberculosis Block had its camp
child (*Lagerkind*), a four-year-old Spanish girl named Stella. Her
father was in Buchenwald, and her mother had died of tuberculosis shortly after arriving in Ravensbrück, so Stella had been
adopted by Claire van den Boom, a Belgian. She became known as
the little girl who sat on the steps of the TB Block, darting inside
whenever she saw authorities, then going back to await the return
of her camp mother. Except for the fact that she had to witness so
much misery in her barracks, she really had it pretty good. She
was everyone's *Liebling*, and all the women in the block who were
able did their part in caring for her. At length, her camp mother
was sent away, but others stepped in to take her place.[8] Moreover,
caring for the children became a kind of group project, almost a
mission. The little ones simply *had* to be taken care of. It was a
high priority issue, and it demanded considerable cooperation.
Many women contributed bread and other food items to the little
ones. Women who received parcels were expected to share with
the children, but in late 1944, the receipt of parcels was prohibited. The only packages then were Red Cross packages, and these,
too, were shared with the children. During working hours, it
became part of the routine that the children would be cared for by
the women who remained in the barracks. The older women who
spent much of their time knitting were also expected to knit clothing for the children once they had reached their quota of socks and
caps for the SS.[9]

A five-year-old Jewish boy whose mother was dead and whose
father was in another camp was brought to Ravensbrück (probably in 1944; he was not sure) in the company of his aunt (who he
thought was his mother). During the day, he stayed in the bar-

racks while his aunt worked. There were no toilet facilities in their barracks—they had to go outside and some distance away. He remembers that sometimes at night if he needed to use the toilet, his aunt would not let him, fearing that something might happen to him. Thus, he had no choice but to urinate in his pants. He was "scared to death" of the overseers who once beat him for eating a potato and another time for crying.[10]

Camp authorities at Ravensbrück seem not to have developed a clear and consistent policy concerning children. They did issue a series of regulations governing the behavior of children: They were not to go out on the camp streets unless accompanied by a prisoner official. They were to stay in a corner of the day room and not be in the way of any work crews. They were not to have toys. If a child cried, both the child and its mother were to be beaten by an overseer.[11] However, we know that these regulations were only halfheartedly enforced. Eyewitnesses reported that some children played on the camp streets, doing what children have always done, emulating their role models by pretending to be SS officers and bullying subordinates.[12] And in every barracks, solicitous women fashioned playthings for them out of buttons, matchboxes, blocks of wood, and scraps of fabric.[13] The SS leadership in the camp appears to have adopted an attitude of relative tolerance for the children that was in contrast to their normal demeanor.

Children, to the camp leaders, were unproductive consumers in a system that carefully measured income and output. Where it was possible, children were given work assignments. Some fourteen-year-olds worked in the SS textile factories,[14] but they seem to have been the youngest who were made to do real work. Some of the youngsters who stayed in the barracks volunteered to help the cleaning crew (*Stubendienst*) by performing little chores in the way small children often like to do.[15] As for those five- and six-year-olds who accompanied their mothers to the Siemens factory, it is doubtful that they did anything more than get in the way.

A small daily allotment of bread and soup was the extent of the camp's provisions for the children, and it was horribly insufficient.

Handcrafted dolls made by anonymous prisoners. Photographs by the author. *Sammlungen Ravensbrück.* Courtesy *Mahn- und Gedenkstätte Ravensbrück.*

Without the supplements of bread, and sometimes potatoes, provided by the camp mothers and other women, often selflessly taken from their own inadequate rations, the children would surely have starved. Some of them attempted to add to their food allowance by stealing or begging, or by performing little dances for a few grams of bread.[16]

Although most of the children arrived dressed in ragged clothing, the authorities provided nothing for them. The women, therefore, took it upon themselves to "organize" what they could, and this mainly consisted of adult garments. Thus, even a child who got "outfitted" was likely to look ridiculous.[17] Eventually, each child was provided with some sort of jacket or pullover for the cold weather. But at Ravensbrück, where people understood such things, the saying was: "Hunger is stronger than the winter." Mothers would sometimes barter away warm clothes for bread.[18]

The 1944 Christmas Parties

In November 1944, an organization known as the International Children's Committee was formed at Ravensbrück. This committee had representatives from almost all the blocks, but as usual the better-organized Communists were the guiding forces. The purpose of the committee was to plan, organize, and put on a Christmas party for the children.

Once the idea was put forth, it created a wave of excitement and anticipation that quickly engulfed the entire camp. No event in the history of Ravensbrück brought forth as much enthusiasm or as much genuine international solidarity as did the 1944 children's Christmas party. Everyone wanted to be part of it; all the women wanted to make sure the event would be a happy and memorable occasion for the little ones.

The planning began in early December. There would be stories and songs. There would be a visit from the "Christmas Man" (the equivalent of Santa). Of course, there would be extra food for the children, as well as little gifts. But the part of the program that most stirred the imagination of the women was planning a puppet show (*Kasparltheater*).

Naturally, a program of this magnitude could not be presented without the knowledge and therefore the approval of the camp authorities. The responsibility for securing this permission was assigned to women who worked in the administrative offices and who were on reasonably good terms with Head Overseer Binz. Somehow—the details of their negotiations are unknown—they were given approval, and the path was cleared. They were allowed to use a barracks that had been recently vacated and disinfected, formerly Block 22.

At this point, the project really moved forward. The woodworking crew constructed the stage and the puppet theater. Both were painted by the painting crew. The technical features and lighting were in the hands of Soviet inmates. A Czech artist made the puppet heads, and French women sewed the costumes. The forestry crew brought in a nice, bushy Christmas tree. Somebody who worked at Siemens secured tinfoil to decorate the tree, and others obtained candles from somewhere.

Meanwhile, in nearly every corner of the camp, women were saving their bread and marmalade, making small gifts out of snippets of cloth (stolen from the SS textile factory), and fashioning toys out of anything they could find. About a week before the party was to take place, the SS, suspecting that workers were stealing fabric and other materials, held a few "controls" and confiscated a number of gifts intended for the children. After this, it was decided to be more careful and not even give the children gifts at the party. Later the Christmas Man would put the children's gifts under their pillows.

For reasons that remain obscure, sometime in December the Polish Blocks decided to break ranks and create their own Christmas celebration for the roughly 95 to 100 Polish children in the camp. The idea came from Marta Baranowska, a veteran leader of the Polish women. In many ways, the planning for this celebration paralleled the more elaborate one being organized by the International Children's Committee, but it would be more of a religious observance, and this is likely the primary reason for the separate gathering. The other party, with its puppet theater, its Christmas Man, and its *O Tannenbaum* music was becoming far too secular. The Polish celebration would have Bible stories, "Holy St. Nicholas," and genuine religious music. Approval for the Polish gathering was secured by Halina Smolinska, who worked in the SS kitchen and had personal influence with Head Overseer Binz. The Polish women again demonstrated that they would not be taken for granted. They would pursue whatever course of action best suited their values and their needs, and they alone would determine what these were.[19] Moreover, they had been organizing Christmas celebrations in the camp since 1940,[20] and no doubt felt they did not need the Communists to show them how to do this.

The fact that there were now two Christmas celebrations being organized did not at all diminish anyone's enthusiasm. On the contrary, by the time the holiday arrived, everyone, it seemed, was filled with a joyful anticipation of the effects all of this would have on the camp children.

On the afternoon of December 23, the larger of the celebrations took place. The children were brought in and arranged according to height, in front of the stage, which held the puppet theater. But the party could only begin when Head Overseer Binz and Camp Leader Bräuning made their grand entrances. Bräuning opened the celebration by saying a few words. Then, when a choir and the assemblage sang *O Tannenbaum*, many children began to cry, some quite loudly. Perhaps they were reminded of their last Christmas at home. In any case, Binz tore out the door, followed by Bräuning. One eyewitness speculated that they were conscience-stricken,[21] but who knows?

The departure of the SS notables did not dampen the festivities. The puppet theater was next on the program. The response of the children was peculiar, and not quite what the organizers had expected. A few children laughed heartily, but many viewed the show with total amazement. They understood very little of what they were seeing. A few children were frightened by the little animal puppets, for the only animals they knew about were guard dogs. Following the puppet show, the Christmas tree was lit, and each child was given two pieces of bread. The remainder of the program needed to be compressed, for the allotted time was running out. The special dispensation granted by the SS to hold the Christmas party did not include a suspension of roll call.[22]

A day or two later, the Polish Block held its celebration. This affair was a bit more traditional, but no doubt equally appreciated by the children. There was a visit from Holy St. Nicholas, played by Joanna Szydlowska, in costume. Then there were 95 small paper bags, elaborately decorated, filled with sweets, one for each child. There were songs and skits and a short talk by Helena Salska, the senior Polish prisoner and the driving force behind their cultural and educational programs. The SS did not attend, but when the celebration was nearly over, Head Overseer Binz made a brief appearance just to remind them to finish shortly.[23]

There were other Christmas celebrations at Ravensbrück in 1944. The infirmary prisoner workers organized an elaborate festival for the sick women of the camp, and there was an abundance of them. The Czech and Polish choirs performed, and other national groups sang their own traditional Christmas music. Following the nearly two-hour gathering, carolers went to the other sick barracks to cheer those who were unable to attend.[24]

Even the SS got into the Christmas spirit. Independently of the other celebrations, the SS leaders brought the children together on Christmas Eve for a little gathering. There were things to eat: extra bread and a juicy knockwurst for each child. There was group singing of songs most of them knew, such as "Stille Nacht, Heilige Nacht." When it was over, the children were all given apples and nuts to take with them.[25]

Cynics, like the Communist Erika Buchmann, believed that all this generosity of the SS at this time was conditioned mainly by their fear of the approaching Soviet army.[26] However, it is possible that some in the SS might well have felt sympathy for the little waifs in their midst and were glad for this seasonal opportunity to do something special for them.

Births in the Camp

Until 1942, pregnant prisoners were sent to local hospitals to have their babies. The newborns were then taken from them, and the prisoners were returned to Ravensbrück. In 1943, pregnant inmates were pressured to have abortions (which were illegal for German women, but not for others), and many abortions were performed at the camp, some of them up to the eighth month. In the fall of 1944, with so many pregnant women arriving at Ravensbrück, the SS suddenly and inexplicably shifted policies and allowed most of the pregnant inmates to be delivered of their babies in the camp.[27]

Between 19 September 1944 and 22 April 1945, there were 551 children born at Ravensbrück and entered into the Book of Births (*Geburtenbuch*), a registry kept by a prisoner official, Lisa Ullrich, which has survived into the postwar period. The registry gives the name of each newborn, the date and time of birth, the mother's name along with her number and classification. The vast majority of the women were Polish Politicals. Going through this registry is a sobering experience, for it also gives the date of death. It quickly becomes clear that in many cases the newborns lived only a few days.[28] By October and November 1944, there

Helen Ernst, "Pregnant." Courtesy *Stadtgeschichtsmuseum Schwerin*.

were so many babies being born that Dr. Treite created a maternity ward and assigned a prisoner nurse, Hanka Houskova, to be a midwife there.[29] It was essentially the only concession the SS made to the mothers and their infants. Shortly after giving birth, the new mother was expected to return to work and to stand roll calls, which meant that the newborn had to go the entire day without a feeding. Most of the mothers were so malnourished they were not able to produce much milk anyway.[30]

German women whose pregnancies were the result of liaisons

with foreign men were forced to have abortions. If the pregnancy was too far along for this, the newborn was generally killed at birth.[31]

The plight of the newborns brought forth considerable sympathy from the other prisoners, especially at first. The Polish Block had initially been quite supportive of these new arrivals, Polish mothers and mothers-to-be. But when it was learned that many of these women had had German boyfriends, attitudes changed.[32] Even so, there was so little that anybody could do. Women who got Red Cross packages were expected to contribute the dried milk to the newborns (if it had not been plundered by the SS), but there was never enough of it.[33] If a new mother had the good fortune to be part of an elite block or the Siemens camp, the chances of her child's survival increased significantly. Anni Hendricks, a Dutch prisoner, delivered a baby in the Siemens camp in February 1945. The baby boy, named Bernt, called the "Siemenskind," was fussed over by the other Siemens workers who shared their provisions with him. Even so, he lived only a few months.[34]

Aat Breur, drawing of Dutch women with their babies. From *Een verborgen herinnering*. Courtesy Dunya Breur.

The infirmary did assign some nurses to care for the newborns, swaddling them and looking after them while their mothers worked. One of these nurses, Eliska Valentova, wrote a short memoir in which she discussed how frustrating it was for her to make every effort to help the children, and yet make no progress. The underlying cause of their demise, malnutrition, was not addressed. "And so there was nothing more that we could do except to watch as the babies lost their appetites, became thin and weak and eventually, but slowly, died."[35]

By the first of the new year, the little bodies of dead infants being taken to the corpse cellar and from there to the crematorium became part of camp routine. A young Polish woman whose infant daughter died continued to carry it with her, refusing to believe all who told her the baby was dead. Finally, an infirmary worker convinced the disoriented mother to give up her child's body.[36]

The Children's Transports

In February and March 1945, orders were received to transport all children and pregnant women out of Ravensbrück. In one of the most chilling chapters of Ravensbrück's gruesome history, hundreds of children, from infants to early teenagers, were sent away. Most were shipped to Bergen-Belsen, and virtually none survived. According to a French report, those children who did not succumb to the −20 to −30°C (−5 to −20°F) temperatures during the train trip died shortly thereafter from starvation.[37] By the spring of 1945, Ravensbrück's "Kinderproblem" had ceased to exist.

The story of children at Ravensbrück is a disturbing one, not only because of the suffering and torment these little folks were put through, but also because we know that almost none of them survived. Of the nearly 900 children registered at Ravensbrück from 1939 to April 1945, perhaps 2 or 3 percent survived the experience. The rest all perished, most of them dying or being killed in the last months of the war.

At the same time, the episode of the children is a heartening, even uplifting one. The period during which the most children were at Ravensbrück, from the fall of 1944 to early 1945, was also the period in which there was significant overcrowding of the barracks, further restrictions of rations, and expansion of work hours. In spite of this, the response of so many of the women to the arrival of hundreds of children who were, after all, no hungrier than they themselves were, was absolutely wondrous. It was a truly remarkable outpouring of caring and nurturing and selfless- ness on the part of thousands of women, and surely ranks as one of the defining moments in the history of Ravensbrück.

CHAPTER

21

The Final Winter

Aat Breur, "Ravensbrück Funeral."
From *Een verborgen herinnering*. Courtesy Dunya Breur.

Nineteen forty-four was a disaster for the German military. In the West, the Allies had successfully launched their cross-channel invasion and were beginning the process of liberating areas of Western Europe from Nazi control. By year's end, they stood ready to pounce on Germany herself. In the east, following their spectacular victories at Stalingrad and Kursk in 1943, the Soviet forces had gained the momentum, and by late 1944 they controlled those areas east of a line drawn roughly from the Baltic Sea through Warsaw and Budapest.

These military setbacks raised enormous questions for the German leadership, one of the most troublesome of which was what to do with all that "human cargo" in the occupied territories that were now being lost. Some of these people, especially Jews in the concentration camps of eastern Poland, were already being killed, and now it was mainly a matter of speeding up the process. But the SS was keenly aware of the potential value of all that labor power, especially as it already owned the facilities for exploiting it. It was theirs for the taking, or rather, for the transporting. So during 1944, the two-edged policy of murdering and transporting prisoners was pursued relentlessly. Millions were killed and hundreds of thousands of others had their deaths postponed while they were transported to camps inside Germany.

Overcrowding

We do not know with certainty how many prisoners arrived at Ravensbrück and were held there during 1944. The SS's own Prisoner Strength Reports, which are so detailed for the period up to mid-1942, are missing for the subsequent period. The most considered estimate was made shortly after the end of the war, apparently by infirmary workers. This gave a prisoner population of 17,300 at the beginning of 1944 and 45,637 at the beginning of 1945.[1] After the war, French military authorities made estimates that were remarkably similar: 18,036 and 46,017.[2] Other estimates put the figure in early 1945 somewhat higher, around 50,000,[3] or even 56,000.[4] However, the issue is somewhat muddled because the French estimate includes the entire Ravensbrück system, subcamps as well as main camp, while the others appear to be based only on the main camp. Prisoners were being dispatched almost daily from the main camp to subcamps, but the numbers are not available. In the absence of solid data, which the SS destroyed, any estimate will be argued over, but the following seems a reasonable calculation: Ravensbrück and its sub-camps had a prisoner population of 45,000 to 65,000 at the end of 1944. Probably 20 to 30,000 were being held in the subcamps, while at the main camp there were between 25,000 and 40,000 women. Even the lower estimate represents significant overcrowding, for we must keep in mind that facilities at the main camp were designed to hold only 8 to 10,000 prisoners.[5]

What is not in doubt is that during 1944, particularly in the last half of the year, the number of transports bringing in new prisoners to Ravensbrück was simply phenomenal. Transport lists that somehow survived in a Polish archives give evidence that in November more than fifty transports arrived at Ravensbrück, adding over 7,000 new inmates in that month alone.[6] In early November, the last gassings of Jews occurred at Auschwitz, and later that month, on orders from Himmler, the gas chambers at Auschwitz II (Birkenau) were destroyed. Meanwhile, on 1 November, 1,717 women and 634 men were sent from Auschwitz to Bergen-Belsen and Ravensbrück.[7] The section of this transport destined for Ravensbrück arrived on 3 November, bringing in 800 Hungarian and 400 Polish Jews.[8]

It is clear that this rapid influx of unfortunate humanity totally overloaded the system. Where could thousands of new arrivals be placed in a camp that was already dreadfully overcrowded? Most of the newcomers were dumped in the blocks that had long been filled to capacity. Inmates who shared a bunk with two or three other women were now the lucky ones, as many women had to sleep on the floor.[9] But even the "better blocks" were affected as

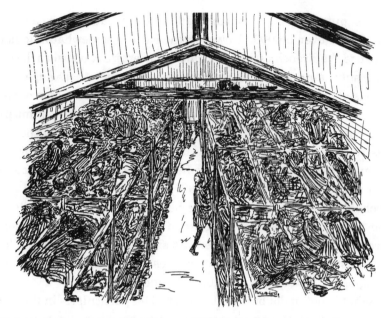

Violette LeCoq, "Domain of Dreams." From *Témoignages.* . . . Courtesy
Mme. Violette Rougier-LeCoq.

they, too, now had to make room for additional residents. At the
very least, this meant losing their day rooms, as these were converted to sleeping areas. Up until this point, the Polish women
had lived in semicomfort (relative to other groups, like the
French), but now they "were invaded by a large number of new
arrivals," who were decidedly not to their liking: "thin, starving
women, all skin and bone, brutalized cattle who pounced like animals on anything edible." Moreover, "the Auschwitz women" as
they were called, "fought over their food,"[10] which the Polish
women had not done.

The Tent

In August 1944, as the inmate population began to get out of
hand, the authorities procured a huge tent from the *Wehrmacht*

and erected it in an open area between Blocks 24 and 26, calling it Block 25.[11] It was to serve temporarily as the new Admissions Block, but "temporarily" in this case was a long time, because there was no letup in the flow of new arrivals and there were apparently no plans to build additional barracks. Because it was to be temporary, neither electricity nor plumbing was installed at first, and the only heat was that generated by the multitude of bodies huddled closely together. There were no toilets—inmates were expected to use latrines dug just outside the tent. Since it was hard to get to them at night, prisoners from other barracks sent them marmalade buckets to use as chamber pots.

Women assigned to the tent did no work. They were not permitted to leave the tent except for morning and evening roll calls, although some inmates did try to sneak into neighboring barracks to use their washrooms. It was treated as an Admissions Block, but there was no pretense at orienting the new prisoners, many of

Aat Breur, "The Great Tent." From *Een verborgen herinnering.* Courtesy Dunya Breur.

whom had previous concentration camp experience anyway. They were being held here until space could be found for them in regular barracks or they could be sent to a subcamp, and in many cases this did happen. A number of prisoners spent only a short time in the tent, then were sent elsewhere.

In the meantime, conditions were so appalling in the tent, particularly once cold weather set in, that prisoners who were sick and weak had almost no chance of survival. The overseers never came inside; they were afraid to.[12] Prisoner officials stayed away, too. There was a block senior, but she didn't stay in the tent. So when the soup tubs were delivered, nobody was in charge of distribution, as in a regular block, and what occurred was that those who were still strong enough fought their way to the food and the rest did without.[13] Annalise Urbye, a Norwegian prisoner who lived in relatively comfortable circumstances, became upset when she learned of conditions in the tent, and went directly to the camp's Communist leaders to see what they could do. Urbye was informed that the previous day the Communists had taken the risk of smuggling five big buckets of soup into the tent. But the soup-carriers had to fight their way in, and as they did, the tent dwellers stormed the buckets, spilling fifty liters of soup.[14] It is impossible not to have sympathy for the young woman, a tent dweller, who tried to volunteer for brothel duty to escape her surroundings. But her mates thwarted her plans by shaving her head to make her less attractive.[15]

The first residents of the tent were Polish women, brought to Ravensbrück in the late summer of 1944, and made to stay in the tent only a short time before space was found for them elsewhere.[16] In October, just as the Mecklenburg weather was turning raw, a large number of Jews from the Budapest Ghetto was brought in. Most of them arrived reasonably healthy, and thus their survival rate for the first few weeks was quite high. Many were given permanent assignments after this,[17] but for those who remained in the tent, survival became precarious at best. Then, in December, a huge transport of two to three thousand Jews was brought in from Auschwitz and dumped into the tent. Many did not have blankets, let alone warm clothes.[18] If they didn't starve, they would freeze. It was at this point that the tent became, in the words of one sympathetic inmate, "the last station on the road to death."[19] Those poor, starving women huddled together, lying in their own straw-soaked excrement, were condemned, and everybody knew it. The senior Russian prisoner doctor, Antonina Nikiforowa, recalled, "They died like flies. Almost the whole transport of about two thousand people died."[20] The tent was guarded by the camp police, whose job it was to keep the tent dwellers inside their compound, and to keep other prisoners out. Denise Dufournier, whose block (26) was right next to the tent, remembered the tent and its inhabitants vividly:

> In the evening, when we were lying two to a berth, we could hear the shrieks which came from the tent all through the night. We were filled with an unutterable shame at the thought that we could not go to the aid of the poor wretches living, if such it can be called, quite close to us in a destitution and misery compared with which our own block, our beds, and our blankets, were the utmost luxury.[21]

Other prisoners were allowed only within a certain distance of the tent, but they could hear the women crying and screaming, and they could smell the "terrible stench" coming from there, according to Dagmar Hajkova. They could witness the bodies being brought out, sometimes as many as thirty or forty in a day, but they were powerless to help these women.[22]

There were both Jews and non-Jews assigned to the tent, but the great majority of inmates living and dying there in the winter of 1944–1945 were undoubtedly Jewish women. However, almost as rapidly as these women were arriving from camps and ghettoes in the east, they were being whisked out of the tent and other makeshift barracks to other destinations, nearly always to one of the subcamps. Conditions there were generally not as dreadful as at the main camp, and chances of survival dramatically improved.

Many women, Jews as well as non-Jews, spent less than a month at Ravensbrück, some of them only a few days, before being transported elsewhere.[23]

Corpses and Cremations

Until 1943, the town crematorium in Fürstenberg was easily able to handle all the bodies brought to them from the camp. To assist them, the camp authorities regularly assigned a work crew of twenty from the men's camp (no women were ever assigned to the crematorium).[24] It was in 1943 that the deaths began to mount, and that year a crematorium with two ovens was built at the camp. The following year, a second oven was built at the town crematorium. By early 1944, these ovens were operating full time, burning two or three bodies at once. In that year, too, the SS ordered the town crematorium to burn five or six bodies at a time.[25] By the end of the year, the ovens could not keep up with the arrival of corpses, and many of the bodies were buried in mass graves on the far

France Audoul, "The Funeral Flames." From
Ravensbrück: 15,000 Femmes en Enfer.

France Audoul, "The Tragic Crew." From *Ravensbrück: 15,000 Femmes en Enfer.*

side of the camp.

The deaths of prisoners had been part of the history of Ravensbrück concentration camp since its beginning, and the "corpse crew" making its daily rounds was a constant reminder of that grisly fact. Before 1942, that crew did not have a lot of work to do, with only a few deaths per day, on average. In 1943, these numbers leaped considerably, and in 1944 with the typhus and tuberculosis epidemics, they increased by a factor of seven or eight. The infirmary's own figures show 116 deaths in January 1944, and 727 in December of that year. But even the Gestapo knew that the infirmary was underreporting deaths.[26] Some prisoners estimated the number to be 25 to 40 per day by the end of 1944.[27] Hildegard Hansche, whose job in the administration offices required her to make the rounds of the barracks each day, recorded her observations:

Aat Breur, drawing showing bodies piled up on the floor of the washroom. From *Een verborgen herinnering*. Courtesy Dunya Breur.

> Today as yesterday, as always the same scene: a two-
> wheeled cart rumbles along the camp street, loaded down
> with several layers of corpses which had been hauled out of
> the barracks. They had been thrown out of their beds, hauled
> to the washroom or wind breaks for storage, then put on the
> carts. The corpse carts, pushed and pulled by two prisoners,
> rattled out of the camp gate since the entrance to the crema-
> tory ovens were outside the camp. For days a haze of the ash-
> es created by the burning of flesh has hung over the camp.[28]

By late 1944, the bodies were sometimes delivered to the corpse
cellar, built against the camp wall behind the infirmary. By then,
women were dying faster than the crematoriums could handle
them. Moreover, since few of the subcamps had their own crema-
toria, they mostly trucked their corpses back to Ravensbrück for
cremation there.[29] However, in some locations, such as Barth, they
had the cremations done locally, then billed the SS at Ravensbrück (RM 35, plus fees).[30] In the main camp, the corpse crew was

expanded, and now went through the camp twice each day picking up bodies.

There were times when numbers of corpses would be stacked outside, next to the door. It was a ghastly sight. Many were nothing but skin and bones, "their pain-distorted faces still betraying the misery of their last hours."[31] At the beginning of 1945, some gruesome news made its way through the camp grapevine: corpses that had been temporarily stored in a washroom were discovered to have been chewed on and partially eaten by people.[32]

There had been a time when each death at Ravensbrück was followed by a

Aat Breur, "Posthumous portait of Jolan Lecovicz." Lecovicz was a fourteen-year-old Jewish girl from Hungary who died on 21 March 1945 at Ravensbrück. Aat Breur drew this portrait as a memento for her family. From *Een verborgen herinnering*. Courtesy Dunya Breur.

death notice sent by the commandant to the next of kin. They were, in fact, form letters, and they bore no resemblance to the truth, but they might have had the effect of consoling a grieving relative. Consider the following example:

Ravensbrück, 3 June 1943

Dear Frau Schulz:

On 24 May 1943, your daughter reported sick and was thereupon taken into the medical building and placed under a physician's care. She was given the best possible medical treatment and nursing care, but in spite of all the medical efforts which were undertaken, the illness could not be overcome.

I extend to you my condolences regarding your loss. Your daughter did not express any last wishes.

I have directed the Prisoners' Property Administration of the camp to send any personal effects to your address.

Suhren (signed)

SS Hauptsturmführer[33]

These were lies, of course. The woman might have been beaten to death in the bunker and given no medical assistance whatever, but her parents were sent this form letter anyway. Sometimes the death notices were not sent out until months later, as the SS apparently gave the matter a low priority.[34] By 1944, these notices were not being sent at all. The number of deaths, no doubt, had something to do with this. Now all that was done was to file an official death notice with the civilian agencies. This form almost always noted that the cause of death was "heart failure." The commandant had a standard form that was sent to civilian authorities along with the death notice, telling them that there would be no sending of the urn (which was probably a good thing, since even the crematorium authorities knew that the names on the urns often did not correspond to the ashes inside)[35] nor would any personal effects be returned. Finally, the form ended with the request that no further inquiries be made.[36]

Uckermark: A Killing Place

Since 1942, the Youth Camp at Uckermark, a small enclosure located on the southern periphery of the main camp, had functioned as a detention center for girls, most of whom were characterized by the welfare system as "hopeless cases." There had all along been organizational ties between the camps, but almost no working connection between them.

In early 1944, Uckermark was ordered to close. Its staff and some of its inmates were transferred to a "transitional camp" (*Übergangslager*) at Dallgow-Döberitz. A handful of inmates was

France Audoul, "Your hour has struck." From *Ravensbrück: 15,000 Femmes en Enfer.*

released, and a carefully selected few were parceled out for house-hold service, mainly to SS personnel. Most, however, were sent back to the main camp.[37] Uckermark now began to be used as an extension of the main camp, and in the last months of 1944, pris-oners began to be sent there. According to rumors, its barracks and other facilities were nicer than in the main camp. Prisoners were told that it was a *"Schönungslager"* (roughly, convalescing camp), and some women volunteered to go there.[38]

In December 1944, a decision was made to evacuate to Uckermark all those prisoners who already held a "bed card," which included all those who were in the Typhus and Tuberculosis Blocks.[39] In addition, block seniors were ordered to turn over lists of those who were incapable of working, implying that they would be allowed to remain in bed and rest. A few of the craftier block seniors saw through this ploy, and reported that all the women in

Aat Breur, untitled drawing of a
woman with an empty drinking cup
standing by an empty soup container
(damaged). From *Een verborgen
herinnering*. Courtesy Dunya Breur.

their blocks were work-capable.[40] But from other blocks there were long lists. Erika Buchmann, a block senior, later acknowledged that on three different occasions in January and early February 1945, she turned over lists totaling 132 women from her block to SS doctors. Once she realized these women were not convalescing, but were being killed, she stopped doing this.[41] By early January 1945, Uckermark held over 3,500 women.[42]

All of this was nothing but a selection, pure and simple: Ravensbrück was being cleared of its old, sick, and weak women in order to make room for the multitudes who were pouring in every day and who might be more able-bodied. Although the SS records are missing, testimony has been given by *SS Obersturmführer* Johann Schwarzhuber, who was transferred from Auschwitz-Birkenau in January 1945 to take over as camp leader (*Schutzhaftlagerführer*). Schwarzhuber recalled that shortly after taking office, he was summoned to a meeting by Commandant Suhren, who informed him and Dr. Trommer (the camp doctor) that Himmler had given the order "that all women who were either sick or were incapable of marching (*marschunfähig*) were to be killed."[43]

The women sent to Uckermark were given hardly any provisions, and many of these already sick prisoners died within a short period of time.[44] But it was a slow process, and Suhren wanted things speeded up. Dr. Trommer had nurses distribute "a white powder" to sick prisoners, and the next morning they were dead.[45] Some prisoners were killed by shooting, carried out by SS *Hauptscharführer* Moll. But to Commandant Suhren, all of these methods were inefficient. In the presence of Schwarzhuber, Suhren ordered the creation of a gas chamber in a barracks close to the crematorium.[46]

The Gas Chamber

The existence and operation of a gas chamber at Ravensbrück are not in doubt. However, there are some uncertainties surrounding this issue, caused in part by the SS's destruction of the gas chamber in the closing days of the war, and by their virtual annihilation of those prisoners who worked in the crematorium and gas chamber.[47] The SS did a quite thorough job of destroying evidence that might be used against them. Following the war, the Russians did not help matters by keeping researchers out of the camp and making sweeping changes, turning it into a military post.

No female prisoners were involved in either the construction or the operation of the gas chamber at Ravensbrück. Rather, inmates from the men's camp were used for both of these purposes.[48] The exact location of the gas chamber has been disputed, but it is now almost certain that it was located just to the west of the crematorium in a refurbished barracks formerly used to store building materials.[49] In other words, it was outside the camp, neither observable nor approachable from the barracks area.

Something about the gas chamber's operations is known from the trial testimony of Camp Leader Schwarzhuber, who was appointed by Commandant Suhren to be in charge of selections. Nearly every afternoon, Schwarzhuber would go to Uckermark to confer with Dr. Treite and other officials about that day's "lists." The women on the lists were told they were being transferred to another concentration camp, one named Mittwerda. No such camp existed; Schwarzhuber invented it in order to deceive the inmates. Only one of these lists has somehow survived. This is a list of 480 women who were to be sent to "Mittwerda" in early 1945. The document lists prisoners by name and number only, so it is necessary to guess at their nationalities based on their names. What seems noteworthy about this list is its heterogeneity: Poles, Czechs, Germans, Jews, French, Russians. Virtually all the national groups in continental Europe are represented, with none being even close to a majority.[50]

The women were assembled in an empty barracks that afternoon, and in the evening were taken by trucks the short distance to the gas chamber. Since the gas chamber was located near the crematorium, and was outside the camp walls, the little convoy would have taken a service road that skirted the perimeter of the camp. Even at a slow pace, the trip would have lasted only ten to fifteen minutes. The stop would not have been unexpected, since the women had undoubtedly been informed that they would need to be deloused before journeying to "Mittwerda."[51] SS officer Schwarzhuber was present at a gassing and has left a description:

> There were always 150 women who were forced into the gas chamber at one time. *Hauptscharführer* Moll ordered the women to undress and told them that they were going to be deloused. They were thereupon sent into the gassing room and the door was closed. A male inmate, wearing a gas mask, climbed onto the roof and threw a canister into an opening, which he immediately closed again. I heard moaning and whimpering from inside. I can't really say whether the women were dead or unconscious because I was not present when the room was cleared out.[52]

In addition to the prisoners being sent through Uckermark, other prisoners, mainly the sick and injured, were being forwarded from subcamps. Subcamps had no gas chambers of their own, and when transports arrived from these camps, the victims were taken directly to the gas chamber without ever entering the camp proper.[53]

Other prisoners heard rumors of the gassings and other killings, and they suspected foul play because of all the clothing that was being returned, some of which they recognized.[54] But the prisoners who were assigned to help with the gassings and shootings were male prisoners rather than females, so the women had no direct contact with these events. Moreover, the killings were carried out with extreme secrecy. Of the dozens of women survivors who wrote about their experiences at Ravensbrück, none had direct knowledge of the gas chambers, and only one was an eyewitness to the SS's killing mechanisms. This was Olga Körner, who in the last days of the camp's existence witnessed 48 women being shot by the SS.[55]

Once begun, the killings went on until nearly the end of the war. The gas chamber was closed down in early April 1945, having been in operation for perhaps two months. It was then destroyed.[56] Suhren himself acknowledged that fifteen hundred women had been gassed at Ravensbrück during this time,[57] but this number seems self-servingly low given the capacity of the facility and the length of time it was in use. Estimates made by Tillion (4,500–5,200),[58] Charlotte Müller (5,793),[59] Hilde Boy-Brandt and Anise Postel-Vinay (both 6,000)[60] are more believable.

The Chaos of Dissolution

The continued dumping of all this human freight (for that is how the prisoners were viewed and handled) from the now-shrinking reaches of the Reich into the already hopelessly overcrowded facilities of Ravensbrück Concentration Camp had consequences that were both devastating and ameliorating. On the one hand, with no increase in provisions or improvement in accommodations, it meant that many would starve or freeze even if they were not directly killed by the SS. But on the other hand, this very over-crowding created conditions that led to a loss of control by the SS, a situation some of the prisoners were quick to exploit for their own purposes.

One of the first indications of the SS's diminished control in the camp is that it became much easier to hide people. New prisoners were being dropped off so fast and in such numbers that it was increasingly difficult for camp authorities to keep track of them. Many of the prisoners who were jammed into the tent had no numbers and had not been registered.[61] Similarly, in the "Auschwitz shed," another makeshift barracks, many inmates were unregistered, apparently because they were destined for imminent transfer or even death. But it was a favorable location for hiding people. Many of the "rabbits" were hidden there, once it was learned that the SS intended to kill them.[62] These victims of the experimental operations still drew sympathy from other prisoners, who showed considerable solidarity in protecting and hiding them.[63]

New prisoners were still arriving almost daily from Poland, while at the same time, others were leaving Ravensbrück for unknown destinations, generally other concentration camps. In one of these transports, a number of women and almost all the children were sent to Bergen-Belsen. Most of the children died en route.[64] On 2 March 1945, nearly two thousand women were tak-en to Mauthausen.[65] This included nearly all the NN (Night and Fog) prisoners who had been living under a death sentence since their arrival.[66] Probably many of the women were relieved at being taken away, for even if they didn't know anything about their destination, there was a prevalent attitude that Ravensbrück was such a "hell hole" that no other place could be much worse.[67] The situation bordered on chaos. Ravensbrück was sending its surplus prisoners to other camps, while these camps were sending their unwanted inmates to Ravensbrück. An example of this is that in February a transport of 992 prisoners was sent to Dora-Mittelbau. A few weeks later, when that camp was closed because of RAF bombings, its approximately forty thousand inmates were packed off to Bergen-Belsen, Sachsenhausen, and Ravensbrück.[68] The numbers are not known because by this time, nobody was bothering to keep accurate head counts.

Ravensbrück in February and March 1945 presented an incredible picture of continued productivity in the workplaces, but growing anarchy in the barracks area. Women still went to work every day in the Siemens factory and in the SS textile plants. In spite of frequent interruptions caused by air raids and power outages, they managed to maintain reasonably high levels of production. Indeed, at the SS textile factory, work was proceeding on an extension of the plant.[69] However, not nearly as many prisoners were taken to work sites outside of the camp as in previous years, and the result was that there were now thousands of women with no work assignments and nothing to do.[70]

Many survivors have commented on how, in the closing months of the war, the SS adopted a much more lenient attitude toward the inmates than before. Discipline "became lax,"[71] as the camp police no longer patrolled the streets. "The strains of existence had sapped the entire system. . . . One no longer saw many SS."[72] At night thieves and even bands of thieves roamed the camp, searching for easy victims to rob. They would sometimes go inside a barracks and attempt to cut away the little bundles of possessions the residents had tied to their beds or to their wrists.[73]

Whereas earlier, displays of homosexual behavior were at least frowned upon, now they were flaunted:

> . . . The *Pärchen* [little couples] proclaimed their natures completely in the open. In men's suits, men's blouses, the 'Max, Fritz, Pete, and Bobby' paraded arm in arm on the camp streets with their lovers. One need not talk about what went on at night in the sleeping rooms. Indeed, the overseers were often organizers and participants in these sorry occurrences.[74]

In the barracks, where bored and desperate women lay around with nothing to do, some lesbians took advantage of the situation and seduced them.[75] There was no need to worry about Reports now. The SS had more pressing matters to attend to. At the little subcamp at Finow, the situation was even freer. There the head overseer lived in an entirely open relationship with a female inmate. Lesbian relationships were widespread and more than tolerated. A survivor complained that the kitchen staff "would choose their partners from our ranks and whoever refused them would go hungry."[76]

Meanwhile, as Ravensbrück drifted deeper into anarchy, the dying and the killings continued. Even the demonstrably under-reported tally of the infirmary showed 3,858 deaths in the first three months of 1945,[77] and the true figures may be many times this.

By the end of March 1945, it made no sense to continue pouring women by the thousands into a facility that could not care for the inmates already there. But this policy, if it can be called that, was principally the result of Hitler's almost hallucinatory refusal to confront reality and to begin the process of ending the war while there was anything left of Germany.

Hitler was at this point sequestered in the Berlin Bunker with what remained of his loyal entourage. He was, on the one hand, dreaming of miracles, and on the other condemning all but himself for the impending defeat. Even his beloved Volk were not spared, as he obstinately refused to order measures that might have ended the war and eased their ordeal.[78] And what about the hundreds of thousands of miscreants whose suffering in the concentration camps surpassed anyone's? The point is easily made that at the highest level of leadership no consideration whatever was being given to them.

CHAPTER

April
1945

22

Violette LeCoq, "The Path to Heaven." From *Témoignages* . . .
Courtesy Mme. Violette Rougier-LeCoq.

Red Cross Transports

By the first of April 1945, everyone, inmates as well as SS, knew the end of the war could not be far off. Naturally, rumors abounded: The camp was going to be torched. They were all going to be evacuated. They were going to be killed.[1] In one case, a Jewish woman was told by an SS guard that "At five minutes before twelve he [Hitler] will kill all the Jewish people. But," the guard added, "not here."[2]

At about this time, with the war clearly in its final stages, prisoners talked about the war ending shortly, most often using the reference of fourteen days. This became a kind of "magic time span" for many of the prisoners. A Polish Jew, Halina Nelken, expressed this idea in the following sprightly verse:

> Hey! Forward march, if you've got feet!
> On toward Cracow, where we'll meet.
> Through woods and fields, a bread with me!
> In fourteen days we will be free![3]

On 4 April, a convoy of trucks from the Canadian and American Red Cross arrived at Ravensbrück. This was the result of negotiations between Professor Carl Burckhardt, President of the International Red Cross, and high-ranking SS leaders, particularly Walter Schellenberg. The next morning, the convoy left for Switzerland with 300 women: 299 French and one Polish.[4] Two days later (7 April), the Danes and Norwegians were evacuated by the Red Cross.[5] Apparently, one of these convoys had dropped off provisions because some of the prisoners later made mention of packages. After SS personnel took their share, the prisoners got what was left. At least some of the prisoners did.[6] The system of haves and have-nots still functioned.

The mood among the inmates changed dramatically. In the first week of April, with the end of the war obviously approaching, some of the prisoners dared to hold a candlelight dance in Block 17, accompanied by an accordion. A French inmate recalled the event: "The 'Jules' held their 'girls', who were all dressed up, on their laps, fondling them. There was a vague smell of greasy humanity in the air. In the darkest corners lovers were kissing."[7]

By the second week of April, shortages of power and materials had forced the closing of both the SS textile factory and the Siemens plant. There was virtually no work being performed except for essential services such as the infirmary and kitchens. Margarete Buber-Neumann, a veteran Political, noted: "We all lay around singing songs and smoking cigarettes stolen from the SS (which the SS had stolen from Red Cross packages). The atmosphere at the camp was alive with the hope of freedom."[8] There were few roll calls by mid-April, and when one was held, the prisoners stood around chatting or sat on the ground, whatever their inclination. The overseers did nothing.[9] Many of the overseers and other SS personnel became noticeably more friendly as the war drew to a close.[10] A few spent their last days in the SS barracks totally drunk, a clear sign to one prisoner that the end was very near.[11]

At about this time, prisoners broke into the SS warehouses, helping themselves to the SS's own plundered goods. There were no repercussions, in part because SS personnel were fleeing the scene themselves. Some of the lower-ranking SS men who were still there handed out Red Cross packages that the SS had earlier confiscated. Unfortunately, some of the sick women ate more than was wise, worsening their condition.[12] As a further act of generosity, the SS on 20 April (Hitler's birthday) made sure that each woman got a little chunk of meat in her soup.[13]

Since February 1945, Count Bernadotte, Chairman of the Swedish Red Cross, had been negotiating with Himmler for the evacuation of women from Ravensbrück. In mid-April, Himmler agreed to their evacuation, apparently hoping this would favorably influence Eisenhower to grant a separate armistice. Bernadotte was trying to assemble all available transport to move as many women out of the camp as quickly as possible, with priorities being given to west European women. On 22 April, a trans-

Count Bernadotte addresses a group of women prisoners who are about to be transported to Sweden by the Red Cross. *Dokumentationsarchiv des Österreichischen Widerstandes.* Courtesy USHMM Photo Archives.

port of two hundred sick French women was taken to Denmark, followed by eight hundred women the next day, almost all from the Benelux countries. In the following days, in a remarkable and inspiring story of humanitarian aid, Red Cross buses, trucks, and ambulances went back and forth between Ravensbrück and Padborg (located on the Danish border), several times, taking out thousands of women, many of them desperately ill.[14]

The rescuers feared that, when the German leadership knew that all was lost, they might give the order to kill all remaining prisoners. The rescuers' awareness of the liquidation of the Maidanek Concentration Camp gave a real urgency to their efforts. For his part, however, Commandant Suhren was extremely cooperative, asking the Red Cross to accept fifteen thousand women instead of the seven thousand agreed upon. But on 25 or 26 April, Suhren received a signed order from Hitler to the effect that concentration camp prisoners were *not* to be evacuated. Suhren hesitated, but a telephone call to Himmler determined that the orders had been changed again. The rescue could proceed. Not only that, but German authorities also put a sixty-car freight train at the disposal of the Red Cross, and on 26 April, the train left Ravensbrück with four thousand women on board. It stopped once, at Lübeck, for food, and was at Padborg the following day. Considering that the roads and rails were choked with German refugees and military units trying to escape the oncoming Russian army, the offer of a train to expedite the movement of women prisoners was a surprising "act of generosity."[15] By 29 April, more than eight thousand women, almost half of them Jews, had been evacuated to the safety of Denmark, from where they were taken mainly to Malmö, Sweden. Tragically, many of the women who were transported there were already in such a debilitated condition that even the genuinely heroic efforts now being made for them proved futile, and in the following weeks, hundreds died.[16]

Meanwhile, the scene at Ravensbrück was one of near total confusion. Transports were leaving, one after the other, for points west, often loaded with prisoners and SS personnel (some of whom were now trying to disguise themselves as prisoners). Nobody was noting names any longer or even counting.[17] The gas chamber had been destroyed in early April, but the SS now made use of the crematorium ovens to burn documents. Virtually the entire collection of official records for the Ravensbrück Concentration Camp went up in smoke. Even more tragic, some of the prisoners who knew too much were shot by SS squads in the closing days of the war.[18]

Camp authorities were already releasing prisoners. On 21 April, a group of about sixty "old Politicals" were given loaves of bread and certificates (proving their identities as former prisoners) and allowed to walk out the gate, still dressed in their uniforms or prison garments. They all walked into Fürstenberg, where some of them banged on doors and demanded food and other items from startled and apprehensive townspeople.[19] Eventually they went to the railroad station where, amid terrible confusion, they managed to get on a train going northwest, joining hundreds of other refugees. Margarete Buber-Neumann related that when they explained to wary fellow travelers what their uniforms and badges signified, most were sympathetic and helpful.[20]

Death Marches

In the closing days of April, the thunder of Russian cannon was moving threateningly close to Ravensbrück, and all who were able were assembled to move out on foot. The International Red Cross sent a representative to Commandant Suhren, attempting to dissuade him from the idea of a forced march. But Suhren would not be deterred. He had orders from Himmler to evacuate the camp, the logistics were already in place to feed and house the marchers, and there would be no turning back.[21]

What the SS hoped to accomplish through the forced marches of thousands of weak and starving prisoners has never been fully explained; the event virtually defies reason. Suhren mentioned at one point that the women would be marched to Malchow, where Ravensbrück had a subcamp.[22] Presumably, the women would be put to work there. But in the closing days of April 1945, did Suhren and others of the SS leadership not know the war was lost, that if Ravensbrück was not safe from the Russians, neither was Malchow, only 70–75 km (45 miles) away? Incredibly, the answer is "no." Suhren believed the war was still to be won, and the "new weapons" touted by Dr. Goebbels would hurl the Allies back.[23]

Before the Death March (as it later came to be called)[24] began, the camp Communists had one more act of political solidarity to fulfill, and they used the prevailing chaos and confusion to carry it out effectively. Because of her age and condition, Rosa Thälmann would have been greatly endangered had she been made to go on the forced march. Thus, certain "comrades" got Frau Thälmann and two Russian companions safely placed in the cellar of a local confidante.[25]

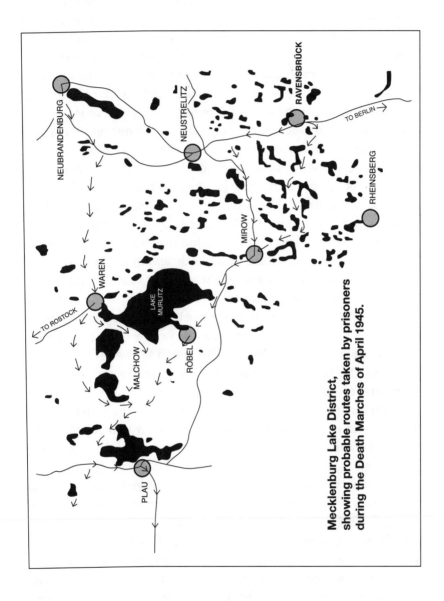

Mecklenburg Lake District,
showing probable routes taken by prisoners
during the Death Marches of April 1945.

On 27 and 28 April all those prisoners who were well enough to walk were led out of the camp. They had each been given bread and Red Cross rations, but under the circumstances this would hardly be sufficient. Moving in a northwesterly direction, they formed long columns, guarded by SS personnel. It was chaotic, in part because of all the other refugees also going in the same direction. The first night, as soon as it became dark, a number of prisoners ran off into the woods. Some of the SS guards, male and female, did the same, almost always in civilian clothes.

The women were not all marched together. Rather, there were a number of separate columns, generally composed of a few hundred prisoners each. These changed size considerably as they moved along, losing marchers who sneaked off in the darkness, but gaining stragglers, too. One column merged with a sizable contingent of male prisoners from Sachsenhausen. In the initial stages of the march, SS personnel were quite brutal in their handling of prisoners, even shooting those who might be trying to escape.[26] But as the march progressed, discipline became more relaxed, as many of the SS personnel were now more scared than the prisoners were. Charlotte Müller noted that after a few days of travel, the SS in her column became transformed into fellow marchers, no longer ordering people around.[27]

Suhren's assurances to the Red Cross official that kitchens and accommodations for the marchers were already in place along the route were empty nonsense. Prisoners slept out in the open, and once their small rations were gone, they had to scrounge. Unfortunately, at that time of year there was virtually nothing to glean from fields or orchards. Some of the already weak women fell by the wayside and were left behind to die. In some cases, SS guards accompanying the marchers shot prisoners who could not go any farther. In a particularly tragic incident in the village of Mirow, well-meaning villagers gave the starving marchers, men as well as women, as much as they could eat. Their digestive systems could not handle all that rich food, and several died.[28]

Inmates at the Neubrandenburg subcamp had begun their

Aat Breur, untitled drawing of a dead woman, covered with a coat. From *Een verborgen herinnering.* Courtesy Dunya Breur.

march at about the same time as those at the main camp. They, too, headed for Malchow, almost directly west. In one column, on the second day, the guards hitched a ride on a westward-bound military convoy, leaving the prisoners to fend for themselves. A group of French women stayed together, continuing west to the town of Waren, where they found refuge in a barn. That night (30 April), the Russian army arrived. Rather than being liberators, they put the French women through a more hellish ordeal than what they had experienced in the camp. The women were raped repeatedly by Russian troops, to the point where some of them were too weakened to continue their journey.[29] When Soviet forces liberated the subcamp at Neustadt-Glewe, "they raped all the women and girls: Jewish, Hungarian, German—it didn't matter."[30] A group of Jewish women from this subcamp believed that their emaciated condition (they weighed on average only 30 kg/66 lbs) would be a deterrent. It was not.[31]

Such behavior by Russian troops was extremely widespread,[32] and as rumors of the rapes spread, many women either hid or tried to make themselves look sick and contagious when they learned of approaching Russian military units.[33] Not all Russian troops acted in such a manner, of course. Many were genuine liberators and were warmly received by the former prisoners. In one case, a group of French women from the Neubrandenburg subcamp met up with a Russian unit, whose officers, upon learning of their identity, took pains to care for them. But that night, two of the French women were raped by drunken Russian soldiers anyway. In the morning, when the offenders could be identified, the rapists were summarily executed by their officers.[34]

The forced march of the prisoners became like some kind of gigantic slime mold, changing size and shape as it lurched onward. By the time the marchers reached Malchow, perhaps a third of the original members had been left behind, either dead or in hiding. A few stayed at Malchow, finding shelter in a now broken down work camp.[35] But most continued moving, trying like all the other refugees to make it to the Allied lines. After Malchow, the goal became anywhere the Americans or British were in control. By now it was no longer a forced march or any other kind of march, but merely a conglomerate of human beings moving in the same general direction. Most of the SS had fled, and any who remained had put on civilian clothes in an effort to appear inconspicuous. A few overseers tried to pass themselves off as inmate refugees.[36]

In the first days of May 1945, refugees from Ravensbrück began to cross into areas held by the American and British forces. At the little town of Lübz, Esther Bejarano and six other *Ravensbrük-kerinnen* met a contingent of Americans. It was a joyous and exhilarating experience for all of them, as the women somehow found the strength to celebrate into the night with their liberators.[37]

Liberation by the Red Army

On the afternoon of 30 April, advance units of the Soviet army rolled into Fürstenberg. Captain Boris Makarow, of the 49th army, of the second Belo-Russian Front, had been ordered to take control of the area and set up a headquarters there. He knew of the concentration camp, but not its exact location. Initially, Fürstenberg seemed like a ghost town. "Everything was very peaceful. The town seemed dead. There was nothing to hear and nothing to see." Finally, a woman appeared, speaking Russian and telling him of the many sick women in the nearby camp, and pointing out the way for him.

Captain Makarow and a detachment went directly to the concentration camp, where they were met by Antonina Nikiforowa, the senior Russian prisoner doctor who was now in charge of the infirmary. She showed him around the camp, and explained to him the dire situation there. There was no electricity, no water, and thirty-five to forty women were dying in the camp every day. Captain Makarow promised his country's help, but first he needed to secure the region militarily. Even before that was done, some of the Politicals took him to Rosa Thälmann, still in hiding. It fell to Makarow to give her the official news that her husband had been killed.

Soviet troops then thoroughly searched the town, looking not only for Nazis and military personnel, but also for women.[38] Few females in this town of four to five thousand escaped being raped. It was a hideous scene, repeated again and again in the Russian-occupied areas of Germany; it was quite obviously part of a policy which was at least semiofficial, designed no doubt to punish the Germans with contempt, while at the same time allowing Russian troops to reward themselves at the expense of the defeated enemy. After about a week, it was stopped abruptly, as the Russian military leadership brought the situation under control.

In the following days and weeks, the Russian military authorities were indeed cooperative with those former prisoner doctors

and other prisoner officials who had stayed behind to help the
sick. There were approximately three thousand prisoners still in
the camp at the time the Russians arrived, and many were
urgently in need of medical treatment. These numbers were being
augmented daily, as some prisoners who had fled in the early part
of the Death March now filtered back into Ravensbrück. Soviet
officials acted promptly and decisively to prevent the further
spread of disease and to slow the death rate. Squads of townspeople (about eight hundred persons) were dragooned into working at
the camp, cleaning barracks and burying the bodies that had been
stacking up for some days.[39] The entire camp was organized into a
hospital, its barracks again arranged by nationality. Medicines
and food were quickly brought in. Within days, electrical power
and running water were restored. Soon the situation was firmly
under control. In June the remaining sick prisoners were moved
elsewhere,[40] and the process was under way to transform the former women's concentration camp into a Soviet military post.

Conclusion

Statues of women prisoners by Will Lammert, in front
of the Wall of Nations at the Ravensbrück Memorial.
Photograph by the author, 1997.

Ravensbrück Concentration Camp was not, in any true sense, a
community. It was too diverse and heterogenous for that. There
were a few cases of campwide cooperation, as we have seen, but
for the most part what prevailed was a series of subcultures,
based largely on language and nationality. Many of these proved
to be amazingly vibrant, providing not only support systems and
survival mechanisms for their members, but also cultural and
educational programs of a high level. Indeed, it appears as one of
the great ironies of twentieth-century history that the Nazis, with
all of their cultural arrogance and intolerant racism, imprisoned
many "inferior peoples," even making slaves of them, and what
did these "inferior peoples" do? At Ravensbrück, they demonstrated, under the most adverse and inhospitable circumstances, an
amazing cultural creativity and intellectual energy.

The National Socialists viewed women of all countries as another group of inferiors, not to be exterminated, but decidedly to be
kept under control and prevented from assuming positions of
influence for which their natures, supposedly, excluded them.
Ironically, at Ravensbrück, a system was created which encouraged women to compete for positions of power and influence, then
fill these positions. Whereas, on the outside, women could not hold
appointments of real influence in the state or party, in the unnat-
ural surroundings of the concentration camp, women could hold
posts such as block senior and prisoner foreman, positions that
potentially held enormous influence. The lives of countless numbers of women were directly affected by a block senior's decisions,
for good or for ill. Additionally, women performed many of the other tasks which made it possible for Ravensbrück to function.
Indeed, with only a few exceptions, such as the motor pool, the
various facilities of the camp were in their hands. True, the male-
dominated SS was in overall command, set general policies, and
decided over life and death, but the day-to-day running of the
camp was very much in the hands of the women prisoners. The
fact that the SS administration allowed as much control to shift
into the hands of the women as they did attests to their general

satisfaction with an emerging *status quo*, regardless of its incompatibility with ideological theory.

For the women prisoners, these were impressive achievements, and rightly deserve our admiration and respect. However, the most significant accomplishment of the women of Ravensbrück may have been something else, a creation more down-to-earth than sensitive poetry, perceptive drawings, or administrative finesse, yet in its own way as noteworthy as any of these. Again and again, Ravensbrück inmates displayed survival skills based upon abilities and outlooks unique to women prisoners.

Sybil Milton has perceptively pointed out that women in their roles as homemakers and caregivers had developed skills that made them better suited than men to withstand the privations and hardships of the concentration camp.[1] Most of them knew how to extend and apportion a restricted food supply, how to darn socks and downsize a jacket, and how to fashion a carry-bag out of rags. Many of the women were mothers, and they had experience in social arbitration, in sorting out differences between squabbling family members, along with counseling distraught children. They knew how to deal with cuts and bruises, and how to make a poultice for a sick child. Skills such as these had direct applications in a concentration camp, and their prevalence in a camp for women made it a more tolerable and survivable place than it might have been otherwise.

Women's survival skills went further. Whether caused by nature or nurture, women have always been better than men at sharing, not just things, but themselves. Women could and did go to other women and cry on their shoulders, opening up and pouring out their hearts to them. Even if the women whose shoulders were being cried on did not dispense much advice, they were nearly always sympathetic listeners. Those nightly delousing sessions at Ravensbrück, where one woman put another's head in her lap and searched for vermin, were certainly as valuable for their emotional support as for hygiene, providing both physical contact and a sense of mutual sharing. There were countless intimate and deep relationships formed at Ravensbrück among women, and for many of them it was their salvation. Without them, they could not have survived, and even with them—given the conditions in the camp—many did not survive.

Ravensbrück was a place where huge numbers of women died, certainly tens of thousands, perhaps many times this number.[2] It is appropriate in this study that we pay tribute to the many women who died or were killed at Ravensbrück. The Third Reich was permeated with Social Darwinist thinking, but we would be making a dreadful error if we fell into this trap ourselves and thought that those who survived were in any essential way superior to those who did not survive. Many factors influenced survival, but as we have seen, only a few of these were under the control of the individual prisoners. That graceless element, pure luck, was ever present.

Today, at the site of the former women's concentration camp at Ravensbrück, there is a *Mahn- und Gedenkstätte* (Memorial/Place of Remembrance) complete with a museum, exhibits, contemplative walkways, and a monument that looks out over the lake toward the town. The atmosphere is somber, as befits a place where such human misery and death occurred, but not morbidly so. In the former Bunker, different nations have been encouraged to create exhibits honoring their compatriots who lived and died at Ravensbrück, and some of these have a decidedly nongloomy character. This is entirely appropriate, for Ravensbrück is now a monument not only to the suffering and death that took place there, but also to the human spirit, and particularly to the courage and enterprise of the women whose wills the Nazis could not subdue.

Notes

Preface

1. Germaine Tillion, *Ravensbrück* (1975).
2. On the provenance of the *Erlebnisberichte* at the Ravensbrück Archives, see Grit Philipp, "Erlebnisberichte als Quellen historischer Forschung," in Eschebach and Kootz, ed., *Das Frauen-konzentrationslager Ravensbrück: Quellenlage und Quellenkritik* (1997), pp. 123-128.
3. Hedda Zimmer, "Legitimer und legitimatorischer Antifaschismus. Zur Aufführungsgeschichte der 'Ravensbrücker Ballade'," in Klaus Jarmatz, ed., *Ravensbrücker Ballade oder Faschismusbewältigung in der DDR* (1992), p. 181.
4. Sigrid Jacobeit, "Fotografien als historische Quellen zum Frauen-KZ Ravensbrück: Das Ravensbrücker 'SS-Fotoalbum,'" in Eschebach and Kootz, eds., *Das Frauenkonzentrationslager Ravensbrück: Quellenlage und Quellenkritik*, pp. 33-45.

Introduction

1. Werner Maser, *Hitler: Legend, Myth and Reality* (1973), p. 200.
2. Comments made on 1 March 1942. *Hitler's Secret Conversations, 1941-1944* (1953), p. 338.
3. David Schoenbaum, *Hitler's Social Revolution: Class and Status in Nazi Germany, 1933-1939* (1966), pp. 187-188.
4. Ibid., pp. 188-189.
5. Max Domarus, *Hitler: Reden und Proklamationen, 1932-1945* (1965), Bd. IB, pp. 530-531.
6. Atina Grossmann, *Reforming Sex: The German Movement for Birth Control and Abortion Reform, 1920-1950* (1995), pp. 14-45.
7. Claudia Koonz, *Mothers in the Fatherland* (1987), p. 112.
8. Ibid., p. 144.
9. Robert G.L. Waite, *The Psychopathic God: Adolf Hitler* (1977), pp. 53-61; see also the brilliant analysis of the sexual nature of Hitler's oratory in Joachim C. Fest, *Hitler* (1974), pp. 323-332.
10. On these issues, see particularly the two pieces by Claudia Koonz: "Some Political Implications of Separatism: German Women Between Democracy and Nazism, 1928-1934" (1986), pp. 270-273, and *Mothers in the Fatherland*, pp. 59-68.
11. Ute Frevert, *Women in German History: From Bourgeois Emancipation to Sexual Liberation* (1988), pp. 218-219; Koonz, *Mothers in the Fatherland*, pp. 144-145.
12. Frevert, pp. 218-219.
13. Schoenbaum, p. 194.

14. Koonz, *Mothers in the Fatherland*, pp. 216-219, 334.
15. Annemarie Tröger, "The Creation of a Female Assembly-Line Proletariat," (1984), pp. 241-245.
16. Frevert, p. 229.
17. Tröger, pp. 249-264.

Chapter 1

1. Wolfgang Sofsky, *The Order of Terror: The Concentration Camps* (1997), pp. 28-29.
2. Jeremy Noakes and Geoffrey Pridham, eds., *Documents on Nazism, 1919-1945* (1974), pp. 180-181.
3. Sofsky, pp. 29-30.
4. Ibid., p. 30.
5. Ibid., pp. 30-34.
6. Sybil Milton, "Deutsche und deutsch-jüdische Frauen als Verfolgte des NS-Staats" (1987), pp. 3-7; Hans Hesse, "Und am Anfang war Moringen....?" (1996), n.p.
7. "Hanna Elling berichtet über das KZ Moringen," in Barbara Bromberger, Hanna Elling, Jutta von Freyberg, and Ursula Krause-Schmitt, *Schwestern, vergesst uns nicht. Frauen im KZ Moringen, Lichtenburg, Ravensbrück, 1933-1945* (1988), p. 13.
8. Ino Arndt, "Das Frauenskonzentrationslager Ravensbrück" (1970), pp. 94-95.
9. Comments by Henry Friedlander, in Esther Katz and Joan Ringelheim, ed., *Proceedings of the Conference on "Women Surviving the Holocaust"* (1983), pp. 105-106.
10. Ibid., pp. 99-100.
11. Raul Hilberg, *The Destruction of the European Jews*, rev. ed. (1985), vol. 3, pp. 961-979.
12. On this issue, see especially Margarete Buber-Neumann, *Als Gefangene bei Stalin und Hitler* (1962) and Charlotte Müller, *Die Klempnerkolonne in Ravensbrück* (1987).
13. Monika Herzog, interviews with the author, September 1994, Ravensbrück.
14. F. Heilman, "KZ Ravensbrück Chronik," n.p.
15. Gefangenen-Stärkemeldungen. RA II/4-6 Ravensbrück Archives.
16. Buber-Neumann, *Als Gefangene bei Stalin und Hitler*, p. 173.
17. Dagmar Hajkova, *Ravensbrück*, p. 21; Margarete Buber-Neumann, *Milena: the Story of a Remarkable Friendship* (1988), p. 168.
18. Buber-Neumann, *Als Gefangene bei Stalin und Hitler*, p. 298.
19. Arndt, pp. 102-103.
20. Monika Herzog and Bernhard Strebel, "Das Frauenkonzentrationslager Ravensbrück" (1994), p. 14.
21. Arndt, p. 106; Irmtraud Heike, "'...da es sich ja lediglich um die Bewachung der Häftlinge handelt...': Lagerverwaltung und Bewachungspersonal" (1994), p. 223.
22. Maria Plura, RA Erlebnis. Bd. 21, No. 210; see the testimony of Anneliese and Gertrud Phillip, who worked there also. RA Erlebnis. Bd. 17, No. 72, RVB Archives.
23. Arndt, pp. 106-107.
24. Heike, p. 222.
25. Karl Heinz Schütt, *Ein vergessenes Lager? Über das Aussenlager Neustadt-*

Glewe (1997), p. 16.

26. Micheline Maurel, *An Ordinary Camp* (1958), p. xv.
27. Català, p. 97.
28. Insa Eschebach, "Die Geschichte einer NS-Täterin: Versuch einer Rekonstruktion nach den Akten" (1994), pp. 28-34; Sofsky, p. 109.
29. See the interesting report done after the war, giving background information on many overseers: "Liste von SA-, SS- and NSDAP Leuten teilweise mit Bildern." RA Erlebnis. Bd. 24, No. 327-328, RVB Archives.
30. Heike, pp. 232-233.
31. Eschebach, pp. 21-27.
32. Gudrun Schwarz, "SS-Aufseherinnen in N-S Konzentrationslagern (1933-1945)" (1994), p. 43.
33. Anna David, "Aussage der ehemaligen SS-Aufseherin Anna David." RA Erlebnis. Bd. 23, No. 251, RVB Archives.
34. Heike, p. 224.
35. Renate Gruber-Lieblich, "...*und Morgen war Krieg.*" *Arado Flugzeugwerke GMBH Wittenberg 1936-1945* (1995), pp. 53, 66; Heike, pp. 233-234.
36. Heike, pp. 234-235.
37. Anna David, "Aussage der ehemaligen SS-Aufseherin Anna David." RA Erlebnis. Bd. 23, No. 251, RVB Archives.
38. Isa Vermehren, *Reise durch den letzten Akt: Ravensbrück, Buchenwald, Dachau: Eine Frau berichtet* (1946), pp. 52-57.
39. Schwarz, p. 43.
40. Eidestattliche Erklärung von Ursula Uthes. RA Erlebnis. Bd. 19, No. 41, RVB Archives.
41. Testimony of Vera Mahnke. RA Erlebnis. Bd. 37, No. 758, RVB Archives; Theolinde Katharina Katzenmaier, *Vom KZ ins Kloster* (1996), p. 77.
42. Deposition of Erna Boehmer, JAG 335 [RVB IV case] Exhibit 13. Public Record Office.
43. Eugenia Kocwa, *Flucht aus Ravensbrück* (1973), pp. 55-56.
44. Schreiben von Glücks an alle Lagerkommandanten. Dated 15 Nov. 1944. RA Erlebnis. Bd. 20, No. 182, RVB Archives.

Chapter 2

1. Letter of 2 June 1939. RA II/6-1-44. (Briefe und Postkarten) RVB Archives.
2. Sunneva Sandoe, *Und doch ist es Wahr* (1993), p. 60.
3. Català, p. 72.
4. "Herr K. erinnert sich an seine Kindheit in Fürstenberg in den Jahren 1939 bis 1945," in *Ravensbrücker Ballade*, p. 118.
5. Lolf Heinecke, RA Erlebnis., Bd. 34, No. 634, RVB Archives.
6. Irma Trksak described to me a similar incident during which she was spat at by townspeople. Interview with the author of 5 September 1997, Ravensbrück.
7. Charlotte Delbo, *Auschwitz and After*, p. 186.
8. This has been a bit of a controversial issue, with a few former prisoners swearing such a sign was there, but the evidence and the consensus of survivor opinion do not uphold this view.
9. See the interview with Dora Freilich, Gratz College (3-2-37); see also Giuliani Tedeschi, *There Is a Place on Earth* (1992), p. 205.
10. Antonia Bruha, *Ich war keine Heldin* (1984), pp. 88-89.
11. Sandoe, pp. 61-62; see also Vermehren, p. 69.

12. Vermehren, p. 69.
13. Katzenmaier, p. 53; Sara Tuvel Bernstein, *The Seamstress* (1997), p. 199.
14. Buber-Neumann, *Als Gefangene bei Stalin und Hitler*, p. 171.
15. Català, p. 113.
16. Bernstein, p. 204.
17. Catherine Roux, *Red Triangle* (1979), pp. 59-60.
18. Silvia Salvesen, *Forgive — But Do Not Forget* (1958), p. 67.
19. Interview with Erika Buchmann, in Zimmer, p. 175.
20. Fanny Marette, *I Was Number 47177* (1979), pp. 104-105; on the issue of the humiliating effects of parading naked in front of strangers, see the testimony of Maria Jarosawa from Lidice, in Loretta Waltz, *Remembering Ravensbrück* (1997 film).
21. Christa Schultz, *Hanka Houskova* (1995), p. 10.
22. Català, p. 38.
23. Marette, pp. 149-151.
24. Bruha, p. 91.
25. Sandoe, p. 69.
26. See Madeleine Jacquemotte-Thonnart, *Ma vie de Militante, 1907-1945*, p. 176; RA Erlebnis, Bd. 39, no. 887. RVB Archives.
27. Schulz, *Hanka Houskova*, pp. 5-7.
28. Müller, pp. 13-15.
29. Maurel, pp. 6-7.
30. Interview with Hardy Kupferberg, Gratz College (3-1-45).

Chapter 3

1. Bruha, *Ich war keine Heldin*, pp. 91-92.
2. Claudia Schoppman, *Days of Masquerade: Life Stories of Lesbians during the Third Reich* (1996), pp. 1-23.
3. See the chart "Kennzeichen für Schutzhäftlinge in der Konz. Lagern," reprinted in Jacobeit and Brümann-Güdter, eds., *Ravensbrückerinnen* (1995), p. 100.
4. Müller, *Die Klempnerkolonne*, pp. 95-96.
5. RA Erlebnis, Bd. 17, No. 72, pp. 1-7. RVB Archives.
6. Berichtungen vom 15 Aug. 1942 and 28 Nov. 1942. Mss. RG-04.006M, Reel 20. U.S. Holocaust Memorial Museum Archives.
7. Esther Bejarano, *"Man nannte mich Krümel"* (1991), p. 28.
8. RA Erlebnis., Bd. 42, No. 1004. Liste über eingelieferte Häftlingsnummern von 1939-1945 und woher. RVB Archives.
9. Roux, p. 65.
10. Brian R. Dunn, "Green Triangles" (1993), pp. 19-22.
11. Ibid., pp. 24-25.
12. Atina Grossmann, *Reforming Sex. The German Movement for Birth Control and Abortion Reform, 1920-1950* (1995), pp. 82-83, 146-152.
13. Ibid., pp. 136-139, 146.
14. RA II/4-6 Gefangenen-Stärkemeldungen. RVB archives.
15. Wanda Kiedrzynska. Auswertung über prozenturale Zusammensetzung der Häftlinge. RA Erlebnis., Bd. 42, No. 1037. RVB Archives.
16. Interview with Clark, in Anton Gill, *The Journey Back From Hell. Conversations with Concentration Camp Survivors: An Oral History* (1988), p. 328.
17. Hajkova, p. 23.
18. Gill, p. 327.

19. Müller, pp. 13-16.
20. Erika Buchmann, "Brief an eine berliner Reporterin" (1992), pp. 32-34.
21. Martina Scheitenberger and Martina Jung, "Fürsorge – Arbeitshaus – KZ: Betty Voss" (1994), pp. 302-304.
22. Sigrid Jacobeit and Elisabeth Brümann-Güdter, eds., *Ravensbrückerinnen* (1995), pp. 83-86.
23. Hajkova, p. 24.
24. Michael Hepp, "Vorhof zur Hölle: Mädchen im 'Jugendschutzlager' Uckermark" (1987), p. 192.
25. Christa Schikorra, "'Asoziale' Frauen. Ein anderer Blick auf die Häftlingsgesellschaft," in Jacobeit and Philipp, eds., *Forschungsschwerpunkt Ravensbrück* (1997), pp. 61-63.
26. Christa Schikorra, "Asoziale Häftlinge in Frauen-konzentrationslager Ravensbrück; Eine Annäherung" (1996), n.p.
27. On this issue, see Klaus Jarmatz, "Gespräche mit Monika Herzog ...", *Ravensbrücker Ballade*, p. 160.
28. Schikorra, "'Asoziale' Frauen," pp. 67-68.
29. Hajkova, p. 24.
30. Nanda Herbermann, *Der gesegnete Abgrund. Schutz-Häftling Nr. 6582 im Frauenkonzentrationslager Ravensbrück* (1959), pp. 88-89.
31. Buber-Neumann, *Als Gefangene bei Stalin und Hitler*, p. 198.
32. Ibid., pp. 178-181.
33. Bruha, p. 99.
34. "Aus dem Tagebuch von Lidia Rolfi," RA Erlebnis., Bd. 26. No. 399. RVB Archives.
35. Dunn, pp. 25-27.
36. Hepp, pp. 200-201.
37. Ibid., p. 200.
38. Ibid., pp. 205-215.
39. Grossmann, pp. 70-74.
40. Ibid., pp. 205-215.
41. Angus Fraser, *The Gypsies* (1992), pp. 7, 260.
42. On this issue, See Donald Kendrik and Grulton Puxon, *The Destiny of Europe's Gypsies* (1972), pp. 13-25; See also David Crowe, *A History of the Gypsies of Eastern Europe and Russia* (1994), passim.
43. Isabel Fonseca, *Bury Me Standing: The Gypsies and Their Journey* (1995), pp. 5-12.
44. Ibid., p. 227.
45. Henry Friedlander, *The Origins of Nazi Genocide: From Euthanasia to the Final Solution* (1995), pp. 248-255.
46. Quoted in Fraser, *The Gypsies*, p. 260.
47. Fraser, pp. 260-265; Kendrick and Puxon, pp. 76-94.
48. Yehuda Bauer, "Gypsies," in *Anatomy of the Auschwitz Death Camp* (1994), p. 446.
49. Romani Rose and Walter Weiss, *Sinti und Roma im dritten Reich* (1991), p. 40.
50. Reimar Gilsenbach, "Wie Lolitschai zur Doktorwürde kam" (1988), pp. 103-115.
51. Crowe, pp. 48-50.
52. Heike Krokowski and Bianca Voigt, "Das Schicksal von Wanda P.—Zur Verfolgung der Sinti und Roma" (1994), p. 263.
53. Kendrick and Puxon, pp. 162-165.
54. Krokowski and Voigt, pp. 264-265.
55. Vermehren, p. 80.

56. Madeleine Jacquemotte-Thonnart, *Ma Vie de Militante, 1907-1945* (1992), p. 180.
57. Käte Roth and Hanna Conrad, RA Erlebnis. Bd. 40, No. 934. RVB Archives. On this general subject, see Guenter Lewy, *The Nazi Persecution of the Gypsies* (2000), pp. 13-14.
58. Wanda Symonowicz, ed., *Beyond Human Endurance: The Ravensbrück Women Tell Their Story* (1970), p. 45.
59. Ceija Stoika, *Wir Leben im Verborgenen: Erinnerungen einer Rom-Zigeunerin* (1988), pp. 15-40.
60. Ibid., pp 41-50.
61. Ibid., pp. 51-53.
62. Krokowski and Voigt, p. 266.
63. Mlada Tauferova, "Die Sterilisiering der Zigeunerinnen im Lager Ravensbrück", RA Erlebnis., Bd. 29, No. 533. RVB Archives.
64. Schulz, *Hanka Houskova*, p. 14.
65. Ibid.
66. Pro-Jag 335, No. 19a, p. 165. Wo 235/531. Public Records Office.
67. Krokowski and Voigt, pp. 266-267.

Chapter 4

1. This incident is put together primarily from the report by a Polish (non-Jehovah's Witness) prisoner, Stanislawa Schöneman-Luniewska, in Ursula Winska, *"Zwyciezyly Wartosci"—Die Werte siegten: Erinnerung an Ravensbrück"* (1985), pp. 136-137.
2. Michael Kater, "Die ernsten Bibelforscher im Dritten Reich, *Vierteljahreshefte für Zeitgeschichte*, Vol. 17 (April 1969), pp. 181-218.
3. Claus Füllberg-Stolberg, "Bedrängt, aber nicht völlig eingeengt—Verfolgt, aber nicht verlassen—Gertrud Pötzinger, Zeugin Jehovahs" (1994), pp. 321-323.
4. Hajkova, p. 26.
5. Buber-Neumann, *Als Gefangene bei Stalin und Hitler*, pp. 205-207.
6. Jack Morrison, "Women of Ravensbrück" (1994), n.p.
7. Charlotte Gross, "Eine Widerstandsaktion der Bibel-forscherinnen," in Bromberger et al., *Schwestern, vergesst uns nicht* (1988), p. 40.
8. Buber-Neumann, *Milena*, pp. 169-170.
9. Buber-Neumann, *Als Gefangene bei Stalin und Hitler*, pp. 197-202.
10. Berta Hartmann, RA Erlebnis., Bd. 25, No. 332. RVB Archives.
11. Müller, pp. 27-28.
12. Bericht von Elisabeth Lynhard, RA Erlebnis., Bd. 17, No. 55. RVB Archives.
13. Wanda Radwanska, RA Erlebnis., Bd. 31, No. 577. RVB Archives.
14. Buber-Neumann, *Als Gefangene bei Stalin und Hitler*, pp. 208-210.
15. Salvesen, pp. 84-91; Annalise Urbye, *Himmlers 100,000 Frauen* (1946), pp. 44-48.
16. Interview with Gertrud Pötzinger, in Füllberg-Stollberg, p. 330.
17. Buber-Neumann, *Als Gefangene bei Stalin und Hitler*, p. 200.
18. Interview with Gertrud Pötzinger, in Füllberg-Stollberg, pp. 331-332.

Chapter 5

1. Karl Schleunes, *The Twisted Road to Auschwitz: Nazi Policy Toward German Jews, 1933-1939* (1972), p. 38.
2. Paul Kosok, *Modern Germany: A Study of Conflicting Loyalties* (1933), p. 252.
3. Schleunes, p. 38.
4. See Yisrael Gutman, "On the Character of Nazi Anti-Semitism," in *Anti-Semitism through the Ages* (1988), pp. 354-363.
5. Friedlander, *The Origins of Nazi Genocide: From Euthanasia to the Final Solution* (1995), pp. 17-20.
6. For a recent concise treatment of the issues surrounding anti-Semitism in Weimar Germany, see Omer Bartov, "Defining Enemies, Making Victims: Germans, Jews, and the Holocaust," *American Historical Review*, vol. 103, no. 3 (June 1998), pp. 776-783.
7. Schleunes, pp. 62-91.
8. Marion A. Kaplan, *Between Dignity and Despair: Jewish Life in Nazi Germany* (1998), pp. 21-22.
9. Yehuda Bauer, *A History of the Holocaust* (1982), pp. 100-101.
10. Ibid., pp. 102-103.
11. Friedlander, *Origins of Nazi Genocide*, pp. 246-247. In 1933, there were 385 of these children, according to the government's figures.
12. Kaplan, pp. 72-73; Rita Steinhardt Botwinick, *A History of the Holocaust* (1996), pp. 119-120.
13. Kaplan, pp. 25-28, 54-59.
14. Ibid., pp. 74-80, 147-159.
15. Bauer, p. 107.
16. Leni Yahil, *The Holocaust: The Fate of European Jewry, 1932-1945* (1990), p. 108.
17. Trude Maurer, "Abschiebung und Attentat: Die Ausweisung der polnischen Juden und der Vorwand für die 'Kristallnacht'" (1988), pp. 52-73.
18. Uwe Dietrich Adam, "Wie spontan war der Pogrom?" (1988), pp. 74-80.
19. Yahil, pp. 110-113; Botwinick, pp. 121-123; Bauer, pp. 108-109.
20. David Bankier, *The Germans and the Final Solution* (1992), pp. 86-87.
21. Kaplan, pp. 145-151.
22. Bauer, p. 107.
23. Schleunes, p. 242.
24. Hanna Sturm, *Lebensgeschichte einer Arbeiterin* (1982), p. 270.
25. RA II/4-6, Gefangenen-Stärkemeldungen. RVB Archives.
26. See Judith Buber Agassi, "Opfer und Überlebende — die jüdischen Häftlinge des Frauenkonzentrationslager Ravensbrück — eine historische und soziologische Studie," Paper presented at the Ravensbrück Kolloquium, Oct. 1996. Agassi has divided this into four periods, rather than three, as I have done.
27. Ibid., pp. 143-149, 266-280.
28. Jack Morrison, "Guide to the Museum at the Ravensbrück Memorial." Exhibit 4-d.
29. Henry Friedlander, *The Origins of Nazi Genocide* (1995), pp. 88-96.
30. Ibid., pp. 144-147.
31. Ibid., p. 284.
32. Hilde Boy-Brandt, RA Erlebnis. Bd. 15, No. 7, RVB Archives.
33. Wanda Symonowicz, ed., *Beyond Human Endurance* (1970), p. 71.
34. See the memoir of Esther Bejarano, a German Jew who was sent from Auschwitz to Ravensbrück in October 1943. Bejarano, *"Man nannte mich Krümel"* (1991), pp. 25-26.
35. Frieda Jaffe, interview (1982). Holocaust Documentation & Education Center

(Miami).
36. Milton, pp. 12-13.
37. Katzenmaier, p. 73; Müller, pp. 73-75.
38. Ada Feingold-Nelson, interview (1995). Holocaust Documentation & Education Center (Miami).
39. Hajkova, pp. 27-28.
40. Luise Gotthelf, interview (1997). Holocaust Documentation & Education Center (Miami).
41. Buber-Neumann, *Als Gefangene bei Stalin und Hitler*, pp. 246-249.
42. RA Erlebnis., Bd. 17, No. 72. RVB Archives.
43. Boy-Brandt, RA Erlebnis., Bd. 15, No. 17. RVB Archives.
44. Tillion, p. 36.
45. Hajkova, p. 252.
46. Bernhard Strebel, "Sabotage ist wie Wein: Selbstbehauptung, Solidarität und Widerstand im FKL Ravensbrück" (1994), p. 182.
47. RAII/4-6. Gefangenen-Stärkemeldungen. RVB Archives.
48. Bernhard Strebel, "'Die Lagergesellschaft': Aspekte der Häftlingshierarchie und Gruppenbildung in Ravensbrück" (1994), p. 82.
49. Jacobeit and Brümann-Güdter, eds., *Ravensbrückerinnen*, p. 152.
50. Alexandra Gorko, interview (1985). Gratz College Holocaust Oral History Archive.
51. Faye Eckhaus, interview. Holocaust Documentation & Education Center (Miami).
52. Yvonne Useldinger, "Aus meinem Tagebuch." RA Erlebnis., Bd. 27, No. 475. RVB Archives.

Chapter 6

1. Kiedrzynska, RA Erlebnis., Bd. 42, No. 1037. RVB Archives.
2. Katzenmaier, pp. 24-27.
3. Andreas Pflock, "Bitteschön, und jetzt können Sie mich verhaften" (1994), p. 292.
4. Hans Hesse, "Und am Anfang War Moringen....", paper presented at the Kolloquium: "Neuere Forschungen zur Geschichte des Frauenkonzentrationslagers Ravensbrück," Oct. 1996.
5. Bericht von Rene Gaston Ferderer, RA Erlebnis., Bd. 20, No. 176. RVB Archives.
6. Müller, p. 37.
7. Buchmann, *Die Frauen von Ravensbrück* (1959), p. 121.
8. Arndt, pp. 94-95.
9. Sigrid Jacobeit, "Lisa Ullbrich, 'Es begann schon in Odessa'", in Jacobeit and Thomas-Heinrich, *Kreuzweg Ravensbrück* (1987), pp. 212-216.
10. Liselotte Thomas-Heinrich, "Olga Körner: 'Lebenslauf mit Lücken,'" in Jacobeit and Thomas-Heinrich, *Kreuzweg Ravensbrück*, pp. 101-110.
11. Liselotte Thomas-Heinrich, "Margarete Jung: In einer kleinen Druckerei," in Jacobeit and Thomas-Heinrich, *Kreuzweg Ravensbrück*, pp. 74-78.
12. Müller, p. 144.
13. Jacquemotte-Thonnart, pp. 175-177.
14. Müller, pp. 71-72.
15. Ibid., p. 42.
16. Ibid., pp. 33-34.

17. Jan Cerná, *Kafka's Milena* (1993), p. 166.
18. Buber-Neumann, *Als Gefangene bei Stalin und Hitler*, pp. 176-179.
19. Anise Postel-Vinay, "A Young Frenchwoman's Wartime Experiences" (1985), p. 226.
20. Martin Broszat, "The Concentration Camps 1933-1945" (1965), pp. 483-486.
21. Müller, p. 33.
22. Maurel, pp. 6-7.
23. Vermehren, pp. 70-71; Bruha, pp. 136-138; Müller, pp. 32-33.
24. Rita Sprengel, RA Erlebnis., Bd. 42, No. 991. RVB Archives.
25. Català, p. 28.
26. Jacobeit and Brümann-Güdter, eds., *Ravensbrückerinnen* (1995), pp. 93-94.
27. Marette, pp. 13-23; Maurel, pp. xiii-xiv; Roux, pp. 17-35.
28. Tillion, pp. 91-92; Hajkova, pp. 22-23; Postel-Vinay, pp. 228-229.
29. Müller, pp. 61-62.
30. Grete Stabey, RA Erlebnis., Bd. 17, No. 63. RVB Archives.
31. Brief an A. Alexandrowna von Olowjannikowa, RA Erlebnis., Bd. 28, No. 492. RVB Archives.
32. Müller, pp. 138-145.
33. M. Wiedmaier, RA Erlebnis., Bd. 34, No. 680. RVB Archives.
34. Boy-Brandt, RA Erlebnis., Bd. 15, No.17. RVB Archives.
35. Sandoe, pp. 99-100.
36. Müller, pp. 95-96.
37. Salvesen, *Forgive—But Do Not Forget* (1958), passim.
38. Gemma La Guardia Gluck, *My Story* (1961), passim. The quote is from p. 40.
39. Margaret Rossiter, *Women in the Resistance* (1986), pp. 204-210.
40. Brandt, RA Erlebnis., Bd. 39, No. 892. RVB Archives.
41. Hajkova, p. 204.
42. Gluck, pp. 53-54.
43. Müller, pp. 131-133.
44. Bericht Rosa Thälmanns, RA Erlebnis., Bd. 25, No. 345. RVB Archives; see also Müller, pp. 128-129.

Chapter 7

1. Wanda Kiedrzynska, "Das Frauenkonzentrationslager Ravensbrück" (1960), p. 84.
2. Annelise and Gertrud Phillip, RA Erlebnis., Bd. 17, No. 72. RVB Archives.
3. Tillion, p. 33.
4. R. L. Ferdonnet-Gay, RA Erlebnis., Bd. 41, No. 978. RVB Archives.
5. Rosa Deutsch, Hungarian Jewish survivor of Ravensbrück, interview by the author (1994); see also *Montluc-Ravensbrück, Record of Imprisonment* (1946), p. 8.
6. Buber-Neumann, *Als Gefangene bei Stalin und Hitler*, pp. 174-177; Vermehren, p. 69.
7. Trude Mittag, RA Erlebnis., Bd., 40, No. 930. RVB Archives.
8. Käte Roth and Hanna Conrad, RA Erlebnis, Bd. 40, No. 934, RVB Archives.
9. Buber-Neumann, *Als Gegangene bei Stalin und Hitler*, p. 295.
10. Poltawska, p. 137.
11. On the nasty behavior of the Ukrainians, see also Giuliana Tedeschi, *There Is a Place on Earth* (1992), p. 206; Tillion, pp. 27-30; Denise Dufournier, *Ravensbrück—The Women's Camp of Death* (1948), p. 56.

12. Marette, p. 175.
13. Maurel, pp. 20-21.
14. Interview with Alexandra Gorko (1985), Gratz College Holocaust Oral History Archive.
15. Bernstein, pp. 240-241.
16. Maurel, p. 21.
17. Roux, pp. 217-222.
18. Urbye, p. 15.
19. Buber-Neumann, *Als Gefangene bei Stalin und Hitler*, p. 270.
20. RA Erlebnis., Bd. 39, No. 879. RVB Archives.
21. Salvesen, p. 153.
22. Jacquemotte-Thonnart, pp. 189-190.
23. Hajkova, p. 262.
24. Rolfi, RA Erlebnis., Bd. 26, No. 399. RVB Archives.
25. Report of Johanne Hansen, RA Erlebnis., Bd. 18, No. 75. RVB Archives.
26. Sandoe, pp. 116-117.
27. Winska, pp. 2-4.
28. Ursula Winska sent a questionnaire to 400 known Polish survivors of Ravensbrück in 1978. She got 158 responses, many quite detailed, and all of them containing information on education, vocation, etc. See also Hajkova, pp. 197-198.
29. Wanda Kiedrzynska, "Introduction," in Wanda Symonowicz, ed., *Beyond Human Endurance* (1970), p. 8.
30. Vermehren, p. 79.
31. Tillion, p. 28.
32. Hajkova, p. 197.
33. Ibid., p. 198.
34. Tillion, p. 28.
35. Testimony of Marta Baranowska and Josefa Karaskiewicz-Kaczmarck, in Winska, pp. 95-96, 116. Another discussion of Boedeker's human side is in Vermehren, pp. 60-61.
36. Salvesen, p. 79.
37. Tillion, p. 28.
38. Hajkova, pp. 73-75; Winska, p. 357.
39. Tillion, p. 28.
40. See Winska, especially pp. 86-87, 97-98.
41. Irmtraud Heike and Bernhard Strebel, "Häftlingsselbstverwaltung und Funktionshäftlinge im KZ Ravensbrück" (1994), p. 96.
42. R. L. Ferdonnet, RA Erlebnis., Bd. 41, No. 978. RVB Archives; actually, I have learned of one French block senior, at the Holleischen subcamp. See Roux, p. 114.
43. Ingo Siegner, "Auf der Suche nach der Wahrheit: Germaine Tillion, eine Französin in Ravensbrück" (1994), p. 269.
44. Dufournier, p. 11.
45. *Les Françaises à Ravensbrück*, pp. 90-91.
46. Tillion, pp. 33-37.
47. Siegner, p. 269; a good example of upper-class representation is Odette Fabius, *Sonnenaufgang über der Hölle* (1997), passim.
48. Roux, pp. 35-36; Maurel, p. xiii; *Montluc-Ravensbrück*, p. 5.
49. Hajkova, p. 23.
50. *Les Françaises à Ravensbrück*, p. 239.
51. Dunya Breur, *Ich lebe, weil du dich erinnerst* (1997), p. 31.
52. Siegner, pp. 269-270.
53. Kocwa, p. 14.

54. Ibid., pp. 123-129.
55. Siegner, p. 270.
56. Fabius, p. 108.
57. Maurel, p. 54.
58. Marette, pp. 203-204.
59. *Les Françaises à Ravensbrück*, pp. 255-260.
60. Ibid., pp. 240-241; Roux, pp. 143-145.
61. *Les Françaises à Ravensbrück*, pp. 243-245.
62. Siegner, pp. 273-274.
63. Sandoe, p. 78.
64. Tillion, p. 24.

Chapter 8

1. Kogon, *The Theory and Practice of Hell: The German Concentration Camps and the System Behind Them* (1950), p. 56.
2. Ibid., pp. 56-58.
3. Testimony of Marta Baranowska, in Winska, pp. 295-297.
4. Testimony of Wanda Radwanska, RA Erlebnis., Bd. 31, No. 577. RVB Archives.
5. Fabius, p. 101.
6. Report of Wanda Kowalska, RA Erlebnis., Bd. 31, No. 579. RVB Archives.
7. Marette, pp. 140-141.
8. Bruha, p. 95. Only one of these Block Books in any complete form has been found, the Book for Block 4. RA II, 4-6. RVB Archives.
9. Simone Lahaye, *Libre parmi les morts, Ravensbrück 1942-1945* (1983), pp. 75-76.
10. Sandoe, pp. 99-100.
11. Ibid., p. 68.
12. Eva Busch, *Und Trotzdem: Eine Biographie* (1991), p. 144. Busch served as camp runner for some time; see also Müller, p. 31.
13. Buber-Neumann, *Milena*, p. 13.
14. Maurel, p. 20.
15. Buber-Neumann, *Als Gefangene bei Stalin und Hitler*, pp. 177-178.
16. Maurel, p. 19.
17. Müller, p. 30.
18. Interview with Denise Clark, in Gill, p. 327; see also Sandoe, pp. 85-87.
19. Katzenmaier, pp. 79-84.
20. See the testimony of Waleria Kowalski, RA Erlebnis., Bd. 31, No. 579. RVB Archives.
21. *Montluc-Ravensbrück*, p. 12.
22. Bettina Durrer, "Ein Verfolgte als Täterin? Zur Geschichte der Blockälteste Carmen Maria Mory" (1997), pp. 86-93.
23. Testimony of Marta Wesolowska-Szarzynska, in Winska, pp. 305-306.
24. Testimony of Stanislawa Schoenmann-Luniewska, in Winska, p. 57.
25. Testimony of Janina Zbik-Fudalej, in Winska, pp. 310-311.
26. Bruha, pp. 136-137.
27. Müller, pp. 32-33; Hajkova, pp. 19-20; Busch, p. 132.
28. Bruha, pp. 137-138.
29. Winska, pp. 329-330.
30. Hajkova, p. 45.
31. Delbo, pp. 193-194.

32. Helen Ernst, RA Erlebnis,. Bd. 40, No. 931. RVB Archives.
33. Elisabeth Lynhard, RA Erlebnis., Bd. 34, No. 634. RVB Archives.
34. Hajkova, p. 46.
35. Marette, pp. 131-132.
36. Helen Ernst, RA Erlebnis., Bd. 40, No. 931. RVB Archives.
37. Hajkova, p. 47.
38. Winska, pp. 293-317; Müller, pp. 31-33; Bruha, pp. 136-138.
39. Vermehren, p. 71.
40. Ernst, RA Erlebnis., Bd. 40, No. 931. RVB Archives.
41. Hansche, RA Erlebnis. Bd. 42, No. 1040. RVB Archives.

Chapter 9

1. Bruha, p. 95.
2. Jacquemotte-Thonnart, p. 180.
3. Vermehren, p. 83.
4. Müller, p. 26.
5. Müller, pp. 25-29; Vermehren, pp. 82-84.
6. Buber-Neumann, *Als Gefangene bei Stalin und Hitler,* p. 201.
7. Testimony of Janina Debska, in Winska, p. 138.
8. Poltawska, p. 42.
9. Sandoe, p. 72.
10. Katzenmaier, pp. 73-75; Tillion, pp. 14-16. Each spent considerable time as an Available.
11. Hajkova, pp. 71-72.
12. Buber-Neumann, *Als Gefangene bei Stalin und Hitler,* p. 181.
13. Katzenmaier, p. 71.
14. Vermehren, p. 85.
15. Testimony of Stanislawa Mlodkowska-Bielawska, in Symonowicz, ed., *Beyond Human Endurance* (1970), p. 34; Hajkova, pp. 14-15.
16. Maurel, p. 29.
17. Barbara Bricks, interview (1982). Holocaust Documentation & Education Center (Miami).
18. Katzenmaier, p. 71.
19. Poltawska, p. 71.
20. Hajkova, p. 126.
21. Katzenmaier, p. 98.
22. Poltawska, p. 54.
23. Halina Nelken, *Freiheit will ich noch erleben. Krakauer Tagebuch* (1996), p. 311.
24. Katzenmaier, p. 105.
25. Müller, p. 187.
26. Maurel, p. 102.
27. Müller, pp. 26-29; Katzenmaier, p. 98.
28. Anne-Katrin Ebert, *Dr. Hildegard Hansche, 1896-1992* (1996), p. 59.
29. Hajkova, p. 15.
30. Kocwa, p. 51.
31. Ibid., p. 16.
32. Buber-Neumann, *Als Gefangene bei Stalin und Hitler*, pp. 183-184; Müller, p. 36.

33. Müller, pp. 36-67.
34. Marette, pp. 159-161.
35. Hajkova, pp. 268.
36. Müller, p. 39.
37. Astral Blumensaadt-Pedersen, RA Erlebnis., Bd. 41, No. 968. RVB Archives.
38. Katzenmaier, pp. 131-132.
39. Testimony of Janina Debska, in Winska, pp. 144-146.
40. Fabius, p. 114.
41. Jacquemotte-Thonnart, p. 179.
42. Dufournier, p.69.
43. Hajkova, pp. 268-278.
44. Kocwa, pp. 51-52.
45. *Les Françaises à Ravensbrück*, p. 98.
46. Buchmann, *Die Frauen von Ravensbrück*, p. 49.
47. Vermehren, p. 85.
48. Ebert, p. 58.
49. Interview with Denise Clark, in Gill, p. 328.
50. Winska, pp. 430-431.
51. Letter from Jeanette van der Berg to Familie Lange in Mülhausen. Date undecipherable. RA II/6-1-66. RVB Archives.
52. Elisabeth Lynhard, RA Erlebnis., Bd. 17, No. 55. RVB Archives.
53. Gluck, pp. 57-59.
54. Sandoe, p. 70.
55. Hajkova, p. 62.
56. Maurel, pp. 13-15.
57. Bruha, p. 99.
58. Müller, p. 39.
59. Maurel, pp. 16-17.
60. See the descriptions by Elisabeth Lynhard, RA Erlebnis., Bd. 34, No. 634, and R.L. Ferdonnet-Gay, RA Erlebnis., Bd. 41, No. 978. RVB Archives.
61. Hajkova, p. 21; see also Buber-Neumann, *Milena*, p. 168; Erika Buchmann, interviewed in Zimmer, *Ravensbrücker Ballade*, p. 183.

Chapter 10

1. Interview with Denise Clark, in Gill, p. 328.
2. Zimmer, p. 185; Miriam Guttmann, interview (1990). Holocaust Documentation & Education Center (Miami).
3. Kupferberg, interview (1988), Gratz College Holocaust Oral History Archive.
4. Regina Kahn, interview (1990). Holocaust Documentation & Education Center (Miami).
5. Vera Unverzagt, "Das soll sich nicht wiederholen: weibliche Kriegsgefangene der Roten Armee im KZ Ravensbrück" (1994), p. 310.
6. Erika Kounio-Amariglio, *Damit es die ganze Welt erfährt. Von Salonika nach Auschwitz und Zurück, 1926-1996* (1996), pp. 118-119.
7. Winska, pp. 74-96.
8. Wanda Buzowska, in Winska, p. 81.
9. Miroslawa Grupinska, in Winska, p. 93.
10. See the testimony of Jozefa Karaskiewicz-Kaczmarck, in Winska, pp. 95-96. She discusses Janina Kiszken-Kalicka, who possessed all these virtues.
11. Ibid.

12. Wanda Wojtasik-Poltawska, in Winska, p. 90.
13. Urzula Wyrwicz-Broniatowska, in Winska, p. 94.
14. Urzula Winska, in Winska, p. 94.
15. Matusiak, in Winska, p. 93.
16. Jozefa Karaskiewicz-Kaczmarck, in Winska, pp. 95-96.
17. George Gibian, "Who was Milena?" in Jana Cerná, *Kafka's Milena* (1993), p. 3.
18. Buber-Neumann, *Milena,* p. 4.
19. Ibid., passim.
20. Jacobeit and Brümann-Güdter, eds., *Ravensbrückerinnen* (1995), pp. 135-138; Margaret Rossiter, *Women in the Resistance* (1986), pp. 138-139.
21. Bernstein, pp. 199-252.
22. Clara Rupp, RA Erlebnis. Bd. 25, No. 361. RVB Archives.
23. There is a very interesting comparison to be made with a group of orthodox Jewish women at the Plaszow labor camp in Poland. In comparison, the Polish women at Ravensbrück were not as exclusive, but then they didn't have the cohesiveness of the Jewish group, either. Judith Tydor Baumel, "Social Interaction Among Jewish Women in Crisis during the Holocaust: A Case Study" (1995), pp. 64-84.
24. Roux, pp. 72-73.
25. Maurel, p. 22.
26. Marette, p. 196.
27. Postel-Vinay, p. 226.
28. Maurel, p. 90.
29. Buber-Neumann, *Milena,* pp. 40-41.
30. Vermehren, pp. 51-52.
31. Buchmann, "Brief an eine berliner Reporterin," pp. 38-39.
32. Marette, p. 175.
33. Poltawska, pp. 57-58.
34. Schoppmann, pp. 15-23.
35. Richard Plant, *The Pink Triangle: The Nazi War Against Homosexuals* (1986), pp. 30, 114.
36. Gluck, pp. 58-59.
37. Sandoe, pp. 88-89.
38. Denise Clark, in Gill, p. 327.
39. Dufournier, pp. 66-69.
40. Fabius, p. 116.
41. David Ward and Gene Kassebaum, *Women's Prison: Sex and Social Structure* (1965), pp. 80-200; see also Allison Sesnon, producer, "Women Doing Time," (1996). The film concerns the Louisiana Correctional Institution for Women.

Chapter 11

1. Letter of April 1944 from Ida van Pachterbeké sent to M. & Mme. Struy in Brussels. RA II 6-1-6. RVB Archives.
2. Katzenmaier, p. 72.
3. Buber-Neumann, *Als Gefangene bei Stalin und Hitler,* p. 183.
4. Elisabeth Lynhard, RA Erlebnis., Bd. 17, No. 55. RVB Archives.
5. This is based on the letters of Paula Lohagen. Some of her letters went well beyond the thirty lines, but she was, after all, a veteran "old Political." Briefe von Paula Lohagen aus dem KZ. RA Erlebnis., Bd. 22, No. 229. RVB Archives.
6. Letter of Nov. 1941 from Ludwika Pretrzak to Frau Agnes Pretrzak. Pretrzak

Sammlung. RA II/6-1 (Briefe und Postkarten). RVB Archives.
7. See the 4 letters from Tone Reiersen from 9.43 to 8.44. RA II/6-1-28. RVB Archives.
8. Letter of October 1942. L. Pretrzak to Fr. Agnes Pretrzak, Pretrzak Sammlung. RA II 6-1. RVB Archives.
9. Letter of April 1944 from J. Kerilis to Mme. Kerilis. RA II/6-1-48 (Briefe und Postkarten). RVB Archives.
10. Letter of Dec. 1941 from Wanda Kozdrun. RA II/6-1-23. RVB Archives.
11. Letter of 14 April 1944 from Peder Sivertsen (Oldereide, Norway) to Nanna Sivertsen. RA II/6-1-29. RVB Archives.
12. Paula Lohagen, Letter of March 1941. RA Erlebnis., Bd. 22, No. 229 (Briefe und Postkarten). RVB Archives.
13. Lohagen, Letter of June 1942. Ibid.
14. Lohagen, Letter of November 1942. Ibid.
15. Müller, p. 40.
16. Letter of 31 March 1945. RA II/6-1-40. RVB Archives.
17. Briefe und Berichte von Rosa Menzer. RA Erlebnis., Bd. 26, No. 405. RVB Archives.
18. Morrison, "Guide to the Museum at the Ravensbrück Memorial." Exhibit 4d.
19. Testimony of Krystyna Czyz-Wilgat, in Symonowicz, ed., *Beyond Human Endurance*, pp. 62-67.
20. Winska, pp. 346-347.
21. Testimony of Willy and Hildegard Dockhorn, RA Erlebnis., Bd. 20, No. 187. RVB Archives.
22. Winska, p. 355.
23. Bejarano, p. 26.
24. Hajkova, pp. 127-129.
25. Letter of Nov. 1942 from Ludwika Pretrzak to Frau Agnes Pretrzak. Pretrzak Sammlungen, RA II/6-1. RVB Archives.
26. Gluck, p. 32.
27. Müller, p. 54.
28. Schreiben vom Chef der Amtsgruppe B, SS Gruppenführer Glücks an die Abwehrbeauftragten über alle Lagerkommandanten. This redirected Pohl's order of 24 July 1944. RA Erlebnis., Bd. 20, No. 182. RVB Archives.
29. Elisabeth Lynhard. RA Erlebnis., Bd. 34, No. 634. RVB Archives.
30. Katzenmaier, pp. 84-85.
31. Müller, p. 55; Hajkova, p. 129.
32. Testimony of Krystyna Czyz-Wilgat, in Symonowicz, ed., *Beyond Human Endurance,* p. 71.
33. Müller, pp. 125-127.
34. Testimony of Zenobia Dubinska, in Winska, p. 198.
35. Winska, pp. 199-200.
36. Jacquemotte-Thonnart, p. 182.
37. Roux, p. 121.
38. Rita Sprengel, RA Erlebnis., Bd. 34, No. 648. RVB Archives.
39. E. Sommer, RA Erlebnis., Bd. 39, No. 886. RVB Archives.
40. Helen Ernst, RA Erlebnis., Bd. 40, No. 931. RVB Archives.
41. Sandoe, p. 68.
42. Maurel, pp. 1-15.
43. Jacquemotte-Thonnart, p. 183.
44. Aus dem Tagebuch von Lidia Rolfi, RA Erlebnis., Bd. 26, No. 399. RVB Archives.
45. Buber-Newmann, *Milena,* pp. 40-41.
46. Delbo, p. 187.

47. See the condemning Erlebnisberichte by Anneliese and Gertrud Phillip. RA Erlebnis., Bd. 17, No. 72. RVB Archives.
48. Urbye, pp. 9-10.
49. Hajkova, pp 75-76.
50. Maurel, p. XIV.
51. Elisabeth Lynhard, RA Erlebnis., Bd. 34, No. 634, RVB Archives.
52. Lynhard, Ibid.
53. Buber-Neumann, *Als Gefangene bei Stalin und Hitler,* pp. 182-183.
54. Elisabeth Lynhard, RA Erlebnis., Bd. 17, No. 55. RVB Archives.
55. Hajkova, p. 127.
56. Busch, *Und Trotzdem* (1991), p. 147.

Chapter 12

1. Christa Schulz, ed., *Der Wind weht weinend über die Ebene* (1991), pp. 8-9. The English translations are my own.
2. Ibid., p. 16.
3. Bruha, p. 111.
4. Schulz, *Der Wind weht weinend über die Ebene,* pp. 21-22.
5. Ibid., p. 40.
6. The poem (in German) is prominently displayed on a wall in the Cell Building Museum at Ravensbrück. Morrison, "Guide to the Cell Building at the Ravensbrück Memorial." English translation by the author.
7. Dufournier, pp. 86-91.
8. Quoted in Monika Herzog, *Ravensbrücker Zeichnungen* (1993), n.p.
9. Buber-Neumann, *Milena,* p. 161.
10. Herzog, *Ravensbrücker Zeichnungen,* n.p.
11. Yvonne Useldinger, "Aus meinem Tagebuch." RA Erlebnis., Bd. 27, No. 475. RVB Archives.
12. Telephone conversation with Dunya Breur of 24 July 1998; See also Breur, *Ich lebe, weil du dich erinnerst* (1997), pp. 9-74; Herzog, *Ravensbrücker Zeichnungen,* n.p.
13. Herzog, *Ravensbrücker Zeichnungen,* n.p.
14. Ibid.
15. Busch, p. 149; Herbermann, pp. 119-120.
16. Fabius, p. 106.
17. Directive from *Oberaufseherin* Mandel, "An alle Blocks" of 2 March 1944. Mss. RG-04.006M, Reel 20. USHMM Archives.
18. Ibid.
19. Renee Salska and Joanna Kukulska, in Winska, p. 191.
20. Herbermann, pp. 116-117.
21. Kocwa, p. 20.
22. Busch, p. 148.
23. "Die Jugoslawinnen in Ravensbrück," RA Erlebnis., Bd. 41, No. 977. RVB Archives.
24. Wanda Kiedrzynska, *Ravensbrück Kobiecy Oboz Koncentracyjny* (1961), p. 240.
25. Susanne Minhoff, "Ein Symbol der menschliche Würde: Kunst und Kultur im KZ Ravensbrück" (1994), p. 212.
26. Jacquemotte-Thonnart, p. 212.
27. A number of the reports in the *Erlebnisberichte* are simply testimonies by Slovak, Yugoslav, Ukrainian, etc., survivors, proclaiming how fervently they

upheld each other and the national culture. See, for example, Mara Cepic, "Die Jugoslavinnen in Ravensbrück," RA Erlebnis., Bd. 41, No. 977. RVB Archives. See also Roux, pp. 199-201; Sandoe, p. 82; Hajkova, p. 268; Maurel, pp. 74-77.

28. Müller, p. 39.
29. Gluck, p. 36.
30. Sprengel, RA Erlebnis., Bd. 34, No. 648. RVB Archives; Jacobeit and Thomas-Heinrich, *Kreuzweg Ravensbrück*, ch. 15.
31. Kiedrzynska, *Ravensbrück Kobiecy Oboz Koncentracyjny*, p. 250.
32. Vermehren, p. 79.
33. In the 1978 survey-questionnaire sent by Ursula Winska to 400 Ravensbrück survivors, there were 158 responses. Of these, 5 were professors or doctors, 33 were teachers, 40 were students (at the time of incarceration).
34. Maria Jankowska-Gabryel and Krystyna Zaremba, in Winska, pp. 64-67.
35. Wanda Wojtasik-Poltawska, in Winska, pp. 205-210; Kiedrzynska, *Ravensbrück Kobiecy Oboz Koncentracyjny,* p. 249.
36. Kiedrzynska, *Ravensbrück Kobiecy Oboz Koncentracyjny*, pp. 247-249.
37. Ibid., p. 241.
38. Kiedrzysnka, "Introduction," in Symonowicz, ed., *Beyond Human Endurance*, p. 13.
39. Jacobeit and Brümann-Güdter, eds., *Ravensbrückerinnen*, p. 64.

Chapter 13

1. Hajkova, pp. 63-65.
2. Jacquemotte-Thonnart, p. 179; Maurel, p. 22.
3. Roux, p. 73.
4. Marette, p. 196.
5. Sandoe, p. 100.
6. RA Erlebnis., Bd. 15, No. 9, RVB Archives.
7. Katzenmaier, p. 68.
8. Sandoe, pp. 98-101.
9. RA Erlebnis., Bd. 15, No. 9, RVB Archives; Sandoe, pp. 100-101.
10. Marina Plura, RA Erlebnis., Bd. 21, No. 210, RVB Archives.
11. Hadina Raczyaska and Waclawa Wojcik. RA Erlebnis., Bd. 31, No. 3. RVB Archives.
12. Poltawska, pp. 137, 139.
13. R. L. Ferdonnet-Gay, RA Erlebnis., Bd. 41, No. 978. RVB Archives.
14. Brief an A. Alexandrowna von Olowjannikowa, dated 1 Feb. 1957. RA Erlebnis., Bd. 28, No. 492. RVB Archives.
15. Marette, p. 61.
16. See the testimony of the following women: Jacqueline Bernard, Barbara Bricks, Margaret Friedman. Holocaust Documentation & Education Center (Miami).
17. Gruber-Lieblich, p. 49.
18. Katzenmaier, p. 67.
19. Janet Anschütz, Kerstin Meier, Sanja Obajdin, "...Dieses leeren Gefühl und die Blicke der Anderen...." (1994), pp. 127-128.
20. Katzenmaier, p. 67.
21. Maurel, p. 39.
22. Bernstein, pp. 212-213.
23. Vermehren, p. 71.

24. Katzenmaier, p. 67; Müller, p. 183.
25. Trude Mittag, RA Erlebnis., Bd. 40, No. 930. RVB Archives.
26. Sandoe, p. 74.
27. Maurel, p. 39.
28. Müller, pp. 19-20; Maria Plura, RA Erlebnis., Bd. 21, No. 210, RVB Archives.
29. Testimony of Conchita Ramos, a prisoner at the Oberschönweide (Berlin) sub-camp, in Català, p. 129.
30. Marette, pp. 205-206.
31. Sandoe, pp. 105-106.
32. Maurel, p. XV.
33. Tillion, pp. 23-24.
34. Testimony of Jozefa Karaskiewicz-Kaczmarek, in Winska, p. 95.
35. Maurel, p. 92.
36. Report of 30 April 1945 from Glen Whisler. Pro FO371/51193. Public Record Office.
37. Heike Krokowski & Bianca Voigt, "Das Schicksal von Wanda P" (1994) pp. 254-267.
38. This comment was made by E.F. in a van with a small group of survivors traveling between Ravensbrück and the former subcamp at Genshagen on 8 October 1994.
39. Sandoe, p. 72.
40. Interview with Hardy Kupferberg (1988), Gratz College Holocaust Oral History Archive (3-1-44.)
41. Sigrid Jacobeit, ed., "Ich grüsse Euch als freier Mensch" (1995), passim.
42. Montluc-Ravensbrück, p. 8.
43. JAG 335 (Ravensbrück IV Case) PRO Ref. No. WO235/531-532. pp. 76-86. Public Record Office; Buber-Neumann, Milena, pp. 182-183.
44. Buber-Neumann, Milena, pp. 40-41.
45. Schulz, "Weibliche Häftlinge aus Ravensbrück in Bordellen der Männerkonzentrationslager" (1994), p. 139.

Chapter 14

1. See the "Letter of Hohberg to Pohl, 10 April 1943, submitting for Himmler a survey of capital and turnover of economic enterprises of WVHA, with a short description of the firms." Trials of War Criminals Before the Nuernberg Military Tribunals, Vol. 5 (1950), pp. 528-536.
2. Enno George, Die wirtschaftliche Unternehmungen der SS (1963), pp. 66-69.
3. Lotte Zumpe, "Die Textilbetriebe der SS im KZ Ravensbrück," Jahrbuch für Wirtschaftsgeschichte (1969), p. 21.
4. Ibid., pp. 27-28; Bericht von Hilde Fischer, Helen Potetzt und Rosa Jochmaun. RA Erlebnis., Bd. 16, No. 31. RVB Archives.
5. Buber-Neumann, Als Gefangene bei Stalin und Hitler, pp. 274-277.
6. Stanislawa Mlodkowska-Bielawska, in Symonowicz, ed., Beyond Human Endurance, p. 34.
7. Alfredine Nenninger, in Morrison, "Guide to the Museum at the Ravensbrück Memorial," 7b.
8. E. Lynhard, RA Erlebnis., Bd. 34, No. 634. RVB Archives; see the discussion of Premiums by Defendant Karl Sommer in Trials of War Criminals Before the Nuernberg Military Tribunals, vol. 5, pp. 597-600.
9. Prämienliste von 3 Feb. 1945. RA Erlebnis., Bd. 44, no number. RVB Archives.

10. Lotte Zumpe, "Arbeitsbedingungen und Arbeitsergebnisse in den Textilbetrieben des SS im KZ Ravensbrück," *Jahrbuch für Wirtschaftsgeschichte* (1969), pp. 15-16.
11. Buber-Neumann, *Als Gefangene bei Stalin und Hitler*, p. 276; Maria Wiedmaier, RA Erlebnis., Bd. 25, No. 331. RVB Archives.
12. Testimony of Friedrika Jaroslavsky, RA Erlebnis., Bd. 17, No. 7. RVB Archives.
13. RA Erlebnis. Bd. 16, No. 31. RVB Archives. See also Alfrieda Nenninger, RA Erlebnis. Bd. 26, No. 397. RVB Archives.
14. Hilberg, *Destruction of the European Jews*, vol. 3, pp. 949-954.
15. Maria Wiedmaier, RA Erlebnis. Bd. 25, No. 331. RVB Archives; Rene Ferderer, RA Erlebnis., Bd. 20, No. 176. RVB Archives.
16. RA Erlebnis., Bd. 39, No. 887, RVB Archives; RA Erlebnis., Bd. 17, No. 70. RVB Archives.
17. Elisabeth Lynhard, RA Erlebnis. Bd. 17, No. 53. RVB Archives; Friederika Jaroslavsky, RA Erlebnis., Bd. 17, No. 70. RVB Archives.
18. F. Jaroslavsky, RA Erlebnis., Bd. 17, No. 70. RVB Archives. In 1944, this was raised to RM 2.50/RM 5.
19. RA Erlebnis., Bd. 19, No. 161. RVB Archives; George, p. 69.
20. Benjamin B. Ferencz, *Less than Slaves: Jewish Forced Labor and the Quest for Compensation* (1979), p. 28.
21. Hajkova, pp. 90-91.
22. Ebert, p. 61.
23. Jacquemotte-Thonnart, pp. 188-189.
24. Edith Sparmann, Ravensbrück survivor, interview by the author, 11 Nov. 1994 at Ravensbrück.
25. Georgia Peet, interview in a Ravensbrück film produced by Ingrid Fliegel (1993).
26. Buber-Neumann, *Als Gefangene bei Stalin und Hitler*, p. 238.
27. Lahaye, p. 47.
28. In the 1960s, the firm of Siemens and Halske agreed to pay claims to Jewish victims through the "Conference on Jewish Material Claims Against Germany." Ferencz, *Less Than Slaves*, pp. 119-122. See also Georgia Peet, interview, 1993. She was extremely bitter that Siemens had paid compensation to Jews because of pressure from the World Jewish Congress, but not to other victims, like herself.
29. Interview by the author, 5 Sept. 1997 at Ravensbrück.
30. Jacquemotte-Thonnart, p. 188.
31. Lahaye, p. 47.
32. Edith Sparmann, interview by the author, 11 Nov. 1994, Ravensbrück.
33. Jacquemotte-Thonnart, p. 191.
34. Yvonne Useldinger, "Aus meinem Tagebuch." RA Erlebnis., Bd. 27, No. 475. RVB Archives.
35. I have taken most of this from interviews with Edith Sparmann (11 Nov. 1994) and Rosa Deutsch (9 Oct. 1994), both at Ravensbrück.
36. Ulrike Brandes, Claus Füllberg-Stolberg, and Sylvia Kenze. "Arbeit im KZ Ravensbrück" (1994), pp. 64-65.
37. Ibid., p. 64.
38. Hajkova, p. 92.

Chapter 15

1. This information has been taken from the *"Arbeitseinteilungslisten"* which are quite complete for 1941 and 1942, then disappear. RA II/8-2. RVB Archives.
2. A complete list of work crews is found in *Frauenkonzentrationslager Ravens-brück: Eine Gesamtdarstellung* (1972), pp. 174-192.
3. It is unlikely that the SS's own correspondence, office files and personnel records were handled by prisoners. See the testimonies of Anneliese and Gertrud Phillip. RA Erlebnis., Bd. 17, No. 72. RVB Archives.
4. Edith Sparmann, interview by the author. 11 Nov. 1994 at Ravensbrück.
5. Sofsky, p. 135.
6. Maria Plura, RA Erlebnis., Bd. 21, No. 210. RVB Archives.
7. Katzenmaier, p. 60.
8. Buber-Neumann, *Als Gefangene bei Stalin und Hitler*, pp. 202-204.
9. This section on the kitchens has been compiled from two main sources: Waleria Kowalski, "Ein Fragment aus der Küche," RA Erlebnis., Bd. 31, No. 578. RVB Archives; see also Hajkova, pp. 73-75.
10. Postel-Vinay, "A Young Frenchwoman's Wartime Experiences," p. 228.
11. Buber-Neumann, *Als Gefangene bei Stalin und Hitler*, pp. 236-237.
12. Agnieszka Glinczanka, in Winska, p. 345.
13. Winska, pp. 342-346.
14. "Friede P. (83) und ihre Schwester (82) haben ihr ganzen Leben in Fürstenberg verbracht," in *Ravensbrücker Ballade*, pp. 119-121.
15. Irma Trksak, interview by the author. 5 Sept. 1997. Ravensbrück.
16. S.M. Kudrijawzewa, in Morrison, "Guide to the Museum at the Ravensbrück Memorial," 6b.
17. Clara Rupp, "Die andere Seite des KZ," RA Erlebnis., Bd. 25, No. 361. RVB Archives.
18. Herbert Steiner, ed., *Käthe Leichter: Leben und Werk* (1973), pp. 201-203; "Frauen aus Ravensbrück 1995" (Calendar), ed. Ravensbrück Gedenkstätte (1994), n.p.
19. Clara Rupp. RA Erlebnis., Bd. 25, No. 361. RVB Archives.
20. Strebel, "Sabotage ist wie Wein," p. 182.
21. See the report by Arno Teubner, a prisoner at Sachsenhausen who kept getting sent to Ravensbrück for various construction projects. Teubner, RA Erlebnis., Bd. 35, No. 692. RVB Archives.
22. Berta Hartman, in Morrison, "Guide to the Museum at the Ravensbrück Memorial," 6a.
23. Bruha, pp. 96-97.
24. Maria Günzl, *Trost im Leid* (1976), pp. 6-10. Susi Benesch apparently had a reputation for talking back to overseers and encouraging others to do the same; see also Hajkova, p. 70.
25. Ferencz, p. 22.
26. Müller, pp. 64-66.
27. This has been put together from three sources which are mostly in agreement: Testimony of Renee Skalska and Joanna Kukulska, in Winska, pp. 191, 337; Buber-Neumann, *Als Gefangene bei Stalin und Hitler*, pp. 270-272; Kocwa, pp. 5-8. Each had been a member of this crew.
28. Katzenmaier, pp. 73-74.
29. Català, p. 33.
30. Käte Roth and Hanna Conrad, RA Erlebnis., Bd. 40, No. 934. RVB Archives.
31. See Christa Paul, *Zwangsprostitution: Staatliche errichtete Bordelle im Nationalsocialismus* (1994), pp. 23-26; Christa Schultz, "Weibliche Häftlinge aus Ravensbrück in Bordellen der Männerkonzentrationslagern" (1994), pp.

135-146.
32. SS Ogf. Pohl: Geheimnis Schreiben von 17 März 1942. RA Erlebnis., Bd. 22, No. 211. RVB Archives.
33. Paul, pp. 23-26.
34. See R. L. Ferdonnet-Gay, RA Erlebnis., Bd. 41, No. 978. RVB Archives.
35. Schulz, "Weibliche Häftlinge aus Ravensbrück in Bordellen der Männerkonzentrationslagern," p. 139.
36. Herbermann, pp. 93-94.
37. Buchmann, *Frauen von Ravensbrück*, p. 85.
38. Mme. Masson, RA Erlebnis., Bd. 30, No. 547. RVB Archives.
39. Astrid Blumensaadt-Pedersen, RA Erlebnis., Bd. 41, No. 968. RVB Archives.
40. Poltawska, p. 104.
41. Fabius, p. 110.
42. Schulz, "Weibliche Häftlinge aus Ravensbrück in Bordellen der Männerkonzentrationslagern," p. 139.
43. Urbye, p. 11.
44. Paul, pp. 49-56.
45. Elisabeth Lynhard, RA Erlebnis., Bd. 34, No. 634. RVB Archives.
46. Hilde Boy-Brandt, RA Erlebnis., Bd. 15, No. 17. RVB Archives; Paul, pp. 41-42.

Chapter 16

1. Ulrike Brandes, "Der Arbeitseinsatz in zwei Aussenlagern Ravensbrücks" (1994), pp. 71-72.
2. This is put together from several sources, chiefly the testimony of Fritz Suhren at Nuremberg on 17 June 1946. RA Erlebnis. Bd. 22, No. 211. RVB Archives; see also RA Erlebnis., Bd. 17, No. 69. RVB Archives; Hajkova, pp. 95-109.
3. Testimony of Antonia Frexendes, in Català, p. 99; Maurelle, p. 71; Montluc-Ravensbrück, p.14.
4. Sandoe, pp. 79-81.
5. Roux, pp. 166-169.
6. "Bericht über Barth", Käte Roth and Hanna Conrad, RA Erlebnis. Bd. 40, No. 934. RVB Archives.
7. Brandes, p. 71.
8. Waltz, *Remembering Ravensbrück* (1997 Film).
9. Maurel, pp. 8-10; Brandes, p. 71.
10. Maurel, pp. 8-9; Marette, pp. 163-214.
11. Maurel, pp. 18-21; Marette, pp. 171-175.
12. Maurel, p. 29.
13. Marette, p. 196.
14. Maurel, p. 29.
15. Brandes, p. 71.
16. Rita Sprengel, "Bericht über Arbeit von Häftlinge aus Ravensbrück bei der Fabrik 'Universelle,'" RA Erlebnis. Bd. 28, No. 487. RVB Archives.
17. "Unterstützung der Zwangsarbeiter durch Genossen and Kollegen unseres Betriebes," n.d. (I would guess about January 1945), RA Erlebnis. Bd. 29, No. 529. RVB Archives.
18. Ilse Hunger, RA Erlebnis. Bd. 20, No. 187. RVB Archives.
19. "Aussagen zum Aussenlager 'Hasag', Leipzig." Willy Dockhorn und Hildegard Dockhorn. RA Erlebnis. Bd. 20, No. 187. RVB Archives.
20. "Bericht der Häftlinge aus dem FKZ Ravensbrück—welche in der Näherei E.

Grahl in Fürstenberg beschäftigt waren." RA Erleb. Bd. 31, No. 580. RVB Archives.

21. Maurel, p. 29; Testimony of Alfonsina Bueno Ester, in Català, p. 81.
22. *Montluc-Ravensbrück*, pp. 10-11.
23. Dufournier, p. 143.
24. Karl Heinz Schütt, *Ein vergessenes Lager? Über das Aussenlager Neustadt-Glewe des Frauen-KZ Ravensbrück* (1997), p. 7.
25. Testimonies of Edith Kaliner-Bulder and Nicolaas Geradus Sloothaak, in Schütt, pp. 53-54, 116-117.
26. Testimonies of Fanny Celgoh-Segal and Serina Rosenberg, in Schütt, pp. 34-35, 89.
27. Schütt, pp. 5, 11.
28. Testimony of Halina Balin-Birenbaum and Regina Goldberg-Blumen, in Schütt, pp. 26-30, 37.
29. Schütt, pp. 34-35, 96, 109.
30. Testimony of Fanny Celgoh-Segal, in Schütt, pp. 34-35.
31. Testimony of Halina Balin-Birenbaum and Edith Karliner-Bulder, in Schütt, pp. 25-30, 53-54.
32. Testimony of Nicolaas Geradus Sloothaak, in Schütt, p. 117.
33. Schütt, pp. 5, 17-23.
34. Erika Myriam Kounio-Amarigio, *Damit es die ganze Welt erfährt. Von Salonika nach Auschwitz and zurück, 1926-1996* (1996), pp. 117-119.
35. Ibid; Tedeschi, p. 207; Rachel Horowitz, interview (1982). Holocaust Documentation & Education Center (Miami).
36. Irma Trksak, interview by the author, 1997, Ravensbrück. Trksak, while harboring bad memories, is understanding and forgiving of her "hosts."
37. Delbo, p. 184.
38. "Friede P. (83) und ihre Schwester (82) haben ihr ganzen Leben in Fürstenberg verbracht," in *Ravensbrücker Ballade*, pp. 119-121.
39. Frau Brunnhilde Reimann, interview by the author, 1997 in Fürstenberg.
40. Aussage vom Herrn August Schmidt, RA Erlebnis. Bd. 26, No. 439. RVB Archives.
41. Daniel Goldhagen, *Hitler's Willing Executioners: Ordinary Germans and the Holocaust* (1996), p. 171.
42. "Friede P. und ihre Schwester...," *Ravensbrücker Ballade*, p. 120.
43. Report: "In Ravensbrück," Häftlingsbefragungen CSSR. RAII/10-15. RVB Archives.
44. Richard Grunberger: *The Twelve Year Reich: A Social History of Nazi Germany* (1971), p. 205. On the conditions of the Germans, see also Earl R. Beck, *Under the Bombs. The German Home Front, 1942-1945* (1986), pp. 99-128, 162-165, 184-188.
45. Grunberger, p. 213.
46. Ibid. pp. 191-192; on the subject of working hours, see the testimony of Oswald Pohl, *Trials of War Criminals Before the Nuernberg Military Tribunals* (1950), p. 436.

Chapter 17

1. Irmtraud Heike and Andreas Pflock, "Geregelte Strafen, Willkürliche Gewalt und Massensterben" (1994), pp. 241-242.

2. Martin Broszat, "The Concentration Camps, 1933-1945" (1968), p. 433.
3. Hajkova, pp. 110-111; Buber-Neumann, *Als Gefangene bei Stalin und Hitler,* p. 174.
4. Buchmann, *Frauen von Ravensbrück*, pp. 18-19.
5. Buchmann, "Brief an eine berliner Reporterin," pp. 35-36.
6. Katzenmaier, pp. 95-97.
7. Buchmann, *Frauen von Ravensbrück*, p. 19.
8. Poltawska, pp. 105-106.
9. Krokowski and Voigt, p. 266.
10. Buchmann, "Brief an eine berliner Reporterin," pp. 36-37.
11. This is pieced together from several sources: Hildegard Brandt, "Bericht über Transport der 'Idioten,'" RA Erlebnis. Bd. 39, No. 889. Ravensbrück Archives; Charlotte Müller, "Bericht über die Idioten von Block 10," RA Erlebnis. Bd. 25, No. 356. RVB Archives; Müller, *Klempnerkolonne*, pp. 115-119; Deposition of Erna Boehmer, PRO JAG 335 [RVB IV case] item no. 13, pp. 129-132, Public Records Office.
12. Marette, pp. 159-161.
13. Buchmann, *Frauen von Ravensbrück*, p. 19.
14. Elisabeth Lynhard, RA Erlebnis. Bd. 17, No. 55. RVB Archives.
15. Hajkova, p. 111.
16. Antonia Frexendes, in Català, p. 98; Fabius, p. 112.
17. Stanislawa Mlodkowska-Bielawska, in Symonowicz, ed., *Beyond Human Endurance,* p. 35.
18. Katzenmaier, p. 110.
19. Helen Ernst, RA Erlebnis. Bd. 40, No. 931. RVB Archives; Dufournier, p. 93.
20. Dufournier, p. 93.
21. Elisabeth Weber, RA Erlebnis. Bd. 36, No. 720. RVB Archives.
22. See the Deposition of Johann Schwarzhuber in Bruha, p. 145.
23. Morrison, "Guide to the Cell Building of the Ravensbrück Memorial," n.p.
24. Buchmann, *Frauen von Ravensbrück*, pp. 21-22; Hajkova, pp. 115-116.
25. Emmi Thoma-Handke, RA Erlebnis. Bd. 17, No. 42. RVB Archives.
26. Elisabeth Lynhard, RA Erlebnis. Bd. 17, No. 55. RVB Archives. See also Müller, pp. 76-80.
27. Urbye, p. 23.
28. Hajkova, p. 93.
29. Rossiter, p. 115.
30. Maurel, p.29.
31. Ulrike Brandes et al., "Arbeit in KZ Ravensbrück" (1994), p. 66.
32. Hajkova, p. 92.
33. Report of Theresa Hader-Resmann, RA Erlebnis. Bd. 26, No. 442. RVB Archives.
34. Vermerhren, pp. 44-45.
35. Tatjana Pignatti-Maikop, RA Erlebnis. Bd. 22, No. 215. RVB Archives.
36. Wasyl Pikula, RA Erlebnis. Bd. 41, No. 953. RVB Archives.
37. Ibid.; see also Aussagen von Dagmar Hajkova, RA Erlebnis. Bd. 29, No. 516. RVB Archives; Mary Fischer, RA Erlebnis. Bd. 26, No. 395. RVB Archives.
38. Kocwa, pp. 59-101; Hajkova, pp. 122-123.
39. Testimony of Renee Skalska, in Winska, p. 337.
40. Ada Feingold-Nelson, interview, 1995. Holocaust Documentation & Education Center (Miami).
41. *Frauenkonzentrationslager Ravensbrück: Eine Gesamtdarstellung* (1972), p. 97.
42. Jacobeit and Thomas-Heinrich, pp. 106-107.
43. Testimony of Wladyslaw Nackowiak, in *Frauenkonzentrationslager Ravens-*

brück: Eine Gesamtdarstellung, p. 101.
44. Testimony of Horst Schmidt, ibid., p. 104.
45. Heike, "...da es sich ja lediglich um die Bewachung der Häftlinge handelt" (1994), p. 228.

Chapter 18

1. RA Erlebnis. Bd. 15, No. 9. RVB Archives.
2. Maurel, p. 54.
3. RA Erlebnis. Bd. 15, No. 9. RVB Archives.
4. Deposition of Helena Goudsmit. RVB IV case. PRO Ref. No. WO235/531 & 532, pp. 125-126. Public Record Office.
5. Hilde Boy-Brandt, RA Erlebnis. Bd. 15, No. 17. RVB Archives.
6. Sandoe, pp. 107-108.
7. Aussage von Max Hamawald. RAII/10-1-5. RVB Archives.
8. Müller, pp. 59-60.
9. Winska, p. 331.
10. Deposition of Ludwig D. Ramdohr. RVB IV Case. PRO Ref. No. WO 235/531 and 532, pp. 123-124. Public Record Office.
11. Statement by Dr. Benno Orendi, Exhibit 38. Ibid.
12. Depositions of Dr. Helena Goudsmit and Annette Heckman, ibid., pp. 125-126, 143-144.
13. Vermehren, pp. 74-76.
14. Hilde Boy-Brandt, "Überlick über die Reviertätigkeit vom März 1942-Ende April 1945," RA Erlebnis. Bd. 15, No. 17. RVB Archives.
15. I have based this figure on twelve selected dates from 24 June 1939 to 22 April 1942 as recorded in the Prisoner-strength Reports, RA II/4-6: Blockver-zeichnisse, Gefangenen-Stärkemeldung. RVB Archives.
16. Sauckel order of 20 April 1942, in Noakes and Pridham, *Documents on Nazism, 1919-1945,* p. 651.
17. Ferencz, p. 22.
18. Depositions of Dr. Helena Goudsmit and Yvonne de Soignies (Ravensbrück IV Case), PRO Ref. No. WO235/531 and 532, pp. 125-126, 139-140. Public Record Office.
19. Elisabeth Lynhard, RA Erlebnis. Bd. 34, No. 634. RVB Archives.
20. Geheime Reichssache vom 15.1.42 an alle Lager-Kommandanten, betrifft das Euthanasieprogramm 14f13. Präsident des Kriegsverbrechergerichts, Hamburg. Beweisstück 32. PRO No. WO234/531-532. Public Record Office.
21. Schulz, *Hanka Houskova,* p. 14.
22. Morrison, "Guide to the Museum at the Ravensbrück Memorial," Exhibit 4d; See also Hildegard Brandt, "Bericht über Transport der 'Idioten'", RA Erlebnis., Bd. 39, No. 889. RVB Archives; Christa Wagner, *Geboren am See der Tränen* (1987), pp. 84-85.
23. Hilde Boy-Brandt, RA Erleb., Bd. 15, No. 17. RVB Archives.
24. Freya Klier, *Die Kaninchen von Ravensbrück: Medizinische Versuche an Frauen in der NS-Zeit* (1994), pp. 76-86, 141.
25. Angelika Ebbinghaus, Karl Heinz Roth, and Michael Hepp, "Die Ärztin Herta Oberheuser und die Kriegschirurgischen Experimente im Frauen-Konzentra-tionslager Ravensbrück" (1987), pp. 250-252.
26. Testimony of Dr. Zofia Maczka, *Trial of War Criminals Before the Nuremberg Military Tribunals,* vol. 5 (1950), p. 1110; see also the deposition of Dr. Maczka.

PRO JAG335 (Ravensbrück IV Case), pp. 152-155. Public Record Office.
27. Klier, pp. 176-182.
28. Ibid., pp. 182-185; see also Dunja Martin, "Menschenversuche im Kranken-revier des KZ Ravensbrück," (1994), pp. 108-109; see also Dr. Maczka deposi-tion: PRO JAG335. pp. 152-155. Public Record Office; see also the testimony of experimentees in Symonowicz, ed., *Beyond Human Endurance*, pp. 37-42, 45-51, 83.
29. Klier, pp. 150-153.
30. Ibid., pp. 167-168, 214-215.
31. Poltawska, p. 102.
32. Testimony of Krystina Czyz-Wilgat, in Symonowicz, ed., *Beyond Human Endurance*, p. 71.
33. Poltawska, p. 138.
34. Ibid., p. 111.
35. Gluck, pp. 67-69.
36. Kiedrzynska, "Introduction," in Symonowicz, ed., *Beyond Human Endurance*, pp. 18-27; Poltawska, pp. 142-160.
37. Robert P. Hudson, *Disease and Its Control* (1983), p. 29.
38. Trude Mittag, RA Erlebnis. Bd. 40, No. 930. RVB Archives; Erika Buchmann, RA Erlebnis. Bd. 16, No. 19. RVB Archives; Müller, pp. 146-148.
39. Buchmann, "Brief an eine berliner Reporterin," p. 46.
40. Winska, p. 378.
41. Müller, p. 147.

Chapter 19

1. Letter of 16 April 1977 from Fritz Schlaak to Fr. Seidel. RAII/10-1-1. RVB Archives.
2. Arno Teubner, RA Erlebnis., Bd. 35, No. 692. RVB Archives; Hajkova, p. 313.
3. Wlodzimierz Kulinski, RAII/10-2-3. RVB Archives.
4. Cited in Arndt, p. 117.
5. Max Hannewald, RA Erlebnis., Bd. 43, No. 940/39. RVB Archives.
6. Report: "In Ravensbrück," RAII/10-1-5. RVB Archives.
7. Ibid.; Report of Karel Frinta. RAII/10-1-5. RVB Archives.
8. Report by Hermann Frobin. RAII/10-1-5. RVB Archives.
9. Report by Emanuel Kolarik (1945). RAII/10-1-5. RVB Archives.
10. Report of 21 Sept. 1970 by Ernst Barthel. RAII/10-2-4. RVB Archives; Karl Strübing, "Bericht über Ravensbrück," RA Erlebnis., Bd. 43, No. 940/38. RVB Archives.
11. Erklärung von Pollak und Ostasz. 28 Feb. 1974. Häftlingsbefragungen—Polen. RAII/10-1-4. RVB Archives.
12. Hajkova, p. 323.
13. Rene Gaston Ferderer, RA Erlebnis., Bd. 20, No. 176. RVB Archives; Hajkova, p. 323.
14. Ferderer, Ibid.
15. Testimony of Joseph Rehwald. Extract from *Erwachet!* of 8 Feb. 1993. Internet: http://www.jznet.org.jzstandhaft/g930802-rehwald.html (14 April 1998).
16. Report: "In Ravensbrück," RAII/10-1-5. RVB Archives; see also Hajkova, p. 324.
17. Willi Kostusiak, RA Erlebnis., Bd. 43, No. 59. RVB Archives.

18. Report: "In Ravensbrück," Männerlager—Häftlingsbefragungen CSSR. RAII/10-1-5. RVB Archives.
19. Langer, "Gendered Suffering? Women in Holocaust Testimonies" (1998), pp. 351-363; see the counterview in the same volume by Joan Ringelheim: "The Split Between Gender and the Holocaust," pp. 340-350.
20. Milton, "Deutsche und deutsch-jüdische Frauen als Verfolgte des NS-Staats," pp. 11-13.
21. Kulinski, RAII/10-2-3. RVB Archives.
22. Bärbel Schindler-Saefkow, "Quellen zur Erstellung eines Gedenkbuches Ravensbrück" (1997), pp. 46-56.
23. Ibid., p. 47.
24. Sara Horowitz, "Women in Holocaust Literature: Engendering Trauma Memory" (1998), pp. 375-376.
25. Bericht von Franz Zelinka, 11 Aug. 1966. RAII/10-1-5. RVB Archives.
26. Arndt, p. 117.
27. Rene Gaston Ferderer, RA Erlebnis., Bd. 20, No. 176. RVB Archives. Ferderer joined, but denied that he volunteered.
28. Arno Teubner, RA Erlebnis., Bd. 35, No. 692. RVB Archives.

Chapter 20

1. Müller, pp. 44-45.
2. Hajkova, pp. 176-177; Britta Pawelk, "Als Häftling geboren—Kinder in Ravensbrück" (1994), pp. 157-160; also, RA Erlebnis. Bd. 26, No. 398. RVB Archives.
3. Buber-Neumann, *Als Gefangene bei Stalin und Hitler*, p. 222.
4. Ibid.
5. Fabius, p. 106.
6. Bruha, p. 113.
7. Buber-Neumann, *Als Gefangene bei Stalin und Hitler*, pp. 222-223.
8. Breur, pp. 84-86; Müller, pp. 111-114.
9. Hajkova, pp. 182-187.
10. Steven Montrose (born Rosenberg), interview. Holocaust Documentation & Education Center (Miami).
11. Pawelk, pp. 161-162; Müller, p. 66.
12. Bruha, pp. 114-115.
13. Müller, p. 47.
14. RA Erlebnis. Bd. 16, No. 31. RVB Archives.
15. Müller, pp. 46-47.
16. Hajkova, p. 177.
17. Müller, p. 46.
18. Hajkova, p. 183.
19. See the testimonies of Stanislawa Schöneman-Luniewsa, Marta Baranowska and Mieczyslawa Jarosz-Czajka in Winska, pp. 156-157; see also Kiedrzynska, *Ravensbrück Kobiecy Oboz Koncentracyjny*, pp. 231-232; Grit Philipp, "Erlebnisberichte als Quellen historischer Forschung" (1997), pp. 126-127.
20. Kriedrzynska, *Ravensbrück Kobiecy Oboz Koncentracyjny*, p. 258.
21. Müller, pp. 177-178.
22. I have reconstructed this event from several sources: Ilse Hunger, RA Erlebnis. Bd. 34, No. 679 and Bd. 26, No. 398. RVB Archives; Müller, pp. 167-170, 177-179; Hajkova, pp. 184-186; Pawelk, pp. 162-164.

23. Winska, pp. 156-157.
24. Jean Divoire, "Weihnachten im Lager des schleichenden Todes," RA Erlebnis. Bd. 41, No. 970. RVB Archives.
25. Stojka, pp. 49-50.
26. Buchmann, *Frauen von Ravensbrück*, p. 135; Müller, p. 168.
27. Dunja Martin, "Menschenversuche im Krankenrevier des KZ Ravensbrück," (1994), p. 104.
28. Liste der in Ravensbrück in der Zeit vom 19 Sept. 1944 bis 22 April 1945 geborenen kinder. RA Erlebnis. Bd. 36, No. 702. RVB Archives; see also Müller, pp. 198-199.
29. Schulz, *Hanka Houskova*, p. 16.
30. Pawelk, pp. 158-159.
31. Schulz, *Hanka Houskova*, p. 15.
32. Poltawska, p. 139.
33. Hajkova, p. 186.
34. Pawelk, pp. 160-161.
35. Hajkova, p. 190.
36. Bruha, pp. 115-118.
37. *Les Françaises à Ravensbrück*, p. 206; Pawelk, p. 164.

Chapter 21

1. Liste der Stand- u. Sterbefälle in Ravensbrück, 1942-1945. RA Erlebnis. Bd. 42, No. 1003. RVB Archives.
2. *Frauenkonzentrationslager Ravensbrück: Eine Gesamtdarstellung*, pp. 157-158.
3. RA Erlebnis. Bd. 19, No. 161. RVB Archives. This is a report done by the "Institut für Marxismus-Leninismus" in Berlin. No date.
4. Erika Buchmann, in Zimmer, *Ravensbrücker Ballade*, p. 183.
5. Some historians, including Ino Arndt, whose 1970 study of Ravensbrück is still among the most useful examinations of the women's camp, believe that ca. 70,000 women arrived during 1944 alone. This number appears to be arrived at by subtracting the highest prisoner registration number in December 1943 from the highest number in December 1944. There are several problems with doing this: 1) Not all the numbers were actually used. The SS often jumped over numbers to begin a new month on a "round number." 2) Prisoners who were returned to Ravensbrück from other camps were issued new numbers, meaning that quite a number of prisoners were actually counted twice. 3) We know that some prisoners were sent to other camps, but again, we have no firm numbers. See Arndt, "Das Frauenkonzentrationslager Ravensbrück," pp. 118-119; see also "Liste über eingelieferte Häftlingsnummern von 1939-1945 und woher." RA Erlebnis., Bd. 42, No. 1004. RVB Archives.
6. Mss. RG-04.006M, Reel 23, Nos. 74-75. U.S. Holocaust Memorial Museum Archives. The agency referred to is the *Glówna Komisja Badania Hitlerowskich w Polsce. Instytut Pamirci Narodowej* [Head Investigative Commission for Crimes of Hitler in Poland. Institute of National Remembrance].
7. Martin Gilbert, "The Question of Bombing Auschwitz" (1984), pp. 470-473.
8. Mss. RG-04.006M, Reel 23, No. 74. U.S. Holocaust Memorial Museum Archives.
9. Lidia Rolfi, RA Erlebnis. Bd. 26, No. 399. RVB Archives.

10. Poltawska, pp. 140-155.
11. Dufournier, p. 81.
12. Müller, p. 174.
13. Buchmann, *Frauen von Ravensbrück*, p. 46.
14. Urbye, pp. 19-20.
15. Schulz, "Weibliche Häftlinge aus Ravensbrück in Bordellen der Männer-konzentrationslagern," p.142.
16. Buchmann, *Frauen von Ravensbrück*, p. 44.
17. Rosa Deutsch, interviews by the author at Ravensbrück and Budapest, 9 and 25 October 1994.
18. M. Wolter, RA Erlebnis. Bd. 17, No. 67. RVB Archives.
19. Buchmann, *Frauen von Ravensbrück*, p. 46.
20. "Die persönlichen Aussagen der Ärtztin A.A. Nikiforowa," reprinted in Bärbel Schindler-Soefkow, "Die Befreiung des KZ Ravensbrück durch die Rote Armee..." (1994), p. 189.
21. Dufournier, p. 109.
22. Hajkova, p. 61.
23. See the following interviews with Jewish survivors who came to Ravensbrück in the winter of 1944-45, then were sent to a subcamp: Jacqueline Bernard, Miriam Guttmann, Rachel Horowitz, Rosel Kopel, Bella Novak, Elizabeth Speiser, Ruth Stahl, Genia Weicenfeld, Frances Zimmerman. Holocaust Documentation and Education Center (Miami). See also Claus Füllberg-Stollberg, "Die Odysee einer ungarischen Judin: Gloria Hollander Lyon," (1994), pp. 285-286; see also Rena Kornreich Gelissen, *Rena's Promise* (1995), pp. 252-266. Kornreich, a Polish Jew, arrived at Ravensbrück from Auschwitz in late January, and after a few days was sent to the subcamp at Neustadt-Glewe.
24. *Frauenkonzentrationslager Ravensbrück: Eine Gesamtdarstellung*, pp. 90-96.
25. Aussage von Herrn August Schmidt. RA Erlebnis. Bd. 26, No. 439. RVB Archives.
26. Liste der Stand- u. Sterbefälle im Ravensbrück, RA Erlebnis. Bd. 42, No. 1003. RVB Archives.
27. Hilde Boy-Brandt, RA Erlebnis. Bd. 15, No. 17. RVB Archives; see also Fabius, p. 111. She estimates the number of deaths at the turn of the year at 400 per day, which seems rather high.
28. Ebert, p. 61.
29. Maurel, p. 100.
30. "Einäscherungsanmeldungen in Barth verstorbenen Frauen," RA Erlebnis., Bd. 36, No. 700. RVB Archives.
31. Müller, pp. 120-122; Hilde Boy-Brandt, RA Erlebnis. Bd. 15, No. 17. RVB Archives.
32. Hajkova, p. 129.
33. Morrison, "Guide to the Museum at the Ravensbrück Memorial," Exhibit 8d.
34. See the case of Emma Murr, who died on 29 May 1942, but whose death notice was not sent out until 24 Feb. 1943. Morrison, "Guide to the Cell Building at the Ravensbrück Memorial," n.p.
35. Aussage von August Schmidt, RA Erlebnis. Bd. 26, No. 439. RVB Archives.
36. RA Erlebnis. Bd. 20, No.172. RVB Archives.
37. Hepp, p. 214.
38. Irma Trksak, interview by the author. 5 Sept. 1997, Ravensbrück.
39. Hajkova, pp. 161-162.
40. Sandoe, p. 111.
41. Erika Buchmann, RA Erlebnis., Bd. 16, No. 19. RVB Archives.
42. Hilde Boy-Brandt, RA Erlebnis. Bd. 15, No. 17. RVB Archives.
43. Deposition of Johann Schwarzhuber. 15 August 1946. Reprinted in Bruha, p. 146.

44. Irma Trksak, interview by the author, 5 Sept. 1997. Ravensbrück.
45. Deposition of Martha Haake. PRO JAG 335 (RVB IV Case) Exhibit 22. Public Record Office. Haake, a nurse, admitted to administering the powder, but claimed she was ill and not on duty the next day, and doesn't know how many died; see also Hajkova, pp. 163-164.
46. Deposition of Johann Schwarzhuber, in Bruha, p. 146.
47. Anise Postel-Vinay, "Gaskammern und die Ermordung durch Gas im KZ Ravensbrück" (1997), pp. 37-40.
48. See the reports by Emanuel Kolarik and Arno Teubner: RA II/10-1-5 and RA Erlebnis. Bd. 35, No. 692. RVB Archives.
49. Postel-Vinay, "Gaskammern und die Ermordung durch Gas in KZ Ravensbrück," pp. 37-39; Hajkova, p. 166; Müller, p. 149.
50. Konzentrationslager Ravensbrück-Kommandatur. "Betr: Häftlings-überstellung nach Mittwerda," dated 6 April 1945. Sent to the main administrative departments at Ravensbrück. Signed by Kommandant Suhren. Records of Nazi Concentration Camps (Mss. RG-04.006M) Reel 20, No. 15. U.S. Holocaust Memorial Museum Archives.
51. Eugen Kogon, Hermann Langbein, and Adalbert Rückerl, eds., *Nazi Mass Murder: A Documentary History of the Use of Poison Gas* (1993), pp. 186-189; Tillion, pp. 147-149.
52. Testimony of Schwarzhuber, in Bruha, pp. 146-147.
53. Postel-Vinay, "Gaskammern und die Ermordung durch Gas in KZ Ravensbrück," p. 40.
54. Hajkova, pp. 164-166; Bruha, pp. 121-122.
55. Jacobeit and Thomas-Heinrich, *Kreuzweg Ravensbrück*, ch. 9.
56. Gluck, pp. 70-71.
57. Tillion, p. 158.
58. Ibid.
59. Müller, p. 149.
60. Hilde Boy-Brandt, RA Erlebnis., Bd. 15, No. 17. RVB Archives; Postel-Vinay, "Gaskammern und die Ermordung durch Gas im KZ Ravensbrück," p. 45.
61. Sandoe, p. 120.
62. Poltawska, pp. 142-160.
63. Stansilawa Michalik and Leokadia Kwiecirska, in Symonowicz, ed., *Beyond Human Endurance,* pp. 60, 94-96.
64. Stanislawa Michalik, ibid., p. 60.
65. Simone Erpel, "Rettungsaktion in letzter Minute," p. 29.
66. Postel-Vinay, "A Young Frenchwoman's Wartime Experiences," p. 229.
67. Bruha, p. 123
68. Karel Margry, "Nordhausen" (1998), pp. 34-35.
69. Buber-Neumann, *Als Gefangene bei Stalin und Hitler*, pp. 295-297.
70. Helen Ernst, RA Erlebnis. Bd. 40, No. 031. RVB Archives.
71. Jacquemotte-Thonnart, p. 203; see also Symonowicz, ed., *Beyond Human Endurance,* pp. 94-96.
72. Delbo, p. 204.
73. Helen Ernst, RA Erlebnis. Bd. 40, No. 931. RVB Archives; see also Elizabeth Sommer-Lefkovits, *Are You in This Hell, Too? Memories of Troubled Times, 1944-45* (1995), pp. 49-50.
74. Eva Laubhardt, RA Erlebnis. Bd. 40, No. 935. RVB Archives.
75. Ernst, RA Erlebnis. Bd. 40, No. 931. RVB Archives.
76. Helene Freldenberg, RA Erlebnis. Bd. 40, No. 932. RVB Archives.
77. Liste der Stand- u. Sterbefälle im Ravensbrück, 1942-1945. RA Erlebnis. Bd. 42, No. 1003. RVB Archives.
78. Fest, *Hitler*, pp. 774-779.

Chapter 22

1. Müller, p. 203.
2. Rosa Haus, interview, 1986, Holocaust Documentation & Education Center (Miami).
3. Halina Nelken, *Freiheit will ich noch erleben* (1996), p. 311. The English translation of the poem is by the author.
4. Erpel, pp. 29-31; Dufournier, pp. 147-149.
5. Sandoe, pp. 126ff.
6. Müller, pp. 188-192.
7. Dufournier, p. 146.
8. Buber-Neumann, *Als Gefangene bei Stalin und Hitler,* p. 297.
9. Delbo, pp. 213-214.
10. Müller, p. 203; Sommer-Lefkovitz, p. 51.
11. Antonia Frexedes, in Català, p. 100.
12. Bruha, p. 126.
13. Testimony of Lidia Rosenfeld, in Schütt, p. 97.
14. Arnold Folke, "Die Rettungs-Expedition nach Ravensbrück in April 1945," RA Erlebnis. Bd. 32, No. 589. RVB Archives. Folke was in charge of one convoy of twenty buses; Erpel, pp. 29-53.
15. Folke, RA Erlebnis. Bd. 32, No. 589. RVB Archives.
16. Martin Gilbert, *The Holocaust: A History of the Jews of Europe during the Second World War* (1985), p. 798.
17. Bruha, pp. 126-127.
18. Jacobeit and Thomas-Heinrich, pp. 106-107.
19. Frau Brunnhilde Reimann, interview by the author, 17 Aug. 1997, Fürstenberg.
20. Buber-Neumann, *Als Gefangene bei Stalin und Hitler,* pp. 302-303.
21. Wolfgang Jacobeit, "Die 'Todessmärsche von Ravensbrück..." in S. Jacobeit, ed., *"Ich grüsse Euch als freier Mensch"* (1995), pp. 80-82.
22. Interview with Maria Plater-Skasa, in Wolfgang Jacobeit, "Todesmärsche...," pp. 99-100.
23. W. Jacobeit, "Todesmärsche...," p. 81.
24. Many years later (1990), when discussing her participation in the march from the Barth subcamp, Miriam Guttmann was asked: "Was this the Death March?" She answered: "No. It was just a march." Guttmann, interview, 1990. Holocaust Documentation & Education Center (Miami).
25. Müller, p. 206.
26. Esther Bejarano, interview with Bärbel Schindler-Saefkow (22 June 1994, Ravensbrück). Reprinted in W. Jacobeit, "Todesmärsche...," pp. 102-103.
27. Müller, pp. 208-212.
28. W. Jacobeit, "Todesmärsche...," p. 104.
29. Maurel, pp. 112-122.
30. Frances Zimmerman, interview, 1987. Holocaust Documentation & Education Center (Miami).
31. Testimony of Salomea Telner-Baum, in Schütt, p. 124.
32. *Montluc-Ravensbrück*, pp. 18-20; Marette, pp. 236-241.
33. Ada Feingold-Nelson, interview, 1995. Holocaust Documentation & Education Center (Miami).
34. Marette, pp. 236-241.
35. Anneliese und Gertrud Phillip, RA Erlebnis. Bd. 17, No. 72. RVB Archives.
36. Katzenmaier, p. 164; Müller, pp. 212-215.
37. Bejarano, interviewed in W. Jacobeit, "Todesmärsche...," p. 121.
38. General Makarow, "Meine Erinnerungen an die Befreiung Ravensbrücks." RA

Erlebnis. Bd. 42, No. 1005. RVB Archives. See also Bärbel Schindler-Saefkow "Die Befreiung des KZ Ravensbrück durch die Rote Armee," in S. Jacobeit, ed., *"Ich grüsse Euch als freier Mensch,"* pp. 149-160.

39. Frau Brunnhilde Reimann, interview by the author, 27 Aug. 1997, Fürstenberg. She was an eighteen-year-old schoolgirl who was conscripted to work at the camp, carrying bodies. She caught typhus herself in the process.

40. Bericht von S.I. Bulanow über das sowjetische internationale Hospital für ehemalige Häftlinge aus Ravensbrück (1960). Reprinted in Schindler-Saefkow, "Die Befreiung des KZ Ravensbrück," pp. 152-155.

Chapter 23

1. I base this partly on a conversation I had with Sybil Milton at Ravensbrück in October 1996, along with her article: "Deutsche und deutsch-jüdische Frauen als Verfolgte des N-S Staats," pp. 11-12.

2. Estimates on the number of deaths at Ravensbrück between 1939 and 1945 vary wildly. There is no "official estimate," but the Ravensbrück Memorial proclaims "tens of thousands." One survivor has put the figure as high as 92,000: Antonia Bruha, *Ich war keine Heldin*, p. 134. No less an authority on the Holocaust than Martin Gilbert has accepted this number: Gilbert, *The Holocaust*, p. 805. Perhaps, with more and better research, we can be more conclusive on this issue, but right now we just do not know what the true numbers are.

Glossary and Abbreviations

Anweisungshäftling – Prisoner foreman.

Appel – Roll call.

Appelplatz – Roll call grounds.

Aufpasserin – Monitor. Prisoner—official whose job it was to watch for sabotage in the workplace.

Aufseherin – Female overseer.

Aussenkommando – A worksite outside the camp.

Aussenlager – Subcamp.

Bifos – Short-hand for *Bibelforscher*, or Jehovah's Witnesses.

Blockälteste – Block senior, a leading prisoner official.

Blockführerin – SS Block Leader (female).

Blockova – Common prisoner term for *Blockälteste*.

Blockschwester – Block nurse. Responsible for minor medical problems, as well as delousing.

Blitzkrieg – Lightning war, the German strategy in 1939–1941.

Bordell – Brothel.

Bunker – Detention cell building.

Einsatzgruppen – SS "special action squads." Used to kill racial and political "undesirables" in Poland and the USSR.

Erlebnisberichte – Reports of experience. Generally written by former prisoners shortly after their liberation.

Fremdarbeiter – Foreign worker (but not a prisoner).

Führer – Hitler's title, literally "Leader."

Funktionshäftling – Prisoner official or prisoner functionary.

Gauleiter – Nazi Party Province Chief.

Gestapo – *Geheime Staatspolizei*. Secret State Police. Part of the RSHA, a branch of the SS.

Häftling – Prisoner.

Hilfsaufseherin – Overseer trainee (female).

Kapo – Prisoner official, generally in charge of a work crew. The term was widely used at concentration camps, but not at Ravensbrück, except for the men's camp.

KL or *KZ* – Abbreviation for *Konzentrationslager,* or concentration camp.

Kameradinnen – Female comrades.

Kaninchen – "Rabbits." Name given to women who were subjected to medical experiments.

Kolonkova – Polish term for "crew chiefs," but generally used by all the inmates.

Kommandant – Commandant.

Kulturkampf – Struggle over culture.

KZ–Inspektion – The SS Directorate of Concentration Camps, with headquarters in nearby Oranienburg.

Lagerälteste – Camp Senior. The leading prisoner official, but not a substantively important position at Ravensbrück.

Lagerartzt – Camp doctor.

Lagerführer – See *Schutzhaftlagerführer*.

Lagergeld – Camp money, scrip.

Lagerläuferin – Camp runner. Used as couriers within the camp.

Lagerordnung – Camp rules and regulations.

Lagerpolizei – Camp police.

Lebensborn – A program for breeding "racially superior" young women with SS personnel. Some *Lebensborn* homes were subcamps of Ravensbrück.

Liebling – Sweetheart, darling.

Mahn- und Gedenkstätte – Memorial, Place of Remembrance.

Meister – Master, usually a civilian foreman.

Mischling – A person of mixed race.

Nacht- und Nebel – Night and Fog. Prisoners who had been in the anti-German resistance in their home countries.

Nebenlager – Another name for a subcamp, although this generally referred to one that was next to a larger facility.

NSDAP – Official name of the Nazi Party: The National Socialist German Workers Party.

Oberaufseherin – Head female overseer.

Ravensbrückerinnen – Women of Ravensbrück.

Reichsführer SS – Reich Leader of the SS, Heinrich Himmler.

Revier – Infirmary. Sometimes called *Krankenhaus* (Hospital).

RSHA – *Reichssicherheitshauptamt* (Main Security Office of the Empire). The main security office of the SS, which included the *Gestapo* and the *SD* (Security Service).

SA – *Sturmabteilung* or Storm Troopers. The private army of the NSDAP. After 1934 it lost a power struggle to the SS.

Sanitätsdienst – Sanitation Service.

Schreibstube – Orderly room.

Schmuckstücke – Malnourished, emaciated women. In other camps, such prisoners were often called "Muslims."

SD – *Sicherheitsdienst* or Security Service.

Selektion – "Selection" for extermination.

Sonderbehandlung 14f13 – Code name for the killing of invalids and "undesirables" by the T4 organization for euthanasia.

Sonderhäftling – Special [privileged] prisoner.

Sonderkommando – Special crew.

SS – *Schutzstaffel*. The elite organization of the Nazi Party. The name means "Defense Guard."

Strafblock – Punishment Block.

Strafstehen – Punishment standing.

Stubenälteste – Room senior. Each block had two of these prisoner officials.

Stubendienst – Barracks assistant. Generally under the room seniors, they were responsible for keeping the barracks clean.

Stubova – Common term for *Stubenälteste*.

T4 – Code name for the euthanasia program. Its office was in Berlin, at Tiergartenstrasse 4, Hitler's Chancellory.

Verfügbar – Available. A prisoner who had no assigned workplace.

Vernichtung durch Arbeit – Extermination through work.

Völkischer Beobachter – The Nazi party newspaper, called the *VB*.

Volksdeutsche – Ethnic Germans from Eastern Europe.

Volksgemeinschaft – Folkish community.

Vorarbeiterin – Female foreman.

Vorkommando – Advance crew.

Waffen SS – The military branch of the SS, literally "Armed SS."

Wehrmacht – The German army.

Zellenbau – See Bunker.

Zigeuner – German word for Gypsy.

Bibliography

UNPUBLISHED MATERIALS

Archives

Mahn- und Gedenkstätte Ravensbrück (RVB Archives)
Public Record Office, London (PRO)
U.S. Holocaust Memorial Museum Archives, Washington, D.C. (USHMM Archives)

Oral Histories: Gratz College Holocaust Oral History Archive (Philadelphia)

Freilich, Dora. Interviewed by Helen Grossman, 24 October 1984.
Gorko [née Paley], Alexandra. Interviewed by Eileen Steinberg, 19 August 1985.
Kupferberg, Hardy. Interviewed by Josie Fisher, 8 June 1988.
Schwimmer, Sarah. Interviewed by Gladys Bernstein, April 1985.

Oral Histories: Holocaust Documentation and Education Center, Inc. (Miami)

Bernard, Jacqueline. Interviewed by Marilyn Potash, 3 April 1981.
Birenbaum, Betty. Interviewed by Bess Selevan, 2 March 1995.
Bricks, Barbara. Interviewed by Roslyn Lebster, 11 May 1982.
Cardini [née Marcheska], Janina. Interviewed by Marilyn Potash, 12 March 1992.
Eckhaus, Faye. Interviewed by Marilyn Potash.
Einstein, Miriam. Interviewed by Adele Morgenstern, 11 February 1982.
Feingold-Nelson, Ada. Interviewed by Marilyn Potash, 12 December 1995.
Friedman, Margarete. Interviewed by Marilyn Potash, 17 July 1995.
Gotthelf, Luise. Interviewed by Bess Selevan, 14 March 1997.
Gottlieb, George. Interviewed by Pat Bidol-Padva, 9 August 1990.
Guttmann, Miriam. Interviewed by Marilyn Klompus, 23 March 1990.
Haus, Rosa. Interviewed by Paul Kaufman, 9 June 1986.

Horowitz, Rachel. Interviewed by Roslyn Lebster, 27 April 1982.
Jaffe, Frieda. Interviewed by Estelle Kohn, 25 August 1982.
Kahn, Regina. Interviewed by Henni Poliankin, 18 January 1990.
Montrose, Steven. Interviewed by Sigmund Silver, 10 August 1994.
Stahl, Ruth. Interviewed by Abe Kushner, 28 February 1990.
Zimmerman, Frances. Interviewed by Marsha Gehrman, 18 March 1987.

Oral Histories: U.S. Holocaust Memorial Museum Archives (Washington, D.C.)

Kaleska, Nina. Interviewed by Linda Kuzmack, 3 January 1990.
(RG50.030*101)
Weintraub, Guta. Interviewed by Linda Kuzmack, 4 January 1990.
(RG50.030*250)

Oral Histories: Interviews by the Author

Breur, Dunya. Telephone interview, 24 July 1998.
Deutsch, Rosa. Interviewed at Ravensbrück, 8-9 October 1994 and Budapest, 25 October 1994.
Fejer, Eva. Interviewed at Ludwigsfelde, 8 October 1994.
Gyulai, Kato. Interviewed at Budapest, 25 October 1994.
Hofman, Ruth. Interviewed at Fürstenberg, 23 June 1998.
Reimann, Brunnhilde. Interviewed at Fürstenberg, 19 November 1994 and 27 August 1997.
Sparmann, Edith. Interviewed at Ravensbrück, 11 November 1994.
Trksak, Irma. Interviewed at Ravensbrück, 5 September 1997.

PUBLISHED MATERIALS

Autobiographies, Memoirs, and Personal Accounts

Audoul, France. *Ravensbrück: 150,000 Femmes en Enfer*. Paris, publisher unknown, 1966.
Bejarano, Esther. *"Man nannte mich Krümel"—Eine jüdische Jugend in den Zeiten der Verfolgung*. Hamburg: Curio Verlag, 1991.

Bernstein, Sara Tuvel. *The Seamstress: A Memoir of Survival*. New York: Putnam's, 1997.

Bruha, Antonia. *Ich war keine Heldin*. Vienna: Europaverlag, 1984.

Buber-Neumann, Margarete. *Als Gefangene bei Stalin und Hitler*. Munich: Deutscher Taschenbuch Verlag, 1962.

————. *Milena: The Story of a Remarkable Friendship*, tr. Ralph Manheim. New York: Schocken Books, 1988.

Buchmann, Erika. "Brief an eine berliner Reporterin," in Klaus Jarmatz, ed., *Ravensbrücker Ballade* (1992), pp. 32-46.

Busch, Eva. *Und Trotzdem. Eine Biographie*. Munich: Albrecht Knaus Verlag, 1991.

Català, Neus. *"In Ravensbrück ging meine Jugend zu Ende"—14 spanisch Frauen berichten über ihre Deportation in deutschen Konzentrationslagern*, tr. Dorothee von Keitz and Andreas Ruppert. Berlin: Edition Tranvia, 1994.

Delbo, Charlotte. *Auschwitz and After*, tr. Rosette Lamont. New Haven: Yale Univ. Press, 1995.

Dufournier, Denise. *Ravensbrück—The Women's Camp of Death*. London: Allen & Unwin, 1948.

Fabius, Odette. *Sonnenaufgang über der Hölle—Von Paris in das KZ Ravensbrück. Erinnerungen*, tr. by Ira and Gerd Joswiakowski. Berlin: Verlag Neues Leben, 1997.

Gelissen, Rena Kornreich, with Heather Dune Macadam. *Rena's Promise*. Boston: Beacon, 1995.

Gluck, Gemma La Guardia. *My Story*, ed. S. L. Shneiderman. New York: David McKay, 1961.

Günzl, Maria. *Trost im Leid*. Stuttgart: Seliger-Archiv, 1976.

Hajkova, Dagmar. *Ravensbrück*. Prague: Nase Vojsko, 1960. [Privately translated into German from the Czech by the Mahn- und Gedenkstätte Ravensbrück.]

Heilman, F. *"KZ Ravensbrück Chronik."* 2 April 1995. Internet: 5J47-geOYCB@gryps-35.gryps.comlink.apc.org. (28 April 1998.)

Herbermann, Nanda. *Der gesegnete Abgrund. Schutz-Häftling Nr. 6582 im Frauenkonzentrationslager Ravensbrück*. Buxheim/Allgau: Martin Verlag, 1959.

Jacquemotte-Thonnart, Madeleine. *Ma Vie de Militante, 1907-1945*. [Vies de Femmes—Mémoires—Tome I]. Brussels: Université des Femmes, 1992.

Katzenmaier, Theolinde Katharina. *Vom KZ ins Kloster: Ein Stück Lebensgeschichte*. St. Ottilien: EOS Verlag, 1996.

Kocwa, Eugenia. *Flucht aus Ravensbrück*, tr. from Polish by Elisabeth Szubert. Berlin: Union Verlag, 1973.

Kounio-Amariglio, Erika Myriam. *Damit es die ganze Welt erfährt. Von Salonika nach Auschwitz und Zurück, 1926-1996*, tr. from Greek into German by Egon Amariglio. Constance: Hartung Gorre Verlag, 1996.

Lahaye, Simone. *Libre Parmi des Morts: Ravensbrück, 1942-1945*. Dijon-Quetigny: Berg International, 1983.

Marette, Fanny. *I Was Number 47177*. Geneva: Fern, 1979.

Maurel, Micheline. *An Ordinary Camp*, tr. Margaret S. Summers. New York: Simon & Schuster, 1958.

Montluc-Ravensbrück: A Record of Imprisonment. (Typed Copy: U.S. State Department Library, 1946.)

Müller, Charlotte. *Die Klempnerkolonne in Ravensbrück—Erinnerungen des Häftlings Nr. 10787*. Berlin: Dietz Verlag, 1987.

Nelken, Halina. *Freiheit will ich noch erleben. Krakauer Tagebuch*, tr. from Polish by Friedrich Griese. Gerlingen: Bleicher Verlag, 1996.

Poltawska, Wanda. *And I Am Afraid of My Dreams*, tr. Mary Craig. London: Hodder & Stoughton, 1987.

Postel-Vinay, Anise. "A Young Frenchwoman's Wartime Experiences," *Dachau Review*, vol. 1 (1985), pp. 213-232.

Rehwald, Joseph, "Im nationalsozialistischen Deutschland die Lauterkeit bewahrt," in *Erwachet*, 8 February 1993. Internet: http://www.jznet.org.jzs-tandhaft/g930802-rehwald.html.

Roux, Catherine. *Red Triangle*, tr. S. & L. Van Vliet White. Geneva: Fermi, 1979.

Salvesen, Silvia. *Forgive—But Do Not Forget*, tr. Evelyn Ramsden. London: Hutchinson, 1958.

Sandoe, Sunneva. *Og dog er det Sandt*. Aarhus: Kammersternes Forlag, 1945. [Privately translated into German from the Danish by Karin Machnitzky as *Und doch ist es wahr*, 1993. There is a copy at the Mahn- und Gedenkstätte Ravensbrück.]

Sommer-Lefkovits, Elisabeth. *Are You Here in this Hell Too? Memories of Troubled Times, 1944-45*. London: Menard, 1995.

Stojka, Ceija. *Wir leben im Verborgenen: Erinnerungen einer Rom-Zigeunerin*, ed. Karin Berger. Vienna: Picus Verlag, 1988.

Sturm, Hanna. *Die Lebensgeschichte einer Arbeiterin—Vom Burgenland nach Ravensbrück*. Vienna: Verlag für Gesellschaftskritik, 1982.

Tedeschi, Giuliana. *There Is a Place on Earth: A Woman in Birkenau*, tr. Tim Parks. New York: Pantheon Books, 1992.

Tillion, Germaine. *Ravensbrück*, tr. Gerald Satterwhite. New York: Anchor, 1975.

Urbye, Annalise. *Himmlers 100,000 Frauen*. Oslo, 1946. [Privately translated from Norwegian by the Mahn- und Gedenkstätte Ravensbrück, where there is a copy.]

Vermehren, Isa. *Reise durch den letzten Akt: Ravensbrück, Buchenwald, Dachau: Eine Frau berichtet*. Hamburg: Wegner, 1946.

Wagner, Christa. *Geboren am See der Tränen*. Berlin: Militärverlag der DDR, 1987.

Secondary Works

Adam, Uwe Dietrich. "Wie spontan war der Pogrom?" in *Der Judenpogrom 1938*, ed. Walter Pehle. Frankfurt: Fischer Verlag (1988), pp. 74-93.

Agassi, Judith Buber. "Jewish Prisoners of the Women's Camp Ravensbrück—A Historical and Sociological Study." Paper presented at the Kolloquium: "Neuere Forschungen zur Geschichte des Frauenkonzentrationslagers Ravensbrück," 30 October 1996.

——. "Opfer und Überlebende: jüdische Häftlinge im KZ Ravensbrück," in Jacobeit and Philipp, eds., *Forschungsschwerpunkt Ravensbrück* (1997), pp. 71-77.

Alt, Betty, and Silvia Folts. *Weeping Violins: The Gypsy Tragedy in Europe.* Kirksville, Mo.: Thomas Jefferson Univ. Press, 1996.

Anatomy of the Auschwitz Death Camp, ed. Yisrael Gutman and Michael Berenbaum (Bloomington, Ind.: Indiana Univ. Press, 1994).

Anschütz, Janet, Kerstin Meier, and Sanja Obajdin. "'...dieses leere Gefühl, und die Blicke der anderen...': Sexuelle Gewalt gegen Frauen," in *Frauen in Konzentrationslagern: Bergen-Belsen, Ravensbrück* (1994), pp. 123-134.

Arndt, Ino. "Das Frauenkonzentrationslager Ravensbrück," in *Studien zur Geschichte der Konzentrationslager* [Schriftenreihe der Vierteljahreshefte für Zeitgeschichte, No. 21.] Stuttgart: Dt. Verlagsanstalt (1970), pp. 93-129.

Bankier, David. *The Germans and the Final Solution.* Oxford: Blackwell, 1992.

Barkai, Avraham. *From Boycott to Annihilation: the Economic Struggle of German Jews, 1933-1943*, tr. William Templer. Hanover, N.H.: Univ. Press of New England, 1989.

Bartov, Omer. "Defining Enemies, Making Victims: Germans, Jews, and the Holocaust," *American Historical Review*, vol. 103, no. 3 (1998), pp. 771-816.

Bauer, Yehuda. "Gypsies," in Yisrael Gutman and Michael Berenbaum, eds., *Anatomy of the Auschwitz Death Camp.* Bloomington, Ind.: Indiana Univ. Press (1994), pp. 441-455.

——. *A History of the Holocaust.* New York: Franklin Watts, 1982.

Baumel, Judith Tydor. "Social Interaction Among Jewish Women in Crisis during the Holocaust: A Case Study," *Gender and History*, vol. 7, no. 1 (1995), pp. 64-84.

Beck, Earl R. *Under the Bombs. The German Home Front, 1942-1945.* Lexington: Univ. of Kentucky Press, 1986.

Bock, Gisela. "'No Children at Any Cost': Perspectives on Compulsory Sterilization, Sexism, and Racism in Nazi Germany," in Judith Friedlander et al., eds., *Women in Culture and Politics: A Century of Change.* Bloomington, Ind.: Indiana Univ. Press (1986), pp. 286-298.

——. "Ordinary Women in Nazi Germany: Perpetrators, Victims, Followers and Bystanders," in Ofer and Weitzman, eds., *Women in the Holocaust* (1998), pp. 85-100.

Botwinick, Rita S. *A History of the Holocaust*. Upper Saddle River, N.J.: Prentice-Hall, 1996.

Brandes, Ulrike. "Der Arbeitseinsatz in zwei Aussenlagern Ravensbrücks," in *Frauen in Konzentrationslagern: Bergen-Belsen, Ravensbrück* (1994), pp. 71-72.

Brandes, Ulrike, Claus Füllberg-Stollberg, and Sylvia Kempe. "Arbeit im KZ Ravensbrück," in *Frauen in Konzentrationslagern: Bergen-Belsen, Ravensbrück* (1994), pp. 55-70.

Breur, Dunya. *Een verborgen herinnering: De tekeningen van Aat Breur-Hibma uit het vrouwenconcentratiekamp Ravensbrück en de gevangenissen in Scheveningen en Utrecht 1942-1945,* 2nd ed. Nijmegen: Sun, 1995.

―――. *Ich lebe, weil du dich erinnerst: Frauen und Kinder in Ravensbrück,* tr. from Dutch into German by Rudie Leikies and Diete Oudesluijs. Berlin: Nicolai, 1997.

Bridenthal, Renate, Atina Grossmann, and Marion Kaplan, eds. *When Biology Became Destiny: Women in Weimar and Nazi Germany.* New York: Monthly Review, 1984.

Bromberger, Barbara, Henna Elling, Jutta von Freyberg, and Ursula Krause-Schmitt. *Schwestern, vergesst uns nicht. Frauen im KZ Moringen, Lichtenburg, Ravensbrück, 1933-1945.* Frankfurt a/M: Verlag für akad. Schriften, 1988.

Broszat, Martin. "The Concentration Camps, 1933-1945," in Hans Buchheim, et al., eds., *Anatomy of the SS State,* tr. Marion Jackson. New York: Walker (1965), pp. 397-504.

Buchmann, Erika. *Die Frauen von Ravensbrück.* Berlin: Kongress Verlag, 1959.

Cerná, Jana. *Kafka's Milena,* tr. A.G. Bain. Evanston, Ill.: Northwestern Univ. Press, 1993.

Crowe, David M. *A History of the Gypsies of Eastern Europe and Russia.* New York: St. Martin's, 1994.

Domarus, Max. *Hitler: Reden und Proklamationen, 1932-1945—kommentiert von einem deutschen Zeitgenossen.* Munich: Suddeutscher Verlag, 1965.

Dunn, Brian R. "Green Triangles," *Scholars,* vol. 4, no. 2 (1993), pp. 19-27.

Durrer, Bettina. "Eine Verfolgte als Täterin? Zur Geschichte der Blockälteste Carmen Maria Mory," in Jacobeit and Philipp, eds., *Forschungsschwerpunkt Ravensbrück* (1997), pp. 86-93.

Ebbinghaus, Angelika, Karl Heinz Roth, and Michael Hepp. "Die Ärztin Herta Oberheuser und die Kriegschirurgischen Experimente im Frauenkonzentrationslager Ravensbrück," in Ebbinghaus, ed., *Opfer und Täterinnen: Frauenbiographien des Nationalsozialismus.* Nördlingen: Delph (1987), pp. 250-254.

Ebert, Anne-Katrin. *Dr. Hildegard Hansche, 1896-1992: Stiftungs-vermächtnis.* [Schriftenreihe der Dr. Hildegard Hansche Stiftung, Bd. 1]. Fürstenberg: Dr. Hildegard Hansche Stiftung, 1996.

Erpel, Simone. "Rettungsaktion in letzter Minute," in S. Jacobeit, ed., *"Ich grüsse Euch als freier Mensch"* (1995), pp. 22-79.

Erpel, Simone. "Zur Befreiung des Frauenkonzentrationslagers Ravensbrück." Paper presented at the Kolloquium: "Neuere Forschungen zur Geschichte des Frauenkonzentrationslagers Ravensbrück," 30 Oct. 1996.

Eschebach, Insa. "Die Geschichte einer NS-Täterin: Versuch einer Rekonstruktion nach dem Akten," in Jen Ebert and Insa Eschebach, eds., *Die Kommandeuse: Erna Dorn Zwischen Nationalsozialismus und kaltem Krieg*. Berlin: Dietz (1994), pp. 15-72.

Ferencz, Benjamin B. *Less Than Slaves: Jewish Forced Labor and the Quest for Compensation*. Cambridge, Mass.: Harvard Univ. Press, 1979.

Fest, Joachim C. *Hitler*, tr. Richard and Clara Winston. New York: Vintage, 1974.

Fisher, Josie G., ed. *The Persistence of Youth: Oral Testimonies of the Holocaust*. Westport, Conn.: Greenwood Press, 1991.

Fleming, Gerald. *Hitler and the Final Solution*. Berkeley, Cal.: Univ. of California Press, 1984.

Fonseca, Isabel. *Bury Me Standing: The Gypsies and Their Journey*. New York: Knopf, 1995.

Françaises à Ravensbrück, Les, ed. Amicale de Ravensbrück et Association des Déportées et Internées de la Résistance. Paris: Gallimard, 1965.

Fraser, Angus. *The Gypsies*. Oxford: Blackwell, 1992.

"Frauen aus Ravensbrück 1995." [Calendar] Ed. Stiftung brandenburgische Gedenkstätten/Mahn- und Gedenkstätte Ravensbrück. Berlin: Edition Hentrich, 1994.

Frauen in Konzentrationslagern: Bergen-Belsen, Ravensbrück, ed. Claus Füllberg-Stolberg, Martina Jung, Renate Riebe, and Martina Scheitenberger. Bremen: Edition Temmen, 1994.

Frauenkonzentrationslager Ravensbrück: Eine Gesamtdarstellung. Mimeographed copy: Ludwigsburg: Zentralstellung der Landes-justizverwaltung, 1972.

Frauenkonzentrationslager Ravensbrück: Quellenlage und Quellenkritik. Fachtagung von 29.5 bis 30.5.1997, ed. Insa Eschebach and Johanna Kootz. Berlin: Freie Universität, 1997.

Frauen-KZ Ravensbrück: Autorenkollektiv unter Leitung von G. Zörner, ed. Kommittee der antifaschistischen Widerstands-kämpfer in der DDR. 2nd ed. Berlin: Deutscher Verlag der Wissenschaften, 1973.

Frevert, Ute. *Women in German History: From Bourgeois Emancipation to Sexual Liberation*, tr. Stuart McKinnon-Evans. Providence, R.I.: Berg, 1989.

Freyberg, Jutta von, and Ursula Krause-Schmitt, eds. *Moringen-Lichtenberg-Ravensbrück. Frauen im Konzentrationslager 1933-1945. Lesebuch zur Ausstellung*. Frankfurt: Verlag für Akad. Schriften, 1997.

Friedlander, Henry. *The Origins of Nazi Genocide: From Euthanasia to the Final Solution*. Chapel Hill: Univ. of North Carolina Press, 1995.

Friedrich, Otto. *Before the Deluge: A Portrait of Berlin in the 1920s*. New York: Harper & Row, 1972.

Füllberg-Stolberg, Claus, "'Bedrängt, aber nicht völlig eingeengt—verfolgt, aber nicht verlassen': Gertrud Pötzinger, Zeugen Jehovas," in *Frauen in Konzentrationslagern: Bergen-Belsen, Ravensbrück* (1994), pp. 321-332.

———. "Die Odyssee einer ungarischen Jüdin: Gloria Hollander Lyon," in *Frauen in Konzentrationslagern: Bergen-Belsen, Ravensbrück* (1994), pp. 279-290.

George, Enno. *Die wirtschaftlichen Unternehmungen des SS*. [Schriftenreihe der

Vierteljahreshefte für Zeitgeschichte, No. 7]. Stuttgart: Deutsche Verlagsanstalt, 1963.

Gibian, George. "Who was Milena?" in Jana Cerná, *Kafka's Milena*, tr. A. G. Bain. Evanston, Ill.: Northwestern Univ. Press (1993), pp. 1-24.

Gilbert, Martin. *The Holocaust: A History of the Jews of Europe during the Second World War.* New York: Holt, Rinehart & Winston, 1985.

———. The Question of Bombing Auschwitz," in *The Nazi Concentration Camps.* Proceedings of the 4th Yad Vashem International Historical Conference, Jerusalem, Jan. 1980 (1984), pp. 470-473.

Gill, Anton. *The Journey Back From Hell: Conversations with Concentration Camp Survivors: An Oral History.* New York: Avon Books, 1988.

Gilsenbach, Reimar. "Wie Lolitschai zur Doktorwürde kam," in *Feinderklärung und Prävention: Kriminalbiologie, Zigeuner-forschung und Asozialenpolitik.* [Beiträge zur N-S Gesundheits- und Sozialpolitik, Bd. 6.] Berlin: Rotbuch Verlag (1988), pp. 101-134.

Goldhagen, Daniel. *Hitler's Willing Executioners: Ordinary Germans and the Holocaust.* New York: Knopf, 1996.

Gordon, Sarah. *Hitler, Germans and the "Jewish Question."* Princeton: Princeton Univ. Press, 1984.

Grossmann, Atina. "*Girlkultur* or Thoroughly Rationalized Female: A New Woman in Weimar Germany?" in Judith Friedlander et al., eds., *Women in Culture and Politics: A Century of Change.* Bloomington, Ind.: Indiana Univ. Press (1986), pp. 62-80.

———. *Reforming Sex: The German Movement for Birth Control and Abortion Reform, 1920-1950.* New York and Oxford: Oxford Univ. Press, 1995.

Gruber-Lieblich, Renate. "...*und Morgen war Krieg!" Arado Flugzeugwerke GMBH Wittenberg, 1936-1945—Ein KZ Lager entsteht.* Wittenberg: Elbe Druckerei—Selbstverlag, 1995.

Grunberger, Richard. *The 12-Year Reich: A Social History of Nazi Germany.* N.Y.: Holt, Rinehart & Winston, 1971.

Gutman, Yisrael. "On the Character of Nazi Antisemitism," in Schmuel Almog, ed., *Antisemitism through the Ages,* tr. Nathan Reisner. Oxford: Pergamon (1988), pp. 349-380.

Heike, Irmtraud. "'...da es sich ja lediglich um die Bewachung der Häftlinge handelt...': Lagerverwaltung und Bewachungspersonal," in *Frauen in Konzentrationslagern: Bergen-Belsen, Ravensbrück* (1994), pp. 221-240.

Heike, Irmtraud, and Andreas Pflock. "Geregelte Strafen, willkürliche Gewalt und Massensterben," in *Frauen in Konzentrationslagern: Bergen-Belsen, Ravensbrück* (1994), pp. 241-258.

Heike, Irmtraud, and Bernard Strebel. "Häftlingsselbstverwaltung und Funkstionshäftlinge im KZ Ravensbrück," in *Frauen in Konzentrationslagern: Bergen-Belsen, Ravensbrück* (1994), pp. 89-97.

Hepp, Michael. "Vorhof zur Hölle: Mädchen in Jugendschutzlager Uckermark," in Ebbinghaus, ed., *Opfer und Täterinnen* (1987), pp. 191-216.

Herzog, Monika, *Ravensbrücker Zeichnungen.* 2nd ed. Ravensbrück: Mahn- und

Gedenkstätte, 1993.

Herzog, Monika, and Bernard Strebel. "Das Frauenkonzentrationslager Ravensbrück," in *Frauen in Konzentrationslagern: Bergen-Belsen, Ravensbrück* (1994), pp. 13-26.

Hesse, Hans. "Und am Anfang war Moringen...?" Paper presented at the Kolloquium: "Neuere Forschungen zur Geschichte des Frauenkonzentrationslagers Ravensbrück," 31 Oct. 1996.

Hilberg, Raul. *The Destruction of the European Jews.* 2nd ed. New York: Holmes & Meier, 1985.

Hitler's Secret Conversations, 1941-1944. New York: Signet, 1953.

Horowitz, Sara R. "Women in Holocaust Literature: Engendering Trauma Memory," in Ofer and Weitzman, eds., *Women in the Holocaust* (1998), pp. 364-378.

Hudson, Robert P. *Disease and Its Control.* [Contributions in Medical History, No. 12.] Westport, Conn. and London: Greenwood Press, 1983.

Jacobeit, Sigrid, ed. *"Ich grüsse Euch als freier Mensch."* Quellenedition zur Befreiung des Frauen-Konzentrationslagers Ravensbrück im April 1945. [Stiftung Brandenburgische Gedenkstätten, Schriftenreihe Nr. 6.] Berlin: Edition Hentrich, 1995.

————. "Fotografien als historische Quellen zum Frauen-KZ Ravensbrück: Das ravensbrücker SS-Fotoalbum," in Eschebach and Kootz, eds., *Das Frauenkonzentrationslager Ravensbrück: Quellenlage und Quellenkritik* (1997), pp. 33-43.

Jacobeit, Sigrid, and Elisabeth Brümann-Güdter, eds. *Ravensbrückerinnen.* [Schriftenreihe der Stiftung Brandenburgische Gedenkstätten, Nr. 4.] Berlin: Hentrich, 1995.

Jacobeit, Sigrid, and Grit Philipp, eds. *Forschungsschwerpunkt Ravensbrück: Beiträge zur Geschichte des Frauenkonzentrationslagers.* [Schriftenreihe der Stiftung Brandenburgische Gedenkstätten, Nr. 9.] Berlin: Edition Hentrich, 1997.

Jacobeit, Sigrid, and Liselotte Thomas-Heinrich. *Kreuzweg Ravensbrück: Lebensbilder antifaschistischer Widerstands-kämpferinnen.* Köln: Röderberg, 1987.

Jacobeit, Wolfgang. "Die Todesmärsche von Ravensbrück in nord-westlicher Richtung und das Erlebnis der Befreiung durch die Rote Armee," in Sigrid Jacobeit, ed., *Ich grüsse Euch als freier Mensch* (1995), pp. 80-129.

Jarmatz, Klaus, ed. *Ravensbrücker Ballade oder Faschismus-bewältigung in der DDR.* Berlin: Aufbau Taschenbuch Verlag, 1992.

Jenks, William A. *Vienna and the Young Hitler.* N.Y.: Columbia Univ. Press, 1960.

Kaplan, Marion A. *Between Dignity and Despair: Jewish Life in Nazi Germany.* New York: Oxford Univ. Press, 1998.

————. "Sisterhood Under Siege: Feminism and anti-Semitism in Germany," in Renate Bridenthal, Atina Grossmann, and Marion Kaplan, eds., *When Biology Became Destiny: Women in Weimar and Nazi Germany.* New York: Monthly Review Press (1984), pp. 174-196.

Kater, Michael. "Die Ernsten Bibelforscher im Dritten Reich," *Vierteljahreshefte für Zeitgeschichte,* vol. 17 (1969), pp. 181-218.

Katz, Esther, and Joan Ringelheim, eds. *Proceedings of the Conference on "Women Surviving the Holocaust."* New York: Institute for Research in History, 1983.

Kenrick, Donald, and Puxon Grulton, *The Destiny of Europe's Gypsies.* New York: Basic Books, 1972.

Kettennacker, Lothar. "Hitler's Final Solution and its Rationalization," in Gerhard Hirschfeld, ed., *The Policies of Genocide.* London: Allen & Unwin (1986), pp. 73-96.

Kiedrzynska, Wanda. "Das Frauenkonzentrationslager Ravensbrück," *Internationale Hefte der Widerstandsbewegung,* vol. 3 (1960), pp. 82-98.

———. *Ravensbrück Kobiecy Oboz Koncentracyjny.* Warsaw: 1961. [Privately translated into German from Polish by the Mahn- und Gedenkstätte Ravensbrück.]

Klier, Freya. *Die Kaninchen von Ravensbrück: medizinische Versuche an Frauen in der NS-Zeit.* Munich: Knaur, 1994.

Kogon, Eugen. *The Theory and Practice of Hell: The German Concentration Camps and the System Behind Them,* tr. Heinz Norden. New York: Berkley Books, 1950.

Kogon, Eugen, Hermann Langbein, and Adalbert Rückerl, eds. *Nazi Mass Murder: A Documentary History of the Use of Poison Gas.* New Haven, Conn.: Yale Univ. Press, 1994.

Köhler, Jan Thomas. "Zur Baugeschichte des KZ Ravensbrück." Paper presented at the Kolloquium: "Neuere Forschungen zur Geschichte des Frauenkonzentrationslagers Ravensbrück," 30 Oct. 1996.

Koonz, Claudia. *Mothers in the Fatherland: Women, the Family and Nazi Politics.* New York: St. Martin's, 1987.

———. "Some Political Implications of Separatism: German Women between Democracy and Nazism, 1928-1934," in Judith Friedlander et al., eds., *Women in Culture and Politics: A Century of Change.* Bloomington, Ind.: Indiana Univ. Press (1986), pp. 269-285.

Kröger, Marianne. "Ravensbrück als Ort der Erfahrung—Leben und Werk der niederländischen Dichterin Sonja Prins," *Dachauer Hefte,* vol. 10 (1994), pp. 50-68.

Krokowski, Heike, and Bianca Voigt. "Das Schicksal von Wanda P.— Zur Verfolgung der Sinti und Roma," in *Frauen in Konzentrationslagern: Bergen-Belsen, Ravensbrück* (1994), pp. 259-268.

Langer, Lawrence. "Gendered Suffering? Women in Holocaust Testimonies," in Ofer and Weitzman, eds, *Women in the Holocaust* (1998), pp. 351-363.

Lewy, Guenter. *The Nazi Persecution of the Gypsies.* Oxford and New York: Oxford University Press, 2000.

Margry, Karel. "Nordheim," *After the Battle,* no. 101 (1998), pp. 2-43.

Marrus, Michael, *The Holocaust in History.* [Tauber Institute for the Study of European Jewry Series, No. 7.] Hanover and London: Univ. Press of New England, 1987.

Martin, Dunja. "Menschenversuche im Krankenrevier des KZ Ravensbrück," in

Frauen in Konzentrationslagern: Bergen-Belsen, Ravensbrück (1994), pp. 99-112.

Maser, Werner. *Hitler: Legend, Myth and Reality*, tr. Peter and Betty Ross. New York: Harper Torchbooks, 1973.

Maurer, Trude, "Abschiebung und Attentat: Die Ausweisung der polnischen Juden und der Vorwand für die 'Kristallnacht'" in Walter H. Pehle, ed., *Der Judenpogrom 1938*. Frankfurt: Fischer Taschenbuch Verlag (1988), pp. 52-73.

McLaughlin, John. *Gypsy Lifestyles*. Lexington, Mass.: Heath, 1980.

Milton, Sybil. "Deutsche und deutsch-jüdische Frauen als Verfolgte des NS-Staats," *Dachauer Hefte*, vol. 3 (1987), pp. 3-21.

Minhoff, Susanne. "'Ein Symbol der menschliche Würde': Kunst und Kultur im KZ Ravensbrück," in *Frauen in Konzentrationslagern: Bergen-Belsen, Ravensbrück* (1994), pp. 207-220.

Mommsen, Hans. "The Realization of the Unthinkable: The 'Final Solution of the Jewish Question' in the Third Reich," in Gerhard Hirschfeld, ed., *The Policies of Genocide*. London: Allen & Unwin (1986), pp. 97-144.

Morrison, Jack G. "For Women Only: The Ravensbrück Concentration Camp," *Proteus*, vol. 12, no. 2 (Fall 1995), pp. 51-55.

———. "Guide to the Cell Building at the Ravensbrück Memorial." (Typed copy, 1994.) [This and the following were created to facilitate self-guided tours of the Ravensbrück Memorial for English-speaking visitors. About twenty pages each, they are available as "hand-outs" at the visitors' center.]

———. "Guide to the Museum at the Ravensbrück Memorial." (Typed copy, 1994.)

———. "Women of Ravensbrück." [Guide to the new exhibit, *"Ravensbrück-erinnen"*]. (Typed copy, 1994.)

Noakes, Jeremy, and Geoffrey Pridham, eds. *Documents on Nazism, 1919-1945*. New York: Viking, 1974.

Ofer, Dalia, and Lenore J. Weitzman, eds., *Women in the Holocaust*. New Haven, Conn.: Yale Univ. Press, 1998.

Owings, Allison. *Frauen: German Women Recall the Third Reich*. New Brunswick, N.J.: Rutgers Univ. Press, 1993.

Paul, Christa. *Zwangsprostitution: staatlich errichtete Bordelle im Nationalsozialismus*. Berlin: Hentrich, 1994.

Pawelke, Britta. "Als Häftling geboren—Kinder in Ravensbrück," in *Frauen in Konzentrationslagern: Bergen-Belsen, Ravensbrück* (1994), pp. 157-166.

Pflock, Andreas. "'Bitteschön, und jetzt können Sie mich verhaften': Ilse Stephan," in *Frauen in Konzentrationslagern: Bergen-Belsen, Ravensbrück* (1994), pp. 291-298.

———. "'Lebens'-bedingungen im Konzentrationslager: Unterbringung und Ernährung, Kleidung und Hygiene," in *Frauen in Konzentrationslagern: Bergen-Belsen, Ravensbrück* (1994), pp. 43-54.

Phayer, Michael. *Protestant and Catholic Women in Nazi Germany*. Detroit: Wayne State Univ. Press, 1990.

Philipp, Grit. "Erlebnisberichte als Quellen historischer Forschung," in Eschebach and Kootz, ed., *Das Frauen-konzentrationslager Ravensbrück: Quellenlage und*

Quellenkritik (1997), pp. 123-128.

Plant, Richard. *The Pink Triangle: The Nazi War Against Homosexuals.* New York: Henry Holt, 1986.

Plewe, Reinhard, and Jan Thomas Köhler. "Die SS-Wohnsiedlung in Ravensbrück," in Jacobeit and Philipp, eds., *Forschungsschwer-punkt Ravensbrück* (1997), pp. 17-32.

Postel-Vinay, Anise. "Gaskammern und die ermordung durch Gas im Konzentrationslager Ravensbrück," in Jacobeit and Philipp, eds., *Forschungsschwerpunkt Ravensbrück* (1997), pp. 35-46.

Ringelheim, Joan, ed. *A Catalogue of Audio and Video Collections of Holocaust Testimony,* 2nd ed. [Bibliographies and Indexes in World History, No. 23.] Greenwood, Conn.: Greenwood Press, 1992.

———. "The Split between Gender and the Holocaust," in Ofer and Weitzman, eds., *Women in the Holocaust* (1998), pp. 340-350.

———. "The Unethical and the Unspeakable: Women and the Holocaust," *Simon Wiesenthal Center Annual,* vol. 1 (1984), pp. 69-87.

Rose, Romani, and Walter Weiss. *Sinti und Roma im dritten Reich: Das Programm der Vernichtung durch Arbeit,* ed. Zentralrat Dt. Sinti und Roma. Göttingen: Lamuv Taschenbuch, 1991.

Rossiter, Margaret. *Women in the Resistance.* New York: Praeger, 1986.

Scheitenberger, Martina, and Martina Jung. "Fürsorge—Arbeitshaus—KZ: Betty Voss," in *Frauen in Konzentrationslagern: Bergen-Belsen, Ravensbrück* (1994), pp. 299-306.

Schikorra, Christa. "'Asociale' Frauen. Ein anderer Blick auf die Häftlingsgesellschaft," in Sigrid Jacobeit and Grit Philipp, eds., *Forschungsschwerpunkt Ravensbrück* (1997), pp. 60-70.

———. "'Asoziale' Häftlinge im Frauenkonzentrationslager Ravensbrück: Eine Annäherung." Paper presented at the Kolloquium: "Neuere Forschungen zur Geschichte des Frauen-konzentrationslagers Ravensbrück," 31 Oct. 1996.

Schindler-Saefkow, Bärbel. "Die Befreiung des KZ Ravensbrück durch die rote Armee und die erste Beweisaufnahme von Verbrechen," in S. Jacobeit, ed. *"Ich grüsse Euch als freier Mensch"* (1995), pp. 137-208.

———. "Quellen zur Erstellung eines Gedenkbuches Ravensbrück," in Eschebach and Kootz, eds., *Frauenkonzentrationslager Ravensbrück: Quellenlage und Quellenkritik* (1997), pp. 46-56.

Schleunes, Karl. *The Twisted Road to Auschwitz: Nazi Policy Toward German Jews, 1933-1939.* London: Andre Deutsch, 1972.

Schoenbaum, David. *Hitler's Social Revolution: Class and Status in Nazi Germany, 1933-1939.* Garden City, N.Y.: Doubleday, 1966.

Schoppman, Claudia. *Days of Masquerade: Life Stories of Lesbians during the Third Reich,* tr. Allison Brown. New York: Columbia Univ. Press, 1996.

Schulz, Christa. *Hanka Houskova.* Ravensbrück: Stiftung Brandenburgische Gedenkstätten, 1995.

———. "Weibliche Häftlinge aus Ravensbrück in Bordellen der Männerkonzentrationslager," in *Frauen in Konzentrationslagern: Bergen-Belsen, Ravensbrück*

(1994), pp. 135-146.

———, ed. *Der Wind weht weinend über die Ebene.* Paris: Éditions Tirésias, 1991.

Schütt, Karl Heinz. *Ein Vergessenes Lager? Über das Aussenlager Neustadt-Glewe des Frauen-KZ Ravensbrück.* Schkeuditz: GNN Verlag, 1997.

Schwarz, Gudrun. "SS-Aufseherinnen in N-S Konzentrationslagern (1933-1945)," *Dachauer Hefte,* vol. 10 (1994), pp. 32-49.

Sesnon, Allison (producer). *Women Doing Time.* Film report narrated by Diane Sawyer. (*ABC News Primetime Live,* 1996.)

Siegner, Ingo. "'Auf der Suche nach der Wahrheit': Germaine Tillion, eine Französin in Ravensbrück," in *Frauen in Konzentrationslagern: Bergen-Belsen, Ravensbrück* (1994), pp. 269-278.

Sofsky, Wolfgang. *The Order of Terror: The Concentration Camps,* tr. William Templer. Princeton: Princeton Univ. Press, 1997.

Steiner, Herbert, ed. *Käthe Leichter: Leben und Werk.* Vienna: Europaverlag, 1973.

Strebel, Bernhard. "Die 'Lagergesellschaft': Aspekte der Häftlingshierarchie und Gruppenbildung in Ravensbrück," in *Frauen in Konzentrationslagern: Bergen-Belsen, Ravensbrück* (1994), pp. 79-88.

———. "Sabotage ist wie Wein: Selbstbehauptung, Solidarität und Widerstand im FKL Ravensbrück," in *Frauen in Konzentrationslagern: Bergen-Belsen, Ravensbrück* (1994), pp. 167-192.

Strzelecka, Irena. "Women," in Yisrael Gutman and Michael Berenbaum, eds., *Anatomy of the Auschwitz Death Camp.* Bloomington, Ind.: Indiana Univ. Press (1994), pp. 393-411.

Symonowicz, Wanda, ed. *Beyond Human Endurance: The Ravensbrück Women Tell Their Story,* tr. Doris Ronowicz. Warsaw: Interpress Pub., 1970.

Trials of War Criminals Before the Nuernberg Military Tribunals Under Control Code Council Law No. 10, vol. 5. Washington, D.C.: U.S. Government Printing Office, 1950.

Tröger, Annemarie. "The Creation of a Female Assembly-Line Proletariat," in Renate Bridenthal, Atina Grossmann, and Marion Kaplan, eds., *When Biology Became Destiny: Women in Weimar and Nazi Germany.* New York: Monthly Review Press (1984), pp. 237-270.

Unverzagt, Vera. "Das soll sich nicht wiederholen: weibliche Kriegsgefangene der Roten Armee im KZ Ravensbrück," in *Frauen in Konzentrationslagern: Bergen-Belsen, Ravensbrück* (1994), pp. 307-312.

Waite, Robert G.L. *The Psychopathic God: Adolf Hitler.* New York: Basic Books, 1977.

Waltz, Loretta (director). *Remembering Ravensbrück.* Film made in collaboration with the Brandenburg Historical Commission, 1997.

Ward, David and Gene Kassebaum. *Women's Prison: Sex and Social Structure.* Chicago: Aldine, 1965.

Winska, Ursula. *Zwyciezyly Wartosci.* Gdansk: Meereeskundlicher Verlag, 1985. [Privately translated from the Polish into German by the Mahn- und Gedenkstätte Ravensbrück as *Die Werte Siegten: Erinnerung an Ravensbrück.*]

Yahil, Leni. *The Holocaust: The Fate of European Jewry, 1932-1945,* tr. from

Hebrew by Ina Friedman and Haya Galai. New York and Oxford: Oxford Univ. Press, 1990.

Zimmer, Hedda. "Legitimer und legitimatorischer Antifaschismus. Zur Aufführungsgeschichte der 'Ravensbrücker Ballade'," in Jarmatz, ed., *Ravensbrücker Ballade oder Faschismusbewältigung in der DDR* (1992), pp. 175-204.

Zumpe, Lotte. "Arbeitsbedingungen und Arbeitsergebnisse in den Textilbetrieben des SS im KZ Ravensbrück," *Jahrbuch für Wirtschaftsgeschichte,* Jg. 52, No. 2 (1969), pp. 11-51.

———. "Die Textilbetriebe der SS im KZ Ravensbrück," *Jahrbuch der Wirtschaftsgeschichte*, Jg. 52, No. 1 (1969), pp. 11-40.

Index

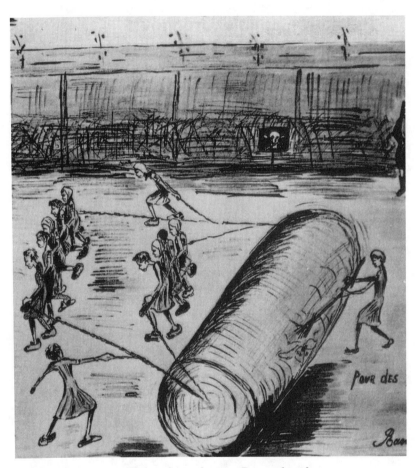

Felicie Mertens, Die Walze, Sammlungen Ravansbruck

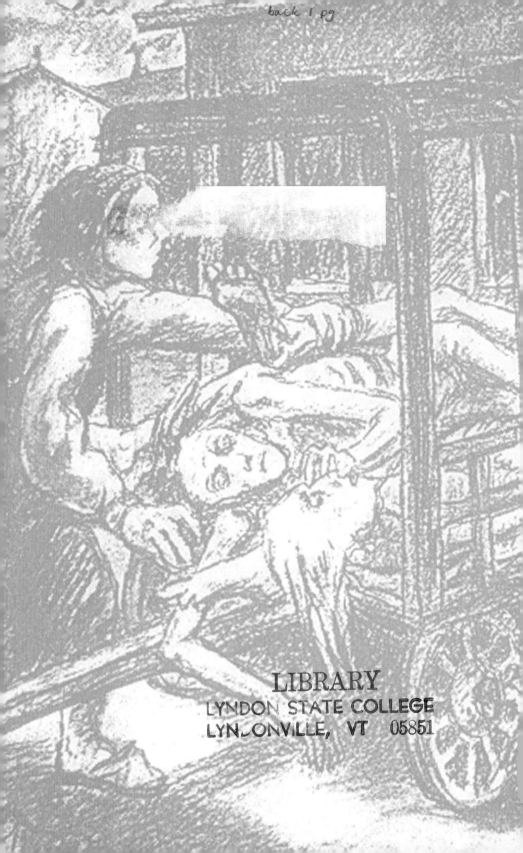

back 1 pg